ALL ABOUT
HEDGE FUNDS

OTHER TITLES IN THE "ALL ABOUT..." FINANCE SERIES

ALL ABOUT
HEDGE FUNDS

The Easy Way to Get Started

ROBERT A. JAEGER, PH.D.

McGraw-Hill

New York Chicago San Francisco Lisbon London Madrid Mexico City
Milan New Delhi San Juan Seoul Singapore Sydney Toronto

Library of Congress Cataloging-in-Publication Data

Jaeger, Robert A.
    All about hedge funds : the easy way to get started / Robert Jaeger.
      p. cm.
    ISBN 0-07-139393-5
    1. . 2. . I. Title.
    HG4661.F34 2000
    332.63'22—dc21   99-39400
                                                 CIP

ISBN 978-0-07-183271-7

10 11 12 13 14 15 DOC/DOC 1 4 3 2 1 0

McGraw-Hill books are available at special discounts to use as premiums and sales promotions, or for use in corporate training programs. For more information, please write to the Director of Special Sales, McGraw-Hill, Two Penn Plaza, New York, NY 10121-2298. Or contact your local bookstore.

This publication is designed to provide accurate and authoritative information in regard to the subject matter covered. It is sold with the understanding that the publisher is not engaged in rendering legal, accounting, or other professional service. If legal advice or other expert assistance is required, the services of a competent professional person should be sought.
—*From a Declaration of Principles Jointly Adopted by a Committee of the American Bar Association and a Committee of Publishers and Associations.*

CONTENTS

Chapter 10

Chapter 11

PART FOUR: SOME OPERATIONAL ISSUES

Chapter 12

Chapter 13

Chapter 14

PART 5: THE MENU OF HEDGE FUND STRATEGIES

Chapter 15

Chapter 16

Chapter 17

Chapter 18

PREFACE

We all enjoy stories in which extraordinary things happen to ordinary people. An unemployed auto worker wins a $100 million lottery jackpot. An 85-year-old mother of five and grandmother of 15 finally goes back to college to complete her degree. We take pleasure in both situations, but the second case is more satisfying since the good news is not the result of luck, but the result of hard work, grit, and courage. We love to see virtue rewarded.

We also enjoy stories in which ordinary things happen to extraordinary people. For example, some member of the rich and famous set has to deal with divorce or major financial reversals. The story is always more interesting when the bad news is not merely the result of bad luck, but is the result of too much self-indulgence, too much power, too much free time, or too much brainpower. Then we can blame the celebrities for the terrible things that happen to them. We love to see vice punished.

Reading about hedge funds in the newspaper is often like reading about celebrity divorce and other miseries. Bad things are happening, but the victims deserve it. After all, hedge funds are generally described in newspapers as secretive, unregulated investment vehicles that enable wealthy individuals to make highly leveraged speculative bets in the global financial and commodity markets. So the people who invest in hedge funds are rich people who can afford the losses and perhaps should have known better. And the people who manage hedge funds are routinely described as investment cowboys who take a healthy percentage of the profits earned by their investors. If a hedge fund is down 50 percent because of bad trading decisions, or if a fraudulent hedge fund manager siphons off the money to buy cars and houses, the story can make entertaining reading. The story is another reminder of the terrible things that can happen to the rich, but usually the story does not affect us directly. The wicked are getting what they deserve, but we don't have to worry because we're in another category altogether.

Hedge funds can be very risky. When things go wrong in the world of hedge funds, they can go very wrong. And when things go very wrong, the stories are very colorful. But the colorful stories are not fully representative of the hedge fund business. They ignore the substantial number of hedge fund managers who labor quietly in the shadows to produce decent returns for their investors. But this kind of low-profile work does not make for colorful newspaper articles. Hence this book, which is designed to present a picture of hedge funds that is more balanced, and more detailed, than the picture you would form from reading the newspaper headlines. But it's natural to begin with some disaster stories.

Long Term Capital Management (LTCM) was a large hedge fund that experienced major financial distress in August 1998. LTCM was formed by an unusually distinguished group of money managers. Many of them had had remarkably successful careers at Salomon Brothers, the major Wall Street investment bank. Others were Nobel Prize–winning academics. This group raised several billion dollars in capital, then used borrowed money to take very large positions designed to exploit small price discrepancies in the financial markets. After several years of stellar returns, LTCM came apart in a very special set of circumstances that unfolded in the late summer and early fall of 1998.

The problems began in Russia, which defaulted on its debt and devalued its currency. This created a panic among investors, who sold anything that had the slightest scent of risk, and then rushed for the complete safety of U.S. Treasury bonds. This global flight to quality put tremendous pressure on LTCM's trading positions, and the unwinding of those positions threatened to destabilize further the financial markets. The Federal Reserve Board was so concerned about the situation that it brought together the major Wall Street firms that were lenders to LTCM and encouraged them to act together in such a way as to minimize further impact on the financial markets, and further damage to themselves. The message from the Fed to the lenders was this: "If each of you pursues your own interests exclusively, the result will be a disaster for every single one of you and for the system as a whole. If you act cooperatively, the results will be better for everyone." The creditors seized control of the LTCM portfolio, thus essentially wiping out the equity investors, and organized a very gradual unwinding of the LTCM positions. Importantly, the government did not "bail out" the investors in the partnership: Those who had money invested in LTCM lost their investment. What the government did was to organize the creditors to act with "enlightened self-interest," rather than a more narrowly focused self-interest that would have been bad for the lenders and bad for the rest of us.

The LTCM debacle, like the crash of 1987, created a market crisis that wound up affecting all sorts of people who have no interest in, or knowledge of, hedge funds. The LTCM debacle was also a vivid reminder of one of the most fascinating facts about the investment management business: Brainpower is no guarantee of success. Indeed, too much brainpower can be a bad thing if it leads the owners of those brains to overestimate their understanding of what is always an inherently uncertain situation. The Greeks had a word for it: *hubris*, excessive pride or self-confidence. The markets always have ways of making the proud humble.

The markets gradually recovered from the LTCM debacle, but then the newspapers were filled with the travails of two other illustrious hedge fund managers: George Soros and Julian Robertson. In 1999 and early 2000 the U.S. stock market entered a completely manic phase in which investors became totally enamored with Internet stocks and anything else connected with "the new economy." This mania created a major problem for Soros and Robertson, both of whom were extremely astute investors who had put together very long and successful track records. Though both investors are too smart and too subtle to fit into simple boxes, Robertson often tended to be a "value investor," whereas Soros often tended to be more oriented toward growth, or momentum. Robertson refused to play the Internet sector in any significant size, his performance lagged, investors redeemed, and Robertson shut down his various Tiger funds on a low note rather than a high note.

The Soros organization recognized that the Internet craze was just a craze but thought that they could make money off the craze without getting hurt. That turned out to be a fatal mistake. When the Internet bubble burst, the Soros funds were caught with too much exposure. The result was big losses, and Soros decided to restructure his investment funds. Soros's predicament was analogous to the predicament of somebody whose house is on fire. You are standing safely on the lawn, but you want to retrieve a few items of sentimental value. You know the risks, but you think that you can rush quickly into the house, retrieve the few items, then rush out. So you run into the house. And you never come back.

The Robertson and Soros situations did not threaten the stability of the financial markets, but they illustrate vividly how fickle markets are and how fickle hedge fund investors are. The market shifted back and forth between new-economy stocks and old-economy stocks with breathtaking speed, and hedge fund investors thought that Robertson and Soros should be able to keep up with all those shifts. When the managers failed to keep up with all the shifts, investors bailed out. But it is doubtful whether any mere human being could have played all those shifts correctly.

And so we come to the early part of 2001, and another hedge fund disaster. This time the problem was not investment misjudgment but plain old fraud. Michael Berger was a short seller who ran a hedge fund called the Manhattan Fund. The job of the short seller is to make money from falling stock prices. Berger's record was remarkable, because he claimed to have made enormous sums of money shorting stocks during a period when most stocks were going up. Finally it emerged that the record depended more on fabrication than on skill. Once again, allegedly sophisticated investors lost a lot of money, this time from elementary fraud.

So much for the disaster stories, in which hedge funds figure as risky investment vehicles managed by cowboys on behalf of investors with more money than sense. If this characterization is unfair, what's a better description? Here is a provisional definition:

> A hedge fund is an *actively managed* investment fund that seeks attractive *absolute return*. In pursuit of their absolute return objective, hedge funds use a *wide variety of investment strategies and tools*. Hedge funds are designed for a *small number of large investors*, and the manager of the fund receives a *percentage of the profits* earned by the fund.

Hedge fund managers are *active managers* seeking *absolute return*. Active managers stand in contrast to passive managers: Passive managers run index funds designed to track the market, whereas active managers try hard to beat the market. But many active managers care only about delivering a good *relative return*: They want to beat the S&P 500 Index, or some other passive benchmark. If the S&P 500 Index is down 20 percent, and the active manager is only down 15 percent, then the active manager feels pleased with himself. The clients are supposed to feel pleased too, but they have lost real money. Hedge fund managers are active managers whose basic objective is to deliver a positive return, no matter what the background market environment may be like.

To achieve their objectives, hedge fund managers draw on an extensive tool kit. They use leverage, they sell short, and they use options, futures, and other hedging devices. They take advantage of a degree of investment freedom unavailable to more conventional investment managers.

Hedge funds also have distinctive business practices. Unlike mutual funds, which are usually designed to serve a large number of small investors, hedge funds are designed to serve a small number of large investors. The minimum investment may easily be $1 million or more, so the investors will be wealthy individuals or institutions, who are supposed to be "sophisticated investors." Moreover, the manager's fee is not merely based on the size of the asset base, but on the performance of the assets. In a typical case, the money manager may charge 1 percent of the assets under management, plus 20 percent of the profits generated.

The title of this book is *All About Hedge Funds*, which sounds as if it will tell you everything you always wanted to know about hedge funds. But the book won't tell you everything that you want to know. And it will tell you some things that you need to know, even though you may not want to know them.

As for the first point, the main thing that you won't find in this book is a lot of stories. This book is not an "invest-and-tell" exposé. We will make no attempt to go behind the scenes as Long Term Capital Management unraveled. We will have no colorful tales about George Soros's speculation against the British pound, or about what really happened inside the Internet funds as the technology bubble collapsed. Why this reticence?

The author of this book is the chief investment officer of a firm that has been involved in the world of hedge funds for more than 25 years. Our business is to invest in hedge funds on behalf of large clients seeking attractive absolute returns. A typical client portfolio will be invested in 20 or more hedge funds, diversified across a range of strategies and styles. Some of the hedge funds in which we invest are high-profile firms whose names appear from time to time in the newspaper; others are low-profile firms who struggle to remain below the radar screen of the press and the investment community. The low-profile firms labor quietly in the shadows while other firms grab the headlines. To invest effectively for our clients, we need to pre-

serve the best possible relationship with the hedge fund community—hence our reticence with regard to names, stories, and so forth.
We will leave the colorful stories to others.

As for the second point, you cannot understand hedge funds
by looking only at hedge funds. Hedge funds are an essential part of
a larger financial environment. To understand hedge funds, you have
to understand how they fit into that environment. People often say
that Wall Street is a jungle, meaning that it is a highly competitive, kill-
or-be-killed environment. But Wall Street is also a jungle in a more fundamental sense: It is a complicated system in which there are many
different kinds of firms, each playing a different role, or occupying a
different "ecological niche." The competition is fierce. But there is
also cooperation and many symbiotic relationships—situations in
which firms, and people, depend on each other for survival. Part of
the strategy of this book is to use the hedge fund community as a
lens through which to view the larger system.

The book is divided into many bite-sized pieces, to facilitate
easy digestion. In the introduction we concentrate on the differences
between hedge funds and mutual funds, with special attention to
the contrast between absolute return and relative return and the very
wide variety of investment tools and techniques required to pursue
absolute return. Part One places hedge funds within a broader historical and institutional context. Why are people so interested in
hedge funds after the extraordinary bull market in U.S. equities that
ran from 1982 to 2000? How did hedge funds get started? How do
hedge funds fit into the financial community? Who invests in hedge
funds, and why? Who manages hedge funds, and why? How do
hedge funds fit into the larger community of stockbrokers, investment bankers, and other denizens of Wall Street? Part Two places
hedge funds within the context of a larger debate about active investment management, passive management (the world of index funds),
and efficient financial markets. The active versus passive debate has
been raging for many years, and you can't understand hedge funds
without understanding how to place them within that debate. Part
Three looks inside the hedge fund tool kit at leverage, short selling,
futures, options, and some of the specialized trading strategies practiced by hedge funds. Part Four looks at some peripheral issues that
are not strictly investment related but have an impact on investment
issues. The list here includes performance fees, legal and regulato-

ry structures, and tax issues. Finally, Part Five takes a look at the full menu of hedge fund strategies, with special attention to the great diversity that exists within the world of hedge funds.

Every book is based on certain beliefs, convictions, and prejudices. There are three main convictions that I should declare forthrightly upfront.

First, hedge funds are an essential part of the global financial system, not just a sideshow that occasionally makes for entertaining reading. Hedge funds represent the cutting edge of active investment management. Some people say that passive management is the only money management strategy that makes sense, that active management is no better than astrology. But this can't be right. If markets are efficient, it's only because a lot of smart people, investing a lot of money, are actively seeking attractive investment opportunities. If index funds make sense, it is only because index funds can take advantage of prices that have been set by active managers. If every single equity investor became a passive investor, markets would become ludicrously inefficient.

Second, hedge funds can be an extremely useful portion of a broadly diversified portfolio that also includes stocks (both domestic and foreign, both large and small), bonds, and other investments. The main advantage of hedge funds is that the sources of return and risk are very different from the factors that drive return and risk in a more conventional stock and bond portfolio. Bond returns are driven entirely by the course of interest rates. Stock returns are driven partly by interest rates but also by economic growth, growth of corporate profits, and related factors. Hedge funds have the ability to sell short and to engage in other hedging strategies, so they have the potential to do well when conventional stock and bond portfolios are not doing so well. Their diversification potential can be quite powerful.

Hedge funds are not for everybody. Most investors are ineligible to invest in hedge funds. Other investors, including those who have a long investment horizon and a high tolerance for the volatility of standard equity investing, will have no need for the higher fees and additional complexities of hedge funds. In effect, these investors do not need the diversifying power of hedge funds. But many investors are thinking about allocating 5 percent of their assets to hedge funds, and many other investors have had 25 percent allocations to hedge funds for many years.

Third, the category of hedge funds is remarkably diverse. The term *hedge fund* is like the term *mutual fund*: Each term covers a wide and varied territory. There are high-risk hedge funds that charge outrageous fees and are managed by people who have a dangerously high opinion of themselves. There are lower-risk funds with less outrageous fees, run by people who worry constantly that their information, or analysis, may be flawed. There are hedge fund managers that push the legal and regulatory envelopes in their pursuit of exceptional returns and hedge fund managers that look like Boy Scouts in comparison. Some people will tell you that hedge fund managers are automatically smarter than mutual fund managers, or more aggressive, or greedier. None of this is true.

This book is written for two main types of reader. First, the book should be of interest to "the general reader": the intelligent layperson who wants to know more about hedge funds. Given the increasing amount of attention being paid to hedge funds and their growing role in the financial world, an informed citizen needs to know more than what can be learned from newspapers.

Second, the book should be helpful to the individual who is thinking about making an investment in a hedge fund, or a portfolio of hedge funds. Thanks to the bull market in U.S. equities that began in the early 1980s, more and more individuals are wealthier than they ever expected to be. Many of these individuals satisfy the financial requirements for investing in hedge funds. At the same time, the financial community is likely to become more and more innovative in bringing hedge fund strategies to the ordinary retail investor. Even now, mutual fund regulations allow a mutual fund manager to exploit, within well-defined limits, strategies that are normally associated with hedge funds. And there are more complicated mutual fund structures that permit the ordinary investor to get closer and closer to pure hedge fund investing. The person who is thinking about investing in hedge funds needs solid information about the return potential, and the risk profile, of hedge funds. This book is designed to provide that information.

We have already warned you that this book is not a collection of juicy stories. This book is also not a get-rich-quick book or a book on how to survive the coming financial disaster. The title is not "How to Double Your Money in Two Years with Your Own Portfolio of Hedge Funds," or "How to Survive the Coming Depression with

Hedge Funds," or "How to Survive the Coming Hyperinflation with Hedge Funds." Readers have an insatiable appetite for such books, but this book isn't one of them. Indeed, this book does not really offer any "investment advice" in the usual sense. There are no exhortations to favor stocks over bonds, or value over growth, or small cap stocks over large cap stocks. The book will not even encourage you to put 10 percent (or 5 percent, or 25 percent) of your assets into hedge funds. In general, you should be suspicious about books that claim to offer "investment advice." Wall Street professionals often point out that most investments are sold, not bought. And most dispensers of investment advice have something to sell. The best investment advice is to be very wary of all investment advice. So the object of the book is to give you some information and a framework for thinking about the issues. The rest is up to you.

Finally, this book is not a mathematical treatise filled with complicated formulas bristling with Greek letters. It is a book written for the general reader. But even the general reader needs to understand, and can understand, some basic statistical concepts that have become an essential part of investment thinking. The investment business has become increasingly quantitative and mathematical in the last 50 years or so, so it is hard to understand what is going on in the business without spending at least a little time on the arithmetic. But there is no higher mathematics in the book, and the patient reader should be able to understand everything in these pages.

Still, some parts will be harder than others. Part Two, which focuses on the efficient market theory and related ideas, will be tough sledding for some readers. But if you take your time, you'll understand everything. The other chapters worth mentioning are Chapter 9, which includes an explanation of short selling, and Chapter 17, which includes an explanation of convertible hedging. These two topics have an unusual ability to turn people's brains to jelly. But the basic ideas are very simple, so even here you'll do just fine.

A little arithmetic can be very useful, but too much arithmetic can be dangerous. That is the clear lesson of the Long Term Capital Management crisis. Extreme mathematical sophistication is not sufficient for investment success, and it can even breed a particularly dramatic kind of failure. Nor is extreme mathematical sophistication necessary for successful investing. Investing is not mathematics, but it isn't magic either. Successful investing requires common sense, a healthy degree of skepticism, and a powerful respect for the ability of markets to punish those who think that they have everything figured out.

In the end, what protects you from your mistakes is humility and diversification. Companies go bankrupt, but people still invest in stocks and bonds. The failure of Enron is a dramatic reminder of the need to be cautious, not a reason for avoiding all investments in stocks and bonds. Similarly, the various well-publicized hedge fund disasters do not provide a general argument against investing in hedge funds. The disasters provide an argument for caution, careful due diligence, plus diversification to protect you from your inevitable mistakes.

George Soros, one of the great hedge fund investors of all times, is responsible for one of the great investment observations of all time: "It's not whether you're right or wrong, but how much money you make when you're right and how much you lose when you're wrong." Only the most aggressive and competitive investors spend a lot of time thinking about how much they make when they're right. But all of us need to worry about how much we lose when we're wrong.

One final point, related to men, women, and hedge funds. The hedge fund world, like many other parts of the investment world, is still a male-dominated world. But that is gradually changing. There are many hedge funds where the key investment personality is a woman. And there are many funds where the senior business-person is a woman. In describing the world of hedge funds, it would be misleading to say "he" all the time, even if you explicitly state that "he" means "he or she." The same problem applies to "she." And it's very cumbersome to say "he or she" all the time. So we'll go back and forth between the two. Some readers will find this solution annoying, but it is less unsatisfactory than the alternatives.

ACKNOWLEDGMENTS

This book was written by one person to share a body of knowledge and experience that belongs to a team of people. Our firm has been active in hedge fund investing since the 1970s, when the hedge fund team consisted of one person, Bill (William J.) Crerend, who founded the firm. The team now comprises about 35 people, many of whom have helped with this project. I owe special thanks to Bill Crerend, Phil Maisano, Joe McGowan, and Anna Meena. Each of them has been indispensable, in different ways. I also thank Bill (William C.) Crerend, Tracey Hayes, Andrew Mylott, Mark Burston, Patrick Moriarty, and Peter Gwiazdowski for various kinds of help.

Numerous experts, and nonexperts, outside our firm have also been helpful. The expert category includes Tom Schneeweis and George Martin, of the Center for International Securities and Derivatives Markets at the University of Massachusetts at Amherst, who have been in the middle of many conversations about hedge funds and efficient markets. The nonexpert category includes several friends, who are not in the investment business, who volunteered to act as experimental subjects in determining how the mythical "general reader" would react to this book. I thank Russ Abrams, John Bahde, Holbrook Robinson, and Jane Taylor for helpful comments on earlier versions of this book.

There is a familiar kind of horror movie in which a friendly stranger turns up on the doorstep of an unsuspecting family. The family welcomes the stranger into the household, whereupon the stranger gradually turns into a monster who terrorizes the entire family. I thank my wife, Patricia, for heroic levels of patience and courage as this book, which initially seemed to be such a friendly visitor, gradually took over our household. We are both very pleased that the visitor has moved from our house to your house.

The Basic Themes

Hedge funds represent a distinctive investment style. Their investment objectives, and their strategies, are very different from more traditional funds. They emphasize absolute return rather than relative return, and they use a very wide range of investment techniques—including leverage, short selling, and other hedging strategies—in the attempt to achieve their objectives.

Hedge funds also represent a distinctive investment culture. Hedge fund management firms tend to be small firms dominated by one or two key investment people. The hedge fund culture is part of the "smaller-is-better" culture. In addition, hedge funds give a new twist to the relationship between the money manager and the client. The client does not merely hire the manager. Instead, the client and the manager become partners, coinvesting in situations that the manager finds attractive.

Finally, hedge funds often use distinctive "delivery systems" to make their strategies available to investors. The hedge fund could take the form of a limited partnership, an offshore fund, a commodity pool, or a specialized kind of separate account. Hedge funds do not typically use the mutual fund structure since this structure does not give the hedge fund manager enough freedom.

To introduce the basic themes that separate the world of hedge funds from the world of traditional investment management, we will focus on hedge funds that are structured as limited partnerships and traditional money management strategies that are delivered in the form of a mutual fund. (Table I–1.) As we mentioned in the preface, both of these categories are quite broad and include extremely diverse investment opportunities. Within the mutual fund universe, there is a world of difference between a money market mutual fund and an equity fund that specializes in small cap Latin American equities. Within the hedge fund universe, there is a world of difference between a market-neutral equity hedge fund that specializes in U.S. utility stocks and a trend-following global asset allocator who takes highly leveraged positions, either long or short, in global financial markets as well as physical commodity markets. But there are nonetheless some basic differences that separate the two worlds. This chapter is a quick review of the basic contrasts.

INVESTMENT OBJECTIVES

Most equity mutual funds and most hedge funds are designed to deliver long-term growth of capital. The fundamental objective is to

TABLE I–1

Hedge Funds Versus Mutual Funds

	Hedge Funds	Mutual Funds
Objective	Absolute return	Relative return
Strategies	Wide freedom, including leverage, short selling, other hedging strategies	Limitations on leverage, short selling, etc.
Primary sources of return and risk	Strategy and manager	Market
Cultural style	Lean and mean	Large and cumbersome
Liquidity	Limitations on investment and redemption	Daily liquidity
Marketing	Limitations on marketing and selling	Broad access to retail market
Business relationship	Manager and client coinvest as partners	Manager is agent for client
Fees	Asset-based and performance-based	Asset-based only
Taxation	Pass-through entity, no tax at fund level	No tax at fund level if all income distributed

deliver a return that will exceed the inflation rate over the investment period, so that the real purchasing power of the investment will increase over time. Some funds are more aggressive than others, some are more tolerant of volatility than others, but the basic idea is to make the investors' assets grow. Equity mutual funds do this by investing in the stock market, which has an upward bias over long time periods.

The investment management business is a very competitive business in which the objective is to beat some target rate of return. For an equity mutual fund, there are two targets: first, the rate of return achieved by competing money managers and second, the return of some relevant market index.

Thus the money manager first wants to do better than other managers, or, more specifically, he wants to do better than other managers who belong to his "style category" or "strategy category." The large cap value manager wants to beat other large cap value managers but doesn't mind lagging behind some small cap growth managers. Second, the money manager wants to beat some passive benchmark, such as the S&P 500 or the Wilshire 5000. The *passive benchmark* represents the performance of the basic market that the fund is investing in. If the manager earns 10 percent when the passive benchmark earns 8 percent, he feels good. If the manager loses 8 percent when the index loses 10 percent, the manager also feels good, even though the investor has lost money. What this means is that the money manager is trying to deliver good relative performance: performance that is good relative to a passive benchmark that may, in fact, experience negative returns. But you can't spend *relative performance:* If the index is down 10 percent and you, the investor, are down 8 percent, you have still lost money.

What defines the hedge fund business is that the hedge fund manager cares only about *absolute return.* The purpose of a hedge fund is to earn a positive return, which is totally different from beating a benchmark. A risk-averse manager might be trying to earn 10 to 12 percent annually (after all fees), while a more aggressive manager might be trying to earn 15 to 20 percent. But in both cases the object of the game is to generate a positive number. Sometimes the hedge fund manager may say that he is trying to earn a premium over some short-term interest rate, such as the rate paid on Treasury bills or the London Interbank Offered Rate (LIBOR) or something similar. But these short-term interest rate benchmarks will always be positive numbers. The hedge fund manager who is trying to beat those benchmarks is automatically committed to delivering a positive rate of return.

The hedge fund manager wants to deliver a positive rate of return, while standard market benchmarks are sometimes positive and sometimes negative. So the hedge fund manager is looking for returns that do not depend on what the standard markets are doing. If a hedge fund manager is successful in delivering this objective, then that manager's fund will be an "all-weather fund," or "good for all seasons." Statisticians will say that the objective of the hedge fund manager is to deliver returns that have a *low correlation* with the standard stock and bond markets. (We will return to the concept of correlation in Chapter 7.) Needless to say, this is a tall order, and many hedge fund managers fail to deliver the goods. But at least everybody agrees from the start what the objective is: to earn an attractive positive return. If a hedge fund manager is down 12 percent, he cannot point to some benchmark and say, "Well, the index was down 15 percent, so I beat the index by 3 percent." That excuse is removed from the start. The hedge fund manager walks the tightrope without a safety net.

INVESTMENT STRATEGIES

The basic business of the equity mutual fund manager is to buy good stocks, so that the fund will beat the passive benchmark and beat the competition. But mutual funds operate under specific rules defined by the Securities and Exchange Commission (typically referred to as the SEC), and these rules limit the manager's freedom of movement. The most important limitations relate to leverage, short selling, and diversification. *Leverage* is buying stocks on margin—that is, using borrowed money to buy more stock than you can pay for with your own money. *Short selling* is a strategy designed to take advantage of falling prices: You borrow stock, sell it, then buy it back at a lower price and return the stock you borrowed. *Diversification* is not putting all your eggs in one basket. Mutual funds must follow SEC rules of diversification, and they must observe limitations on leverage and short selling.

In contrast, the hedge fund manager can do almost anything that she wants to do. (I say "almost" because the hedge fund manager is still subject to other rules, separate from the SEC's mutual fund rules.) She can use leverage, she can sell short, she can use other hedging strategies, or she can take very concentrated positions in single stocks, or industries, or trading ideas.

Just as mutual fund managers set out their investment objectives and strategies in a *prospectus*, hedge fund managers set out their objectives and strategies in an *offering memorandum*. But mutual fund prospectuses tend to define the fund's mission fairly narrowly. For example, a mutual fund objective might be to achieve long-term growth of capital by investing in growth stocks in the United States. The offering memorandum for a hedge fund, in contrast, will define its mission very broadly: The mission is to make money by taking long or short positions in stocks, bonds, and related instruments.

Since mutual funds are regulated by the SEC and hedge funds are not, it may seem that hedge funds are automatically more risky than mutual funds. This is not necessarily so. In the final analysis, the risk of a portfolio is determined by the skill and the risk tolerance of the person, or team of people, managing the portfolio. It is possible to build a very risky portfolio that conforms to all applicable SEC regulations, and it is possible to build a very risk-averse portfolio using the freedom afforded in the world of hedge funds. So the challenge for the hedge fund investor is to make sure that he invests with managers who know how to use the freedom that is available to them. And, ultimately, even the best managers may misuse the freedom that is available to them. So diversification across multiple managers is an essential form of protection.

SOURCES OF RETURN AND RISK

For an equity mutual fund, return is determined largely by three factors: the performance of the *market* that the manager invests in; the performance of the manager's *strategy* (sometimes referred to as *investment style*); and the level of *skill* that the manager brings to bear. The most important single factor is the performance of the market. When stocks, in general, are down, most equity managers have a tough time making money. But investment outcomes may still vary according to the various styles and strategies used by different managers. For example, 2001 was a difficult year for U.S. stocks: The S&P 500 was down 11.9 percent. But the Nasdaq Composite, which had more exposure to the technology sector, was down 20.7 percent, and the Russell 2000, representing the small cap sector, was up 2.5 percent. As a matter of fact, the Russell 2000 Value Index was up 14.0 percent. Value managers did much better than growth managers in 2001, unlike prior years in which growth did much better than value.

For a hedge fund manager, the market drops out as a source of return, leaving just two factors: *strategy* and *skill*. The market drops out largely because the hedge fund manager has the ability to take either long positions or short positions. *Long positions* are positions that make money when the price of the security goes up, while *short positions* are positions that make money when the price goes down. Short selling gives the hedge fund manager the ability—or at least the opportunity—to make money in down markets. And this means, of course, that the hedge fund manager also has the ability (or at least the opportunity) to lose money in up markets. So even if a hedge fund manager makes money in an up market, the reason that she made money was not that the market went up. She made money because she decided to be invested in a portfolio of long positions, poised to make money from a rise in prices. Equity mutual fund managers don't *decide* to be long. Being long is their business.

CULTURAL STYLE

There are some very large hedge funds and some very small mutual funds, but in general, hedge funds are smaller than mutual funds. The size difference emerges in two ways: Hedge fund *portfolios* tend to be smaller than mutual fund portfolios, and hedge fund *firms* tend to be smaller than mutual fund firms.

There are many mutual funds with asset bases in the range of $50 billion to $100 billion. But there are no hedge funds in that size category. In the hedge fund world, $5 billion is an unusually large amount of money. Most managers are running funds in the range between $100 million and $1 billion. And there are many funds under $10 million. However, the basic economics of the hedge fund business are such that small funds can still be extremely profitable for the small number of people involved in running the fund. The compensation arrangement in hedge funds is designed to further a smaller-is-better philosophy.

Because hedge funds are smaller than mutual funds, they can trade more nimbly than their larger counterparts, and they can take positions in small situations that would be off limits to very large funds. This does not mean that all hedge funds are hyperactive traders; there are funds specializing in classic long-term, low-turnover investing. But most hedge funds are fairly active traders, making a sustained effort to respond quickly to new information. Large mutual funds are like aircraft carriers, hard to maneuver in tight spaces. Indeed, until 1998 the Securities and Exchange Commission placed a definite limitation (the so-called *short short rule*) on the ability of a mutual fund to seek short-term trading profits.

Hedge fund management firms also tend to be smaller than mutual fund management firms, with an organizational structure that is very flat and designed to enable the firm to respond quickly to new information. Most hedge funds are organized around one or two key investment professionals who are the "stars" of the investment show. Although some mutual funds are managed by small firms organized around one or two stars, more commonly the mutual fund is managed by a larger organization whose performance is attributed to "the company" or "the process," not to a star investor. Indeed, in many cases mutual funds are managed by large banks, insurance companies, or brokerage firms, with elaborate committee structures specifically designed to prevent the emergence of a star system.

BUSINESS RELATIONSHIP

When you invest in a mutual fund, you are hiring somebody to manage your money. When you invest in a hedge fund, you are entering into a partnership with the manager of the fund: You and the money manager are coinvestors. The mutual fund manager may have no personal assets at all invested in the fund that he is running. In contrast, the hedge fund manager should have a major personal investment in the fund that he is running. Part of the allure of hedge funds is the opportunity to "invest alongside a star." The fundamental premise of hedge fund investing resembles a caveat from another industry: You should eat only in those restaurants where the chef eats his own cooking.

Most U.S. hedge funds are organized as *limited partnerships*. The hedge fund manager acts as the general partner of the partnership and bears the ultimate responsibility for managing the portfolio and managing the business of the partnership. The investors in the partnership are the *limited partners*. The limited partners are called "limited partners" because their liability is limited: They can lose their entire investment, but they cannot lose anything more than that. Their liability is limited to the amount of their investment. The *general partner*, in theory, bears unlimited liability. For this reason, most hedge fund managers form corporate entities to serve as the general partner of their hedge fund partnerships. This is merely a prudent business practice, not an evasion of responsibility. After all, most doctors set up their businesses as "professional corporations" precisely to avoid the unlimited personal liability that would otherwise arise.

The manager of a hedge fund should have a substantial portion of his net worth invested in the fund. Ideally, the general partner will have no outside equity investments. The manager might own a portfolio of Treasury bonds, or municipal bonds, or real estate, but he will have no equity investments outside the fund. In particular, investors should be cautious about hedge fund managers who invest actively outside the fund that they manage. Situations like this create opportunities for *front running*, which is a specific conflict-of-interest abuse. For example, the manager might buy stock in XYZ company in his own account, then buy XYZ in the hedge fund, thus driving up the price. Then the manager can sell XYZ at a profit in his own account, and finally sell XYZ in the fund, either at a profit or at a loss. In this situation the manager is illegally using client assets to create personal trading profits.

In most successful hedge funds, the general partner is a wealthy individual whose investment in the fund is a significant portion of the fund. In many cases, the general partner of the fund is the single largest investor in the fund. When a young money manager starts a new hedge fund, the manager's personal investment may be small when measured in dollars, but it should still be significant relative to the manager's net worth. Individuals and institutions who invest in hedge funds should be very careful to examine the level of the manager's personal investment in the fund. If the money manager is not willing to take the risk of the fund, the investor shouldn't either. The chef should enjoy his own cooking.

When investors analyze the stocks of ordinary operating companies, they often look for situations in which management has a substantial ownership stake in the company. This equity stake should be in the form of real equity, not just stock options. When management owns real equity, management is exposed both to the rewards of success and to the penalties of failure. Stock options reward success, but they do not penalize failure. The hedge fund manager should have both "upside risk" and "downside risk."

Even when the hedge fund manager has a substantial personal investment in his own fund, it still cannot be guaranteed that the fund will do well or will avoid unnecessary risks. There are hedge fund managers whose risk tolerance is greater than that of their clients. These managers are willing to take risks with their own capital that the limited partners are not willing to take. The hedge fund manager's substantial personal investment in the fund is not an infallible risk control mechanism.

LIQUIDITY AND MARKETING

The mutual fund manager makes a deal with the general public and the SEC. She wants to sell her fund to the broadest possible audience. In exchange for this freedom, the mutual fund manager is required to offer daily liquidity and is required to operate within SEC limitations on investment strategies and activity. In other words, the mutual fund manager wants to have the broadest possible freedom in *marketing* and must therefore accept substantial limitations in *investing*.

Mutual funds offer the ultimate in liquidity. Investors can put their money in, and take their money out, on a daily basis. And the funds can advertise their strategies, and their results, to a broad market of retail investors who can contribute small amounts of money and do not have to satisfy any specific requirements of wealth or financial sophistication.

The price of access to the retail market is adherence to a complex set of restrictions on investment freedom. There are restrictions regarding leverage, short selling, and concentration (the opposite of diversification). And there are restrictions on investing in illiquid securities because the mutual fund is itself a totally liquid investment that offers its investors access to their capital on a daily basis, with no advance notice.

The SEC imposes these restrictions to protect the investing public. The restrictions do not eliminate risk: An emerging-markets equity fund can be very risky, even while following all the SEC rules.

But the rules do at least attempt to limit activities that would increase the risk of the portfolio.

The hedge fund manager makes a deal that is exactly opposite to the mutual fund deal. The hedge fund manager wants maximum freedom in investing the assets of the fund, in exchange for which he accepts very substantial limitations on marketing and liquidity. As for liquidity, some hedge funds allow money to come in and go out only annually. Indeed, some very successful funds require that capital be committed for two or three years or more. Other funds are geared to a quarterly or monthly cycle. Daily liquidity does not exist in the hedge fund universe. As for marketing, the basic objective of the hedge fund manager is to attract a small number of large investors rather than a large number of small investors. The investors will be wealthy individuals, or institutions, that satisfy specific net worth requirements.

Although the hedge fund manager accepts marketing restrictions, these restrictions have definite marketing advantages. The liquidity restrictions mean that the investors' capital is "locked up" for longer time periods. And the small number of large investors means that the hedge fund is an "exclusive" investment vehicle that has some special cachet. On top of all this, the hedge fund manager gains the freedom to use leverage, to sell short, to hedge with a wide variety of derivative instruments (options, futures, and so on), to hold concentrated positions, to hold illiquid investments, and so forth. No wonder money managers dream about setting up their own hedge funds.

PERFORMANCE FEES

In most mutual funds, the money manager earns a fee based entirely on the size of the assets under management. In an equity fund, for example, the fee might be between 0.5 and 1.0 percent of the assets in the fund. This arrangement is great for the money manager since the cost of running a $2 billion portfolio is not 10 times the cost of running a $200 million portfolio. The money management business is a clear example of *operating leverage*. When assets grow, the revenues grow faster than the expenses, so profit growth can be very handsome indeed. But this also means that the mutual fund business rewards size more directly than it rewards performance. A fund that performs well will attract additional assets, but there is no direct financial link between the fund's performance and the manager's compensation. This means that the mutual fund business is sometimes more focused on *gathering* assets than on *managing* assets.

In the hedge fund business there is a direct connection between performance and the manager's compensation. The hedge fund manager does earn an asset-based fee, which is typically 1 percent of the assets under management but which can sometimes be higher or lower. But the hedge fund manager usually also earns a performance-based fee: a percentage of the profits earned by the partnership. This fee is usually 20 percent of the profits, but it can be higher or lower. So, for example, if a hedge fund is up 20 percent in a single year, then the hedge fund manager would earn 20 percent of 20 percent, which is 4 percent of the underlying assets. If a hedge fund manager is successful, he has the potential to earn very handsome fees on a relatively small asset base. The performance fee arrangement means that the hedge fund manager has a greater incentive to keep an eye on managing assets rather than gathering assets.

The question naturally arises whether the performance fee creates an incentive to take undue risk. After all, performance fees are like management stock options. In each case, the manager (of the hedge fund or the corporation) can reap huge rewards without taking on the risk of real loss. The hedge fund manager can earn millions of dollars if returns are strong. If returns aren't strong, the manager may lose investors and may jeopardize the business, but he will not have to write a check for millions of dollars. So it might seem that the manager has a substantial incentive to take big risks. In fact, however, most hedge fund managers are "long-term greedy" rather than "short-term greedy." They want to earn a performance fee based on many years of annual profits, not a quick hit on outsized returns in the first year or two. Making a quick hit usually requires taking a level of risk that the manager would prefer not to take. We will return to this question later, in Chapter 13.

TAXATION

Mutual funds and hedge funds are both "pass-through entities" with respect to taxation. The funds themselves do not pay taxes, but investors in the funds pay taxes on their share of interest, dividends, and realized gains. Mutual funds earn this pass-through status by distributing annually to their investors 95 percent of the taxable income earned by the fund. The investors then have a choice: They can keep the distribution, or they can reinvest the distribution in the fund. In either case, the mutual fund investor owes taxes on the distribution. If the mutual fund does not distribute its taxable income, then the mutual fund itself will be vulnerable to taxes, which is an outcome that no mutual fund manager wants.

A limited partnership is, by its very nature, a pass-through entity that owes no taxes on the taxable income that it produces. This is true even if the hedge fund does not distribute any of its taxable income. And, generally speaking, hedge funds do not make regular distributions to their investors. Interest income, dividend income, and realized gains are retained within the fund. But the hedge fund investor owes taxes on her share of the taxable income even if that amount is not literally distributed. If a hedge fund investor wants access to her invested capital, she must redeem some or all of her ownership interest in the fund.

Many years ago, when the tax laws were very different from what they are today, limited partnerships were often designed to serve as tax shelters. The basic idea was to produce an investment that generated large tax deductions without necessarily generating large economic returns. In some circumstances, the value of the tax deductions was even greater than the value of the original investment. These limited partnerships generally had high investment management fees and sales commissions, produced no real economic return, and, in the worst case scenario, left the investor arguing with tax authorities about the legitimacy of the deductions. In short, limited partnerships got a very bad reputation.

A hedge fund is a totally different kind of animal. It is a limited partnership, but it is designed to produce an economic return, not a tax benefit. Indeed, hedge funds have to struggle against various built-in tax disadvantages. First, hedge funds generally trade more actively than mutual funds. This is part of the nimbler-is-better approach. Most hedge funds do not strive for high tax efficiency because they think that the skill of the manager will produce a pretax return high enough that the after-tax return will still be attractive. We will return to this topic in Chapter 14, where we will distinguish between *annual tax efficiency* and *total tax efficiency*. A fund with high annual efficiency builds up unrealized appreciation from year to year. But most investors realize the appreciation sooner or later. Total tax efficiency takes into account the impact of that final sale. A fund that looks inefficient on an annual basis can be highly efficient when you include the impact of the final sale. In fact, the recent obsession with "low-turnover, tax-efficient investing" tends to overlook the long-term picture.

Second, tax accounting for hedge fund investments can be cumbersome. Mutual funds report their taxable income to investors on a Form 1099 DIV, which is generally available within a month or two of the end of the calendar year. Hedge funds, on the other hand, produce a Schedule K-1 (Form 1065), which can be a multipage document reporting a large number of taxable items. The complexity of a K-1 reflects the fact that the hedge fund investor is, in effect, investing in a business, not merely investing in a portfolio. Moreover, some hedge funds experience substantial delays in producing their K-1s. These delays may be traced to the complexities of the fund's investing or the fund's failure to manage the tax process properly or other causes. In any event, the K-1 may not arrive in time for the standard April 15 filing deadline, forcing the investor to file for an extension. Taxable investors who are fastidious about avoiding extensions should either avoid hedge funds altogether or question their hedge fund managers very closely on their ability to deliver K-1s in a timely fashion.

We have covered a long list of features that distinguish hedge funds from mutual funds. To organize these contrasts better, in Table I–2 we have separated the hedge fund features into advantages and disadvantages, benefits and costs. Those who invest in hedge funds are willing to pay the costs in order to enjoy the benefits.

And so we face the classic investment problem: Are the benefits worth the costs? There is no general answer to this question. The object of this book is to enable you to form a clearer picture of the benefits and the costs. Then you will have to decide for yourself. And the decision will depend, in part, on the performance of the standard investment markets. When stocks and bonds are performing well, it is easy to conclude that the benefits are not worth the costs. When conventional markets are less friendly, the balance begins to tip in favor of hedge funds.

When the great bull market of 1982 to 2000 was roaring ahead, hedge funds were of interest mainly to ultra-aggressive investors, who wanted returns even higher than those available in a red-hot

TABLE I-2

TABLE I-2

Benefits and Costs of Hedge Funds

	Benefits	Costs
Objective	Absolute return objective: opportunity to outperform in down market.	May underperform in up markets.
Strategies	Manager has total freedom.	There is a high degree of manager-specific risk.
Cultural style	Small organizations can respond quickly to changes.	Results are highly dependent on one or two key people.
Fees	Performance fee creates incentive to emphasize performance over asset growth.	Performance fee may create incentive to take risk.
Liquidity	Money manager does not have to cope with daily cash flows.	Some investors prefer daily access to capital.

equity market, or to risk-averse investors, who wanted some protection from a change in the broader market environment. Change is now upon us. The tech bubble started to deflate in March 2000, and the attacks in September 2001 created tremendous geopolitical uncertainty. In 2002, the Enron scandal and subsequent episodes of corporate misbehavior undermined investor confidence even further. In this new environment, many investors are less willing to believe that the standard markets will deliver returns that meet their objectives. Hence the growing interest in hedge funds.

PART ONE

The Historical and Institutional Context

CHAPTER I

The Historical Context

This chapter provides some historical background for what is now going on in the world of hedge funds. The first part of the chapter focuses on how hedge funds fit into the recent 20-year bull market in U.S. equities. The last part of the chapter is a brief history of hedge funds.

ECONOMIC CYCLES FROM 1926 TO 2001

To understand the current level of interest in hedge funds, both among individuals and institutions, it is essential to appreciate the extraordinary bull market in U.S. equities that began in 1982. And to appreciate that bull market, it is necessary to consider its historical context. We will begin our story in 1926 since the required data are either nonexistent or of low quality prior to that date.

Investors worry about all sorts of economic and financial variables, but two of the most important variables are inflation and growth. The *inflation rate* is the rate at which the cost of living is going up. Inflation is a critical variable for two reasons. First, most investors' goals are related to inflation. They want their investments to do at least as well as the inflation rate so that they will at least preserve the real purchasing power of their assets. Second, financial markets respond to changes in the level of actual and expected inflation.

Growth is the rate of economic expansion. The broadest measure of growth is growth of *real gross domestic product* (GDP). GDP is the total value of all the goods and services produced by the economy. *Real GDP* is GDP measured in a way that takes into account the impact of inflation. To make a long story very short, GDP growth is driven by the growth of the workforce and the productivity of that workforce. The growth of the workforce is driven by population growth and the percentage of the population that is gainfully employed. The productivity of the workforce is determined by two factors: how hard people are working (for example, the number of hours people work per week) and how efficiently they are working.

Figure 1–1 shows the history of growth and inflation from 1926 to 2001. As you can see, growth and inflation rarely stand still. They move up and down in cycles. The inflation cycles are longer than the growth cycles. In Figure 1–1 you will see four very long cycles of rising and falling inflation. From 1926 to 1947 the economy moved from *deflation* (falling prices) to high inflation. Then inflation fell from 1948 to 1965. This was a period of *disinflation*: The inflation rate was positive, but trending downward. Then the inflation rate rose from 1966 to 1980, and fell from 1981 onward. The growth cycles are shorter, with multiple growth cycles falling within a single period of rising or falling inflation. In the 1930s and 1940s there were periods of severe contraction, but in the post–World War II era the contractions have been much more shallow. Notice that the expansion that lasted from 1991 to 2001 was unusually long and steady. Table 1–1 shows the relevant economic and financial data for the four main subperiods and the full period.

Figure 1–2 shows inflation and the level of the stock market, both before and after adjusting for inflation. This time, rather than showing the *rate* of inflation, we are showing the actual increase in the general level of prices. Then we show the level of the stock market, both before and after inflation. What we are showing is the value of $1 invested in the S&P 500 on January 1, 1926. The change in value reflects the impact of dividends, and the reinvestment of those dividends. The stock values are shown on what is called a *logarithmic scale*, where equal vertical distances represent equal *percentage* changes. The period from the mid-1960s through the 1970s is especially noteworthy since high inflation meant that the real return of stocks, after inflation, was close to zero.

In Figure 1–3 you will see inflation again, plus three new variables: short-term interest rates, long-term interest rates, and the earnings yield on U.S. equities. The *earnings yield* of a stock equals the current annual earnings on a share of a company's stock divided by the current price of a share of that stock. It is the inverse of the more

FIGURE 1–1

Year-over-Year Inflation and Real GDP
January 1926 through December 2001

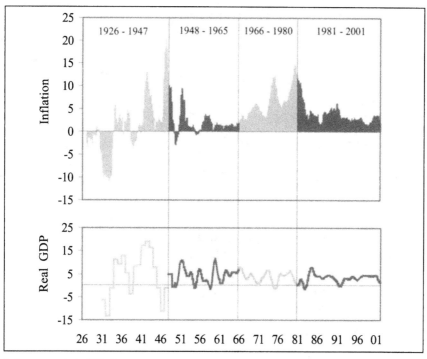

Performance results for GDP reflect data beginning January 1931.
Source: Ibbotson Associates and Bloomberg.

TABLE 1–1

U.S. Financial Markets Annualized Performance
January 1926 through December 2001

	1926–1947	1948–1965	1966–1980	1981–2001	1926–2001
U.S. stocks, nominal	6.3%	15.7%	6.7%	14.2%	10.7%
U.S. stocks, real	5.0	13.7	–0.1	10.3	7.4
U.S. bonds	3.5	2.4	5.5	9.9	5.3
U.S. T-bills	1.0	2.1	6.3	6.5	3.8
Inflation	1.2	1.7	6.9	3.5	3.1
Real GDP[*]	4.1	4.0	3.2	3.1	3.6

[*]Performance results for GDP reflect data beginning January 1931.
Source: Ibbotson Associates and Bloomberg.

FIGURE 1-2

U.S. Equity Versus Inflation
January 1926 through December 2001

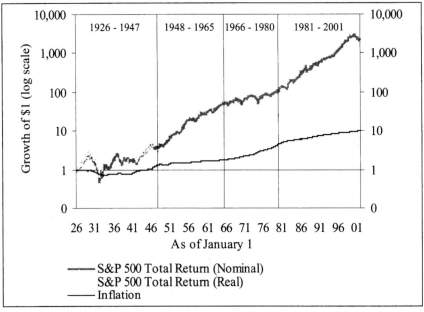

familiar price/earnings ratio. The advantage of thinking about earnings yield is that earnings yield is directly comparable to the yield on bonds and money market instruments.

The first period, from 1926 through 1947, includes both the Great Depression and World War II. During the depression, the economy contracted and prices fell. But gradually the country got back on its feet, the war began, the economy expanded, and inflation rose. At the end of the war the annual inflation rate was over 10 percent. But interest rates trended generally downward throughout this period, so that at the end of the period the prevailing interest rates were well below the level of inflation. This means that the *real yield* on fixed income investments was negative. During this period stocks returned 6.3 percent (annually compounded), compared to an inflation rate of 1.2 percent.

FIGURE 1–3

Inflation Versus Yields
January 1926 through December 2001

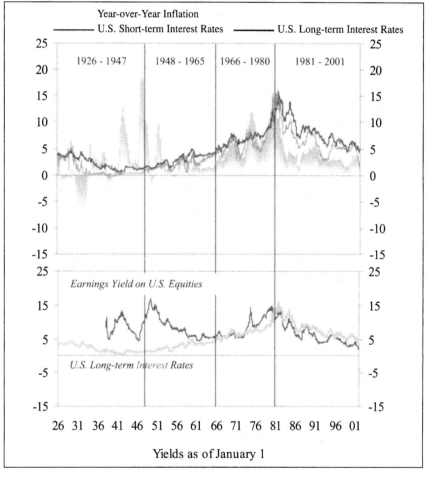

Source: Ibbotson Associates, Standard & Poor's, and Bloomberg.

The second period, from the end of World War II through the early 1960s, was a period of generally falling inflation. Inflation peaked at 20 percent immediately following the war and gradually worked its way below 2 percent by the early 1960s. But interest rates drifted upward despite the decline in inflation, so that real interest rates (that is, interest rates minus the inflation rate) rose slightly over this period. Notice the sharp decline in the earnings yield on equities during this period. Stocks performed exceptionally well, returning 15.7 percent, compared to an inflation rate of 1.7 percent.

From the mid-1960s through the early 1980s, inflation turned upward again. This was due partly to massive government spending earmarked for the war in Vietnam and for a broad variety of government-sponsored social programs. And then came the energy crises of the 1970s, when oil prices—and the prices of gold and other "hard assets"—shot up dramatically. In 1979 and 1980 the inflation rate exceeded 10 percent, and interest rates had moved up with the inflation rate. But, remarkably, interest rates never delivered any premium over the inflation rate. Even when inflation seemed to be totally out of control in the early 1980s, investors in fixed income instruments did not receive any *real* yield—that is, no yield after adjusting for the impact of inflation. Moreover, the earnings yield on equities rose steadily. A rising earnings yield means a falling price/earnings ratio, which means downward pressure on stock prices. Stocks returned 6.7 percent during this period, slightly below the inflation rate of 6.9 percent.

THE GREAT BULL MARKET

And so we come to the most recent period, from 1981 through the present, when the general trend in inflation has been downward. And, not surprisingly, the general trend in interest rates has also been downward. But as interest rates moved lower, they continued to deliver a premium over the inflation rate. What happened, in effect, is that a generation of investors was so traumatized by the inflationary 1970s that they said to themselves, "Never again." Thus was born the "bond market vigilante," the bond investor who is highly sensitive to the risk of inflation and demands a real premium for bearing the risk of inflation. The combination of bond market vigilantes with a Federal Reserve Board that was also highly sensitive to the risks of inflation kept inflation under control and kept economic growth within a relatively narrow band. Stocks performed exceptionally well over this period, delivering an annualized return of 14.2 percent. As the bull market persisted, the earnings yield on equities moved lower and lower, both in absolute terms and relative to the prevailing level of interest rates. The earnings yield on equities moved below long-term interest rates, and sometimes even moved below short-term rates. This phenomenon was one sign of a "shrinking risk premium" for owning equities.

The period from 1981 through 2001 includes the extraordinary bull market that ran from late 1982 into the early part of 2000, and then the more recent environment that includes both the "tech wreck" that began in early 2000 and the terrorist attacks of September 2001. Figure 1–4 shows annual returns for the S&P 500 and the Nasdaq Composite during this period.

During the first period, from 1981 through the early part of 1989, the driving theme was the end of inflation. The Federal Reserve moved decisively in the late 1970s to attack inflation, and when the new strategies showed signs of success in the early 1980s, financial markets rejoiced. The inflation rate came down, interest rates fell, and stock prices rose. Though there was a market crash in October 1987, the general investment environment was refreshingly benign.

Then, in December 1989, the environment got even better. The Berlin Wall came down, the cold war ended, and the world entered a new period of political stability. The new theme was "the peace

FIGURE 1–4

U.S. Equity Market
Annual Returns: January 1981 through December 2001

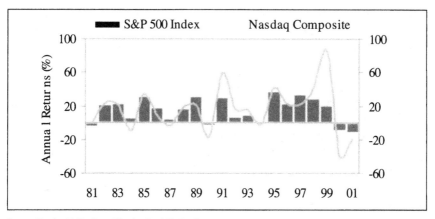

Source: Standard & Poor's and Nasdaq Stock Market, Inc.

dividend," as all the resources that had been devoted to the cold war were freed up for more peaceful purposes. Emerging markets investing became a major fad as investors foresaw that capitalist democracy would sweep across the world during an extended *Pax Americana*.

And then the environment got even better in the mid-1990s as the bull market entered a final manic phase driven by technology stocks. Investors embarked on a torrid affair with personal computers, the Internet, and other technological marvels that would boost productivity and generate outrageous profits for tech companies that were in the right place at the right time. Companies that were unlikely to show a profit for many years nevertheless attained absurd levels of valuation. The valuation bubble was threatened by anxiety about the so-called Y2K problem, which prompted the Federal Reserve Board to make available more than the usual amounts of liquidity. Thus reassured, the stock market held a colossal "end-of-the-millennium" party. The last years of the bull market were accompanied by repeated warnings from skeptics, including Alan Greenspan's famous "irrational exuberance" warning in December 1996. But the exuberance lasted for more than three years after the warning.

There is a venerable Wall Street saying: What can't go on forever, won't. And so it didn't. The technology euphoria came unglued in March and April of 2000. The Nasdaq fell 60.5 percent (unannualized) between April 2000 and August 2001. And then the coup de grace was administered by the terrorist attacks in September 2001. Stock markets were shut down for four days after the attacks, then declined 11.6 percent in the five days after reopening. The era of political tranquility that began with the fall of the Berlin Wall was decisively finished.

The stock market found a bottom on September 21 and performed well into early 2002. Then the Enron/Arthur Andersen scandal, and a string of similar corporate scandals, created a crisis of confidence. Many investors think that making money in a conventional stock portfolio will be harder for the next several years than it was during the great bull market. Over the full period from 1926 to 2001, stocks returned about 11 percent annually before inflation, about 7 percent after inflation. These figures include the two major disinflationary periods, 1948 to 1965 and 1981 to 2001, when returns (both nominal and real) were much higher than the long-term averages. Many observers think that returns will "revert to the mean," or go even lower. Hence the current interest in hedge funds, which offer the possibility of decent returns that do not depend on the performance of the broad U.S. stock market.

HEDGE FUNDS AND THE BULL MARKET

Making money in the bull market was easy, so vast portions of the U.S. population got hooked on the stock market. Some of this new interest in stocks was part of a healthy and growing "equity culture," in which more and more people invested in diversified stock portfolios through their individual retirement accounts (IRAs), 401(k) plans, and other investment accounts. But some of this interest was not healthy. Some people became obsessed with the stock market, even giving up their more conventional jobs to become day traders. The United States became a market-obsessed culture, in which people watched financial news on television and spent time at parties swapping stories about stocks, mutual funds, star portfolio managers, and so forth. Newspapers advertised mutual funds run by investment wizards who had compiled dazzling performance records. The financial pages became an extension of the sports pages as investors pored over the statistics, and the paychecks, of celebrated financial athletes.

This obsession with financial celebrities coexisted with an opposite phenomenon: the rise of the index fund. An index fund makes no attempt to outsmart the market. Its sole objective is to track the market. Index funds have extremely low investment management fees, and they appeal to investors—both retail and institutional—who are cynical about the ability of "active managers" to outperform the markets in which they invest. In a bull market, even an index fund will produce decent returns. And, in a certain kind of bull market, index funds will produce exceptional returns, even better than the typical active manager. And this is exactly what happened in the final stages of the recent bull market. The technology sector became a larger and larger component of the S&P 500, the most widely followed stock index. And the technology sector became increasingly dominated by a small number of extremely large companies: Microsoft, Intel, Cisco, Dell, and so forth. Many active managers were nervous about the tech sector, especially the "mega cap" tech stocks. So they built portfolios that were more conservative than the index, and, during the growth-obsessed stage of the bull market, the performance of the active managers lagged the index.

As the bull market rolled on, the indexes became increasingly important even to those managers who ordinarily would not be caught dead running an index fund. Industry sources estimate that roughly $1 trillion of assets became indexed to the S&P 500. This represents about 10 percent of the total market value of the S&P 500. And another $1 trillion was tied to "closet index funds," or other funds that try hard not to stray too far from the S&P 500. In other words, many portfolio managers began to spend a lot of time worrying about small differences between their portfolios and the S&P 500. To these managers, for example, holding cash became increasingly dangerous. Index funds are fully invested at all times, and in a market whose general trend is up, cash is a drag on performance.

Similarly, portfolio managers worried increasingly about their exposure to specific industries and stocks. As the bull market unfolded, the technology sector of the S&P 500 moved from less than 10 percent of the index to more than 30 percent. Normally, a portfolio manager who was worried about technology valuations would want to be "underweight" in technology. But, in the highly regimented world of institutional portfolio management, hesitation about technology valuations might have translated into a 20 percent weight, rather than a 30 percent weight. Even if the portfolio manager's basic instinct was to hold no technology stocks at all, acting on that instinct would likely have presented too much career risk. And thus we have one of the paradoxes of the investment management business: It rewards independent judgment but simultaneously exerts powerful pressures to conform. As Lord Keynes observed somewhere, it is better to fail conventionally than to succeed unconventionally.

The story of Jeff Vinik and Fidelity's Magellan Fund is a perfect example of the extent to which the equity mutual fund business became obsessed with benchmarks. The Magellan Fund was an extremely successful fund that compiled an extraordinary record under the leadership of Peter Lynch. Lynch was more than willing to "make bets" relative to the index. Although his portfolio always contained many hundreds of stocks, Lynch was willing to make big bets at the industry level. But these bets usually worked out, and in Lynch's day investors were less concerned with tracking error relative to benchmarks.

After Vinik took over the Magellan Fund, he performed well, but he then became concerned that stocks were generally overvalued.

So he built up a big position in bonds, which turned out to be a mistake. The Magellan Fund lagged behind the indexes, and Vinik left Fidelity in 1996 to start his own hedge fund. As a hedge fund manager, Vinik delivered four years of stellar performance and then retired from the business. Vinik could not fit into the benchmark-obsessed world of institutional portfolio management, but he thrived in the absolute-return world of hedge funds. The Vinik saga is a perfect illustration of the brain drain that drives talented people from the highly structured world of institutional portfolio management into the freer world of hedge funds.

So the great bull market provided fertile soil for two radically opposed investment options: the index fund and the actively managed fund run by an investment star. When the bull market ended, index funds became unappealing. Investors became concerned about owning "generic stocks," and they became more interested in portfolio managers who may have some superior skill in running money. Enter the hedge fund: the small, nimble investment vehicle run by a talented portfolio manager who has real investment skill. Or seems to have skill. Or claims to have skill. And there's the investor's problem: How can you identify the skilled portfolio manager and protect yourself from the inevitable situations in which the manager's skill turns out to be less than what it appeared to be?

A BRIEF HISTORY OF HEDGE FUNDS

The traditional story about the origin of hedge funds is that they were invented in the late 1940s by Alfred Winslow Jones. Jones began life as an academic, pursuing a Ph.D. in sociology at Columbia University in the late 1930s. He worked as a writer for *Fortune* in the 1940s, where he became increasingly interested in the workings of the financial markets. In 1949 he formed an investment partnership, A.W. Jones & Co., which lays claim to being the first hedge fund. His fund kept going at least through the early 1970s, compiling an impressive long-term record.

Jones's fund was what we will later classify as an "opportunistic equity hedge fund." Jones's strategy was to invest in individual stocks, taking either a long position (a bet on rising prices) or a short position (a bet on falling prices), depending on the results of his analysis. The total portfolio could be *net long* (the value of the longs would exceed the value of the shorts) or *net short* (shorts would exceed longs) or *net neutral* (equal value). And the portfolio employed leverage to increase return. So, in theory, Jones's fund had the potential to do well even in difficult market environments, which, of course, brings with it the possibility of doing not so well in friendly market environments.

Although it is traditional to consider Jones as the founder of the hedge fund business, this view has to be taken with at least two grains of salt. First, it is likely that there were investment partnerships prior to Jones's that engaged in one or more hedge fund strategies but did not attract the attention that Jones's fund attracted. We know, for example, that Benjamin Graham (who became famous partly because of Warren Buffett's early admiration for Graham's approach to value investing) formed an investment pool in 1926. Although this pool was oriented mainly toward long-term investments in severely undervalued stocks, Graham may also have done some shorting. And even if Graham did not short, there is a decent chance that others were shorting in a way that did not attract as much attention as Jones did.

Second, even if we regard Jones as the founder of the hedge fund business, other organizations were using hedge fund strategies outside the hedge fund arena. The preeminent examples of this phenomenon are the Wall Street brokerage and trading firms, who practiced (and continue to practice) a wide variety of hedge fund strategies for their own accounts. Some of these strategies were essentially "riskless arbitrage": buying gold in New York at one price while simultaneously selling gold in London at a better price. Other strategies involved hedging with some element of risk, and still other strategies were more "directional" or "speculative." Some of this type of trading may have relied on information that today would be regarded as "inside information." This activity took place long before the development of the apparatus now used for defining, and detecting, insider trading. *Insider trading* is trading on the basis of information that is not available to the general investing public.

Jones's success attracted imitators. One source estimates that in 1970 there were approximately 150 hedge funds, with about $1 billion in aggregate assets. Even Warren Buffett was an early participant in the hedge fund business. Buffett Partnership, Ltd., started in the mid-1950s and compiled an excellent record that lasted through most of the 1960s. Buffett dissolved the partnership in 1969, observing that he no longer understood the stock market and recommending that his investors place their money elsewhere. In the 13 years through 1969, he produced a 24 percent annualized return, with no down years. In the mid-1960s Buffett used his partnership as the vehicle with which to buy Berkshire Hathaway, an undervalued textile company that remained undervalued for years. But Buffett was able to transform the undervalued textile company into the modern Berkshire Hathaway, which is simultaneously a major insurance company and an investment company that owns stakes in both public companies and private companies. (For further details on the early days of hedge funds, see the articles by Carol Loomis mentioned in Appendix II.)

The list of early practitioners also includes George Soros and Michael Steinhardt, whose names will be familiar to many readers. George Soros started his hedge fund career in 1969, launching a fund within a Wall Street brokerage firm, Bleichroeder & Co. Soros left Bleichroeder in 1974 to "go independent" and form his Quantum Fund. Soros went on to many successes, leading ultimately to some of the problems in 2000 that we mentioned in the preface. Steinhardt was a well-respected special-situations analyst at Loeb Rhoades. He and his partners formed Steinhardt, Fine & Berkowitz, a hedge fund, in 1967. Then the three partners unwound their partnership and went their separate ways. Fine and Berkowitz maintained a relatively low profile afterward, but Steinhardt maintained a relatively high profile well into the 1980s.

The decade of the 1970s saw high inflation, rising interest rates, falling bond prices, and falling stock prices. But commodities performed well. Oil, gold, and other "hard assets" went into a bull market of their own as stocks and bonds languished. During this period, many wealthy individuals began to trade futures in brokerage accounts located either at the major brokerage firms or at specialized futures brokerage firms. Sometimes the account holder made his own trades, based on his own ideas or on trading recommendations generated by the research department of the brokerage firm. In those days, major brokerage firms retained a staff of in-house research analysts to cover precious metals (gold, silver, platinum, palladium), industrial metals (copper, nickel, zinc), agricultural commodities (corn, wheat, soybeans), and the energy complex (oil, natural gas). Alternatively, the account might be a discretionary brokerage account over which the account representative held trading authority. Because futures contracts permit a great deal of leverage, customers were attracted to the possibility of huge profits. And, if they maintained a long bias in a market of mainly rising prices, there were huge profits to be made. So the customers were happy. And the futures brokers were happy because the commissions on futures trading were very high.

In the late 1970s and early 1980s, the business of running separate futures trading accounts gradually evolved into the futures fund business. The futures fund, or commodity pool, is essentially a mutual fund that invests in futures instead of stocks and bonds. Some of these futures funds were "multimanager funds," in which the assets of the fund were allocated to several commodity trading advisors (CTAs), each of whom took long or short positions in the various commodity markets. Commodity pools were created to enable small retail investors to gain access to a diversified futures portfolio managed by a professional commodity trader. Paul Tudor Jones is perhaps the most familiar example of a CTA who wound up running commingled investment vehicles available to the small investor. John Henry and Louis Bacon also fall in this category. Major brokerage firms, such as Merrill Lynch, Dean Witter (which later acquired Morgan Stanley, thus forming Morgan Stanley Dean Witter, now known simply as Morgan Stanley), and Prudential, offered commodity pools to their customers as a way of profiting from rising commodity prices and skilled money management.

Equity hedge funds of the A.W. Jones style did not take positions in the physical commodity markets, either long or short. So they did not own oil, gold, or other physical assets whose prices were moving relentlessly upward. But they could own stock in commodity-oriented companies: gold mining companies, oil companies, and so forth. And, of course, they could take short positions in companies that were being victimized by rising inflation and interest rates. So even a fund like the Jones fund had the potential to perform well during the 1970s.

The financial environment changed dramatically in the early 1980s, as rising inflation gave way to falling inflation and strong commodity prices gave way to a strong stock market. At the same time, the futures markets were evolving to include futures contracts on financial assets: foreign currencies, bonds (both in the United States and abroad), and stock market indices (both in the United States and abroad). During the 1980s and 1990s, the equity hedge fund community and the futures trading community began to merge along the edges. Hedge fund managers who had begun their careers focused mainly on U.S. equities became more active in non-U.S. equities, U.S. and non-U.S. bonds, foreign exchange, and sometimes even physical commodities. At the same time, CTAs who had begun their careers focused mainly on physical commodities became more active in financial futures, and ultimately became active in the stock, bond, and currency markets directly, without relying on futures contracts. So, on the one hand, funds managed by people like Michael Steinhardt and Julian Robertson evolved from being pure equity hedge funds into being global asset allocators, for which managers survey the entire universe of stocks, bonds, currencies, and physical commodities. On the other hand, managers like Paul Tudor Jones, Louis Bacon, and Bruce Kovner, having begun as pure commodity traders, became increasingly involved in the stock and bond markets. George Soros was apparently a global asset allocator right from the start, equally at home with stocks, bonds, currencies, and physical commodities.

The 1980s saw the emergence of the junk bond market, a market for the publicly traded debt of companies whose finances were not strong enough to enable them to qualify for investment-grade status. Michael Milken, of Drexel Burnham Lambert, was the driving force behind the creation of this market. Originally, junk bonds were designed to provide financing for real operating companies. But gradually junk bonds were used for a much different function: to provide the main financing vehicle for the leveraged-buyout (LBO) boom of the 1980s. In a *leveraged buyout*, the acquisition of a publicly traded company is financed with money borrowed against the equity in the company being bought. In the process, the public company "goes private." Many of these transactions were highly leveraged. For example, a group of investors might have acquired a company for $1 billion, of which perhaps $100 million (or less) represented equity, while the remainder was financed with various levels of debt. The LBO maneuverings produced a number of abuses in the way in which companies were operated, as well as abuses in the way certain types of investments were handled. Many of these abuses related to insider trading. At a time when companies were being taken over every day, investors competed with one another to get advance information about which companies were going to be "put into play" next.

The LBO era ended badly in a series of insider-trading scandals featuring such figures as Ivan Boesky, Dennis Levine, and Martin Siegel. Boesky represented himself as a hedge fund manager with a special focus on risk arbitrage. He formed an investment partnership in 1975 whose official purpose was to invest in risk arbitrage situations on the basis of legally available information. But evidence revealed later suggested that insider trading was an important component of the investment activity. Boesky's investment career ended in 1986, when he agreed to stay out of the investment business for life.

The history of hedge funds also includes such figures as Julian Robertson, who was a stockbroker at Kidder Peabody in the late 1950s. Robertson formed a family of hedge funds that were all named after the big cats: tigers, jaguars, and so forth. His flagship fund, the Tiger Fund, compiled a long and distinguished record until it came to grief in 2000 when the tech bubble burst. Not only was Robertson an excellent investor in his own right, but he also had an excellent eye for talent in others. Many "Tiger cubs" learned the hedge fund business at Tiger and then went on to form their own hedge funds.

Hedge fund failures often generate more news copy than hedge fund successes. Julian Robertson and George Soros made the headlines when they experienced difficulties in 2000, but their earlier successes often attracted less attention. The story of Long Term Capital Management (LTCM) is another example of this phenomenon. Its collapse was a media event of the first order, while its earlier successes generally went unreported. And there are many successful hedge funds that manage to stay out of the headlines altogether. The challenge for the ordinary investor is to develop an understanding of the hedge fund business that goes beyond the stories generated in the inevitable, and very colorful, hedge fund crises.

CHAPTER 2

Hedge Fund Managers and Clients

A hedge fund brings together three very different types of individuals and organizations. First, there are the individuals and organizations who invest in the fund. These are the *owners* of the assets. This category covers a wide range, including high-net-worth individuals, large pension funds and endowments, and others. Second, there is the *manager* of the fund, who buys and sells securities on behalf of the owners of the assets. This category also covers a wide range, all the way from small firms managing a few million dollars to large organizations managing billions of dollars. Third, there is a category of *financial intermediaries*, which includes small and specialized firms, as well as financial powerhouses like Goldman Sachs, Morgan Stanley, Merrill Lynch, and others. These firms deliver a broad range of financial services, many of which are indispensable for the hedge fund manager. And the hedge fund manager has become an increasingly important client of these firms.

In this chapter we will concentrate on the owners of the assets and the managers of the assets. The next chapter will focus on the many links that bind the hedge fund community to the broker-dealer-bank community.

INDIVIDUAL VERSUS INSTITUTIONAL INVESTORS

Businesses need customers, so hedge funds need investors. The community of investors includes both individual investors and

institutional investors. *Individual investors* are "real people." In the
case of hedge funds, these people will generally be wealthy individuals who comprise the so-called *high-net-worth market*. The
assets that they own fall into two categories: taxable assets and tax-
exempt assets. The tax-exempt category has become increasingly
important over the years as individual investors have taken advantage of individual retirement accounts (IRAs), 401(k) plans, 403(b)
plans, and other forms of tax-advantaged investing.

Institutional investors are large pools of capital that belong to
"entities," not flesh-and-blood people. The universe of institutional investors also divides into taxable and tax-exempt investors. The
taxable group includes insurance companies, banks, and more familiar types of companies engaged in nonfinancial businesses: auto
manufacturers, computer makers, and the like. These companies
will typically have portfolios of short-term money market instruments to facilitate their normal operations, but they may also have
bond and stock portfolios.

But the most important institutional investors are the large
tax-exempt institutions: pension funds, endowments, and foundations. *Pension funds* are funds formed by employers to make sure
that the employer will be able to pay the retirement benefits it has
promised to employees. For example, the General Motors pension
plan is a pool of assets designated for the payment of benefits to
current and future retirees. These assets are owned by a legal entity separate from General Motors itself, and these assets are not
available to meet the daily operating needs of the corporation.
Similarly, the state of California has a pension plan for state
employees. The plan assets total roughly $150 billion. The purpose
of that pool of money is to make sure that state employees will
receive their promised retirement benefits. The California pension
plan is an example of a *public pension plan*: a plan formed by a state,
county, or municipality. *Private pension plans* are plans formed by
corporations, like General Motors.

Endowments and foundations are the other major tax-exempt
institutions. *Endowments* are designed to support the activities of a
particular college, university, or similar nonprofit institution.
Foundations are designed to support a broad range of nonprofit
activities carried out by multiple institutions. Some of these institutions are very large. For example, the Harvard endowment and

the Bill and Melinda Gates Foundation both have assets of about $20 billion.

There is a subtle difference between the investment profile of a pension fund and the profile of an endowment or foundation. A pension fund faces definite payment obligations. A pension fund that experiences disappointing returns can't simply reduce the level of benefits paid to retirees. But an endowment or foundation does, in theory, have the ability to reduce its level of spending. Many endowments and foundations have a *spending policy* in which the level of spending is linked to the performance of the assets, thus creating some room for year-to-year declines in the level of spending. This means that endowments and foundations are sometimes more aggressive than pension funds in their investment activities, which often translates into higher allocations to equities, nonliquid "alternative investments," and hedge funds.

Institutional investors are not individuals. They are large groups of people. But every institution will have a small group of people who bear the ultimate responsibility for the investment activities of the institution. These people act as *fiduciaries* for the institution. They do not own the assets for which they are responsible. They are acting on behalf of the owners, and their responsibilities are similar to those of a lawyer who serves as the trustee of an estate or trust. The fiduciary responsibility typically resides in a *board of directors*, which normally forms an *investment committee* to assume detailed responsibility for investment decisions. The job of the fiduciary is extremely complicated since it is invariably easier to make decisions about your own assets than to take responsibility for somebody else's assets.

Fiduciaries for tax-exempt institutions typically do not get involved in day-to-day investment decisions. They delegate that responsibility to an in-house investment staff, or to a group of external money managers, or to some combination of the two. Hedge funds fall within the category of external money managers.

Newspapers routinely describe hedge funds as secretive and unregulated investment vehicles for very wealthy individuals. It is true that the high-net-worth community has been an important source of assets for hedge fund investments. But the level of participation on the part of U.S. institutional investors has increased dramatically, and this interest has translated into a large volume of dollars flowing into hedge funds.

It is a matter of public record that some of the major U.S. universities have become very active hedge fund investors. Harvard, Yale, Princeton, Stanford, MIT, Duke, and many others have invested a portion of their endowments in hedge funds. In some cases the allocation to hedge funds may be 20 percent or more of the total endowment. Yale has been a particularly visible investor in hedge funds. David Swensen, Yale's chief investment officer, has written a book, *Pioneering Investment Management*, that lays out some of the reasons for Yale's use of hedge funds and other "alternative investments." The basic idea could not be simpler: Yale wants good returns that will not depend on the returns of the U.S. stock market. Hedge funds are a natural candidate for that role.

More recently, the California Public Employees' Pension System (CalPERS) has become actively and visibly involved in hedge fund investing. The CalPERS board has decided to allocate an initial $1 billion (out of the $150 billion total) to hedge funds, with the expectation that more money will be allocated to hedge funds as CalPERS acquires more experience in the area. As with Yale, the investment objective is to generate attractive returns that are not closely linked to the returns of the standard stock and bond markets.

The growing interest among very large institutions raises important questions about the ability of the hedge fund community to absorb the new assets. According to plausible estimates, the hedge fund community now controls about $500 billion in assets. This sounds like a lot of money, but that amount needs to be put in perspective. The pool of tax-exempt institutional assets is about $7 trillion, the U.S. stock market has a total capitalization of about $12 trillion, and the largest U.S. company has a market capitalization of about $400 billion. If the entire U.S. institutional investment community decided to invest 5 percent of its assets in hedge funds, the total amount would be $350 billion, which is only slightly less than the current size of the business. As we review the various hedge fund strategies in Chapters 15 through 18, we will ask whether the strategies have the ability to absorb the assets that may be headed in their direction.

NON-U.S. INVESTORS

The hedge fund community has attracted assets both from inside and outside the United States. Non-U.S. investors typically invest in *offshore funds*, which are domiciled in "tax haven" countries like Bermuda and the Cayman Islands. These offshore funds may be managed by firms that are located in the United States, but the assets of the funds are located outside the United States. These offshore funds may accept assets from wealthy non-U.S. individuals, as well as non-U.S. institutions. As in the United States, the list of institutions includes pension funds, foundations, and other pools of capital whose investment activities are directed by a group of fiduciaries. Offshore funds may also accept assets from U.S. tax-exempt institutions.

Some people think of offshore funds as tax-evasion devices, but this is not the case. Offshore funds accept assets that are already not liable for taxes in the investor's home jurisdiction. No doubt, there are situations in which investors are using offshore funds as a place to invest "flight capital" that should not have left the home jurisdiction. And no doubt there are situations in which investors are failing to pay taxes in their home jurisdictions that they ought to pay. Due in part to the terrorist attacks in September 2001, there is increased concern about money laundering and tax evasion, so offshore funds are under increased pressure to observe one of the basic rules of the money management business: Know your customer.

Offshore funds operate on the assumption that the underlying assets are not liable for taxes, so they do not gather or distribute the information that an investor would require to calculate and pay taxes. An investor could, in theory, invest taxable assets in an offshore fund, but the investor would have to report and pay tax on any taxable income earned in the fund. Since the offshore fund manager is probably unwilling to provide the relevant information, the U.S. taxable investor is effectively locked out of offshore funds.

FUNDS OF FUNDS

Many individuals and institutions invest directly in hedge funds. Since the level of fund-specific risk can be very high if the investor uses only one hedge fund, informed investors prefer to invest in a diversified portfolio of hedge funds, often encompassing multiple hedge fund strategies. Depending on the circumstances, the investor may use as few as 4 or 5 funds, or as many as 20 or more. If the hedge fund portfolio includes a large number of managers, then the job of monitoring and managing that portfolio can become a very demanding task. In addition, since hedge funds often have high minimum investments, only very large institutions and very wealthy individuals can afford to be genuinely diversified.

This background creates a role for "managers of managers," specialized investment firms that create funds of funds. Just as mutual funds offer diversification and professional management for investors who do not have the resources to manage a diversified stock portfolio, so a *fund of funds* offers diversification and professional management for investors who are unable, or unwilling, to construct their own portfolios of hedge funds. Some funds of funds are offered by small specialist firms (such as the author's firm), while others are sponsored by large banks and brokerage firms, who offer these funds both to their high-net-worth and institutional clientele. (There is some evidence that even A.W. Jones placed some money with "outside managers," thus anticipating some aspects of the fund-of-funds business.)

The manager of managers will typically charge an investment management fee on top of the fees charged by the underlying hedge funds. The fee charged by the manager of managers may be a pure asset-based fee, or it may combine asset-based and performance-based elements. In some situations, the fund-of-funds manager does not charge a separate fee but instead receives a portion of the fees charged by the underlying hedge fund managers. This fee-sharing arrangement can create conflict-of-interest issues since the fund-of-funds manager has an incentive to hire only hedge fund managers that will enter into fee-sharing arrangements. Choosing from that list of hedge funds may not be in the ultimate best interest of the investors in the fund of funds.

WHO WILL INVEST IN HEDGE FUNDS?

The big question in the hedge fund business now is who will be investing in hedge funds over the next few years. It seems likely that the level of institutional participation will increase, especially if the standard markets do not deliver returns that meet the needs of the large institutions. The great unknown is the extent to which the individual investor will participate in the hedge fund arena, and that depends in large part on what happens—and what does not happen—in the legal and regulatory arenas.

There is currently a fairly sharp divide between the world of hedge funds and the world of mutual funds. Hedge funds are generally organized as limited partnerships that offer a great deal of investment freedom and very little marketing freedom. Mutual funds offer a great deal of marketing freedom and much less investing freedom.

But the lines between hedge funds and mutual funds can get blurred. We noted earlier that SEC regulations already allow mutual funds to buy on margin and to sell short. The SEC imposes limitations, but it does not forbid these activities. Yet many mutual funds do not take advantage of this opportunity. That is likely to change if index returns are lackluster and ordinary investors demand higher levels of active management.

In addition, SEC regulations permit the creation of a certain kind of *closed-end fund* whose purpose is to invest in hedge funds. Most familiar mutual funds are organized as *open-end funds*, which have no fixed number of shares. When new investors contribute capital to the fund, the number of shares goes up; when current investors withdraw assets, the number of shares goes down. A typical closed-end fund has a fixed number of shares. New investors enter the fund by buying shares from existing investors, and departing investors sell their shares to other investors. Alternatively, there might be a *tender process* in which the closed-end fund periodically offers to buy shares from investors in the fund. A number of investment firms are now looking at closed-end structures that would use a tender process to give the investors some kind of liquidity but something well short of the daily liquidity available in an open-end fund. These funds would enjoy substantial freedom regarding leverage, short selling, and so forth. And these funds would be available only to high-net-worth investors. Again, if the background investment environment is one that makes hedge funds attractive, it is safe to assume that mutual fund companies will become more aggressive in making hedge fund strategies available to a wider audience.

WHO MANAGES HEDGE FUNDS?

The people who own assets, or who serve as fiduciaries for the owners, usually do not have the time, or the interest, or the expertise, to manage the assets themselves. So they hire outside experts to assume day-to-day investment authority over the assets. The owner, or fiduciary, delegates authority over the details but retains oversight over the money manager. And so we come to the community of money managers.

Money managers buy and sell stocks, bonds, and other instruments on behalf of the clients whose accounts they manage. Money managers are available in all shapes and sizes. There are large firms that manage hundreds of billions of dollars. This group includes familiar names in the universe of banks, insurance companies, and brokerage firms. It also includes large independent money management firms that were started many years ago by people who left the large banks and insurance companies. And then there are the small independent money managers, the so-called *boutiques*. Hedge funds are an important part of the boutique money management business.

Money managers make a distinction between separate accounts and commingled accounts. *Separate accounts* have just one investor, while *commingled accounts* have two or more investors. Even if the separate account is a joint account belonging to Mr. and Mrs. Jones, there are no other couples invested in that account. In a commingled account, Mr. and Mrs. Jones will invest alongside Mr. and Mrs. Smith. Most money management firms will have a minimum size requirement for setting up a separate account. In some firms, this minimum account size may be as small as $100,000. In other firms whose business is oriented mainly to large institutional investors, the minimum may easily be as much as $10,000,000 or higher. For clients who do not meet the minimum size requirement, commingled accounts are the only available option.

Mutual funds and hedge funds are both commingled accounts. Many underlying investors pool their assets to create a single larger pool of assets that can be properly diversified and that is large enough to command the attention of a skilled money manager.

The job of the money manager is not to hold the assets or to execute trades but to exercise trading authority over the account. The assets will typically be held at a bank or a brokerage firm.

Trade execution will be provided by stockbrokers, bond dealers, and similar providers. The job of the money manager is to decide whether to buy or sell IBM, whether to be long or short U.S. Treasury bonds. In the next chapter we will take a closer look at the ways in which the hedge fund manager interacts with other financial intermediaries.

Hedge funds are available from four different kinds of organizations. First, there are focused and specialized hedge fund managers who offer just one hedge fund "product." The manager may offer a U.S. limited partnership and an offshore fund, but the two funds will pursue the same strategy. This type of firm is the true hedge fund specialist.

Second, there are hedge fund managers who offer a small number of related hedge fund products. For example, the firm may offer a risk arbitrage fund, a convertible hedging fund, and a distressed debt fund. Or the firm may offer a globally diversified equity hedge fund as well as a fund focused on Europe or Asia. Again, each strategy may be available in both onshore and offshore versions. But all the strategies fall clearly within the hedge fund category.

Third, there are large money management firms that offer both traditional investment strategies and hedge fund strategies. The emergence of this type of firm is an important development in the hedge fund business, and it is a very understandable development. Large money management firms face two key challenges: They must attract and retain client assets, and they must attract and retain skilled portfolio management talent. As large institutions become increasingly interested in investing in hedge funds and talented portfolio managers become increasingly interested in running hedge funds, the large multiproduct money management firms have become increasingly interested in adding hedge funds to their menus. This strategy keeps the clients happy, and it keeps the portfolio managers happy.

For example, many equity-oriented money managers have elaborate quantitative processes for separating attractive stocks from unattractive stocks. The traditional "long-only" money manager buys the attractive stocks and ignores the unattractive stocks. This type of firm might decide to introduce a market-neutral version of its investment approach, in which the firm buys the attractive names and then takes short positions in the unattractive names. This portfolio is more conservative than the long-only port-folio, with a greater potential for doing well in down market envi-ronments. And the new portfolio takes advantage of research results that were previously discarded. Thus, the new portfolio can help the firm accomplish its two key objectives: Keep the clients happy, and keep the talented portfolio managers happy.

Fourth, and finally, there are money managers who are part of large financial firms that offer multiple financial services: invest-ment management, brokerage, investment banking, lending, and so forth. Sometimes these financial powerhouses offer specific hedge fund strategies: risk arbitrage, market-neutral European equities, currency trading, and so forth. Sometimes these power-houses offer fund-of-funds strategies, in which the firm builds a diversified portfolio of hedge fund investments, some of which are managed by in-house managers (that is, managers affiliated with the firm offering the fund of funds) and some of which are run by external managers. When the financial powerhouses offer hedge fund products to their clients, the products may be based within the asset management division, the brokerage division, the private banking area, or elsewhere in the bank. We shall return to some of these complexities in the next chapter.

As you think about the four different kinds of hedge fund managers, it is important to think about conflict-of-interest issues. Conflicts of interest are unavoidable in most businesses, and the investment business is no exception. In the crunch, there is often a conflict between the interests of the firm and the interests of the client. The best firms realize that, in the long term, the best way to serve the interests of the firm is to advance the interests of the client. But conflicts will still arise along the way. Those conflicts must be disclosed, in accordance with the familiar advice that sun-shine is the best disinfectant. And those conflicts must be man-aged. The key part of the management process is to set up com-pensation policies that align the interests of the firm and the inter-ests of the client.

Hedge fund managers in the first two categories, who offer either a single product or a limited number of related hedge fund products, are comparatively free of conflict-of-interest issues. Or, to put the point more carefully, they face only those conflict-of-interest issues that arise in any business. The situation changes in the third and fourth categories.

For example, consider the traditional money manager who begins to offer hedge fund strategies. The basic obligation of a money manager is to treat all clients fairly and equitably. At the very least, this means that the firm cannot use the assets of one client to benefit the account of another client. For example, a firm cannot take positions in its hedge fund accounts that were designed to "front run" the trading activity of the firm's more traditional accounts. This means that systems have to be put into place to prevent this kind of abuse.

Then there is the question of how people get paid. In the investment business, the annual bonus is much more important than the fixed salary. People spend a good deal of time during the year worrying about the size of the bonus at the end of the year. Since the hedge fund business can be highly profitable, portfolio managers and research analysts may find that they are spending more time, and more intellectual energy, on the hedge fund portfolios than on the traditional portfolios. At some point, the traditional accounts may become second-class citizens, at which point the traditional clients will revolt.

The problem gets more complicated for firms that are involved not just in money management but also in other businesses. Consider the financial powerhouse that combines institutional investment management, money management for wealthy individuals, stock brokerage, lending, trading, and so forth. Suppose, for example, that the firm decides to build a multimanager hedge fund for its wealthy private banking clients. The firm is trying to decide whether to include hedge fund X in the portfolio, and then it turns out that fund X is an important client of some other part of the bank. So there is some pressure to include fund X in the multimanager fund even though fund X might not be the best candidate for the job.

The point behind these examples is not that you should never do business with a firm that faces conflict-of-interest issues. Virtually every firm faces those issues, at some level or another. What distinguishes the good firms is not their freedom from conflict-of-interest issues but their willingness to face those issues, disclose them, and manage them.

CHAPTER 3

Hedge Funds and the Brokerage Community

Money managers cannot do their job without stockbrokers. Hedge fund managers depend more heavily on brokerage firms than more traditional money managers. And they depend on the brokerage firms for a wider variety of functions. The major stock brokerage firms—Merrill Lynch, Morgan Stanley, Goldman Sachs, and so forth—are in fact financial conglomerates that conduct a number of different lines of business. The typical hedge fund needs multiple services from the financial conglomerates, and the typical conglomerate finds that hedge funds are excellent customers for their several lines of business. To understand hedge funds, which tend to be small and specialized, you need to understand the financial powerhouses, which are large and multifaceted.

There are three main lines of business that are directly relevant to hedge funds: *brokerage, trading,* and *investment banking.* The brokerage job divides into several parts: execution, clearing, and prime brokerage. *Execution* is the most familiar brokerage function: buying and selling securities on behalf of the customer in exchange for a commission. *Clearing* is the *back-office function,* related to the processing of trades, but also related to the financing of positions. *Prime brokerage* is a very specialized function that involves holding the assets of the hedge fund, keeping various kinds of records, and lending money and securities to support the hedge fund's leverage and short selling.

Trading is wholly separate from brokerage. The broker is an agent acting for a customer. The trader is taking positions for the account of the firm. Sometimes the trader will take positions for the firm account that are designed to help the hedge fund. For example, the trader will buy shares of IBM from the hedge fund if the hedge fund wants to sell but there is a dearth of willing buyers. At other times, the trader may wind up competing with the hedge fund as it takes positions for the firm's account.

Brokers and traders are dealing with securities that already exist in the marketplace. *Investment banking* is the business of bringing new securities into the marketplace: helping companies to issue new stocks, bonds, or other securities. In addition, investment bankers are key players in the merger and acquisition business, both proposing and implementing transactions in which companies buy, or merge with, other companies.

Brokerage, trading, and investment banking are the three functions most critical to the life of the hedge fund manager, but two other functions have become very important in the last several years. First, the prime brokerage business has come to include a *marketing* element. Prime brokers often help their hedge fund customers to raise money for their funds. Second, major brokerage firms are increasingly involved as *fund-of-funds operators*. That is, the brokerage firm will build a multimanager fund that may have as many as 20 or more hedge funds in the portfolio. In this situation the broker is hiring the hedge fund, rather than the other way around.

INSIDE THE BROKERAGE BUSINESS

When you think about a stockbroker, you might think about making a phone call, or logging onto the Internet, to place an order to buy 100 shares of General Electric. Maybe the broker is a "full-service broker" who advised you to buy the General Electric stock. Maybe the broker is a discount broker, and you made the decision entirely on your own. In either case, this very simple transaction has both a *front-office* side and a *back-office* side. The front office is where the client and the broker make contact, and the back office is where trades are processed, records are kept, and so forth. The front office has clients and brokers meeting in wood-paneled rooms. The back office is the infrastructure, the engine room.

Most stockbrokers are mainly interested in getting clients, making trading recommendations, and earning commissions. They have little interest in "the boring stuff": processing trades, producing statements, and doing all the other back-office chores. Many stock brokerage firms outsource the back-office function to another firm that has the required expertise, computer systems, and so forth. So the *clearing* firm may turn out to be different from the *executing* firm. The major brokerage firms are self-clearing: They clear the trades that they execute. But many small brokerage firms provide execution only, no clearing.

Hedge funds require strong support from the brokerage community, but in return for this they are excellent customers. Hedge funds often trade more actively than more traditional accounts, so they can generate a level of commission dollars that is quite large relative to the size of the asset base. A very large institutional account that has very low turnover might generate, annually, a level of brokerage commissions that is under 1 percent of the assets in the account. For a very active hedge fund, that ratio can get up to 3 to 5 percent or more. Hedge funds are excellent customers of brokerage firms.

In addition to being active traders, hedge funds take pride in their ability to respond quickly to new information and new investment ideas. When an institutional equity broker "pitches" a large institutional account on an investment idea, the pitch often takes the form of a highly organized presentation, which is then followed by committee meetings, deliberation, and quite possibly no action. When a stockbroker pitches an idea to a hedge fund, the pitch may consist of a single phone call, a few key thoughts, that culminate in the hedge fund client's saying, "OK, let's do it." The brokerage business is a transaction-driven business: no trade, no commission. So, when a broker is trying to decide who should get "the first call" on an investment idea, it is natural to favor the client who has the ability, and the inclination, to act quickly.

A few paragraphs ago we looked at the difference between execution and clearing from the point of view of the brokerage firm. Now let's look at the same difference from the point of view of the hedge fund manager. The manager wants access to research and trading ideas from a broad variety of brokerage firms: all the major New York firms, plus a small number of regional firms, and a few non-U.S. firms. Does this mean that the manager has to open accounts at all those firms?

No. The manager wants access to multiple executing brokers. But the manager also wants to keep life simple, which means consolidating all the assets of the fund at a single firm, which acts as the *prime broker* for the fund. The prime broker holds the assets of the fund, clears all the trades, and provides detailed financial reporting: transaction reports, position reports, and so forth. In addition, the prime broker is the lender to the fund: The prime broker lends money to finance long positions and lends securities to finance short positions.

Part of the job of the prime broker is to *hold* the assets of the fund. The prime broker is a *custodian* for the assets. Even the simple custodial function has some interesting angles. In the mutual fund business, fund assets are held in segregated accounts at banks. The assets of the fund are held in the name of the fund. If the Fidelity Magellan Fund owns 1 million shares of Microsoft, then the books and records of Microsoft will show that 1 million shares of the company are owned by the Magellan Fund. Hedge fund assets are typically held at a brokerage firm, and are held *in street name*. Suppose that Jaeger Capital Partners is a hedge fund that owns 20,000 shares of Microsoft in a brokerage account at Merrill Lynch. The books and records of Microsoft will show that Merrill Lynch owns millions of shares of Microsoft on behalf of Merrill Lynch customers, but the books and records of Microsoft will not show Jaeger Capital Partners. Jaeger Capital Partners will, however, show up on the books and records of Merrill Lynch. Merrill Lynch's records will show that, of the millions of shares owned by the firm in customer accounts, 20,000 shares are owned in the account of Jaeger Capital Partners. Jaeger Capital Partners is thus in exactly the same position as any other investor who owns Microsoft in a brokerage account, instead of holding actual stock certificates. If you hold stock certificates, the corporation knows who you are. If you own the shares in a brokerage account, then the corporation "sees" the broker, and the broker "sees" the brokerage customer, but the corporation does not "see" the broker's customer.

The prime broker for a hedge fund will usually be a large Wall Street firm that also offers execution services. But the execution department and the prime brokerage department are really different businesses, with different personnel, different revenue sources, and different expenses. The prime brokerage department may be having a great year while the execution people are in the doldrums, or vice versa.

The hedge fund manager will sometimes execute trades with the prime broker but will often *trade away* from the prime broker. Again, suppose that Jaeger Capital Partners uses Merrill Lynch as a prime broker. And suppose that I want to buy stock in a small Indiana bank that I learned about from a regional stockbroker. I want to reward the Indiana broker for her research by placing the trade through her, so the Indiana broker will earn the commission. But Jaeger Capital Partners does not need to have an account with the Indiana broker. I simply tell the Indiana broker to buy 5000 shares of XYZ Bank for Jaeger Capital Partners, *giving up the trade* to Merrill Lynch. The Indiana broker will earn her commission on the trade, but the trade will take place in the Merrill Lynch account.

The prime broker holds the assets of the fund, the executing broker executes the trades for the fund. A typical hedge fund will have only one or two prime brokers but many executing brokers. The limited number of prime brokers means that the hedge fund simplifies its administration and recordkeeping. The larger number of executing brokers means that the fund maintains relations with many sources of good trading ideas and can reward those sources with commission dollars.

The prime broker also performs another critical function for the hedge fund, which is to provide financing for leveraged long positions and for short positions. We shall return in Chapter 9 to the details of leverage and short selling. The main point for the moment is that both leverage and short selling require *borrowing*. When you use leverage, you buy more than you can afford; when you sell short, you sell what you don't own. In the case of leverage, you borrow the money that you don't have. In the case of short selling, you borrow the securities that you don't own. When hedge funds borrow, they borrow from prime brokers.

Most mutual funds do not need a prime broker since they do not use leverage or sell short. All that the mutual fund needs is a single bank, for custody and recordkeeping, and multiple brokerage firms, for execution services.

Most hedge funds do use leverage, and they do sell short. The prime broker acts as a lender to the hedge fund, charging an interest rate for lending money and for lending securities. For some of the major brokerage firms, such as Merrill Lynch, Morgan Stanley, Goldman Sachs, and Bear Stearns, this sort of lending activity is an important source of revenue. Moreover, this lending-related revenue is especially valuable to the firm because it tends to be a relatively steady stream of income. For the multiservice financial powerhouses, commission revenues and trading profits are very volatile: Great years will be followed by awful years. But the interest charges generated by the lending of money and the lending of securities provide a comparatively consistent income stream. Sometimes boring is beautiful.

Prime brokerage embraces three separate functions: custody (that is, holding assets), recordkeeping, and lending. Lending is the only function that creates revenue for the broker; the other two functions merely create expenses. But lending creates enough revenue to make the whole package profitable for the prime brokerage firms. And there is room left over for other prime brokerage functions. For example, prime brokers often provide office space for their hedge fund customers. There are office suites in Manhattan where you might find 20 or more small hedge funds, all gathered together on a single floor belonging to a major prime brokerage firm. Each fund has a small amount of office space reserved for its own use, plus access to a common receptionist, office machines, conference rooms, and so forth. As long as the investment activities of the hedge fund generate a critical mass of revenue for the prime brokerage firm, the brokerage firm is happy to have the hedge fund as a nonpaying tenant.

Finally, prime brokers often provide marketing services for their hedge fund customers. They try to raise capital for their hedge fund customers by introducing them to important clients of the brokerage firm: very high net worth individuals, large institutions, and so forth. This function is sometimes called *capital introduction* since the prime broker is introducing the hedge fund client to potential sources of investment capital. The capital introduction function has become especially important since the late 1990s as the general level of interest in hedge funds has increased, and the prime brokerage business has become increasingly competitive. If a bright young money manager with a good reputation is starting a hedge fund, he will talk to several brokerage firms about their prime brokerage services. There will be lots of conversation about reporting capabilities, lending facilities, and the like. But at some point the hedge fund manager is sure to ask, "Can you help me find investors for my fund?"

TRADING

Trading and brokerage are worlds apart. A *broker* acts as an intermediary between the buyer and the seller, earning a commission on the transaction. A trader is a *dealer* who buys and sells for his own account, which requires maintaining an inventory. Think of the difference between an automobile dealer and a consignment shop. The auto dealer owns the cars that he is selling. The dealer may receive attractive financing rates from the auto manufacturer, but the owner of the merchandise is no longer the manufacturer, but the dealer. The consignment shop does not own the merchandise that is displayed in the shop. Various people have left the goods in the shop, but they still own the goods, and they will pay a commission to the shop when the goods finally sell. The dealer is taking a risk that the items in his inventory will decline in value. The broker has no inventory, hence takes no such risk.

Major institutional brokerage firms act as both brokers and dealers. While brokers are executing trades for customers, the bond-trading desk will be taking positions for its own account, and the equity-trading desk will have its own inventory of stock positions. An inventory is really a portfolio, or a "book," of positions, that will include both long positions and short positions. Holding an inventory exposes the dealer to the risk of fluctuating prices, so the dealer may undertake various hedging transactions to reduce this risk. But sometimes a dealer might "have a view on the market," in which case the dealer might take an unhedged position for its own account.

Sometimes dealers take positions for their own accounts in order to help their customers. In the jargon of the business, they are *facilitating customer order flow*. Suppose, for example, that a large institutional investor needs to sell 100,000 shares of IBM. The institutional investor calls Goldman Sachs, who might act as a broker in identifying a buyer for the large block of stock. But if IBM stock is acting weak on the day, then Goldman Sachs may sense an opportunity to do two things at once: help a large client and make a prudent contrarian investment. In other words, Goldman may choose to buy the 100,000 shares of IBM for its own account. Goldman now faces the risk of further declines in the stock, but if the stock rallies, then Goldman will have the opportunity to sell the block to somebody else (or perhaps a small number of "somebody elses") at a higher price. So Goldman books a trading profit, and the initial customer got a better price than she would have if Goldman had *gone to the market* on her behalf.

When you look at the trading activities of a large Wall Street financial institution, what you see is essentially a very large hedge fund. On any given day, the Wall Street firm will hold long or short positions in a dizzying variety of stocks, bonds, currencies, and other financial instruments. Sometimes the large Wall Street firms compete with the hedge funds in putting on their positions; sometimes the Wall Street firms can help the hedge funds to put on their positions. But there are no free lunches. If somebody is helping you out today, chances are that you will be repaying the favor later on. Today's free lunch will be offset by next week's overpriced dinner.

TRADING AND LIQUIDITY

The trading function of the major Wall Street firms is important, but much less important than it used to be. Taking large positions for your own account introduces inventory risk. Inventory risk can lead to trading profits, but trading profits are volatile, and managers of large financial institutions do not like volatility of profits. What they like is steady profits and recurring fee income because investors will place a higher value on steady earnings than they will on volatile earnings.

As the large firms have become less willing to take positions for their own account, they have taken an important source of liquidity out of the market. A *liquid market* is a market in which sellers can easily find willing buyers, and buyers can easily find willing sellers. As the major Wall Street firms have pulled in their horns in the trading area, they have removed a massive amount of buying interest and selling interest.

The liquidity problem is aggravated by the fact that there are fewer major Wall Street firms than there used to be. This shrinking population is the direct result of a massive wave of consolidation among the major banks and brokerage firms, both in the United States and elsewhere. This consolidation picked up considerable speed with the repeal of the Glass Steagall Act in 1999. The Glass Steagall Act was passed in 1934 to curb various conflict-of-interest abuses that were viewed as major contributors to the 1929 crash and the subsequent Great Depression. The Glass Steagall Act enforced a strict separation between commercial banking and investment banking, including stock brokerage. So, for example, J.P. Morgan's original firm was forced to divide into two firms: J.P. Morgan, a commercial bank, and Morgan Stanley, an investment bank–stock brokerage firm. But the financial world evolved dramatically between 1934 and 1999, and many people thought that the act had become an anachronism.

Salomon Brothers provides a perfect example of this consolidation. Salomon was once an independent, publicly traded firm well known for its willingness to take risk for its own account. Salomon's trading profits were high, but volatile. Salomon was essentially a large publicly traded hedge fund. Then Salomon merged with other brokerage firms, and it was eventually acquired by the Citigroup financial empire. The Citigroup complex includes commercial banking, investment banking, stock brokerage, insurance, and a host of related financial activities. Most important, Citigroup is a publicly traded company whose investors place a higher value on steady earnings than on volatile earnings. The recurring fee income generated by prime brokerage, investment management, and related activities is much more valuable than trading profits, which are highly volatile.

When there are lots of trading firms, there are multiple opportunities for them to trade with, and against, each other. When Salomon wanted to buy IBM, maybe Smith Barney wanted to sell. But when Salomon and Smith Barney merged, that opportunity disappeared. Thus the present situation: a small number of firms controlling a large amount of capital, less opportunity for divergent views, and hence less liquidity in the marketplace.

This decline in liquidity creates both a problem and an opportunity for the hedge fund community. The problem arises for those hedge funds that *demand* liquidity: They have a tougher time in the new environment. The opportunity arises for those hedge funds that *supply* liquidity: They are in a position to earn better returns because they are delivering a good that is scarcer than it used to be.

Some observers believe that hedge funds have replaced the major Wall Street firms as a source of liquidity in the markets. This idea is often advanced as a reason for investing in hedge funds and a reason that hedge funds should make money. After all, liquidity is valuable, so if hedge funds can provide it, they should get paid.

But here we need to distinguish between two kinds of liquidity, everyday liquidity and heroic liquidity. *Everyday liquidity* is the normal lubrication that markets require in order to function in an orderly fashion. The firms that supply everyday liquidity are the firms that buy and sell securities with a view to earning small spreads over short holding periods. Specialist firms on the New York Stock Exchange are a major source of everyday liquidity. Their business is a high-volume, low-margin business: They make a small amount on each trade, but they do a lot of trades. These businesses usually use fairly high amounts of leverage.

Heroic liquidity is the willingness to "step up to the plate": to buy when everybody else is selling, or sell when everybody else is buying. Heroic liquidity is what the markets demanded in October 1987, and August 1998, and September 2001, when everybody wanted to sell stock and nobody wanted to buy. Heroic liquidity is also what the market demanded during the manic years of the tech bubble. Lots of people wanted to buy tech stocks, few people wanted to sell, and still fewer people were willing to short tech stocks. When there's not much interest in selling, it doesn't take much buying interest to drive prices into the stratosphere.

To provide heroic liquidity, you need to be a long-term investor who can tolerate adverse price moves. If you bought stocks during the panics of 1987, 1998, and 2001, you needed to be able to sustain further declines in price. If you shorted tech stocks in the late 1990s, you needed to be able to live through further expansion of the bubble. And to tolerate losses, you need to be a well-capitalized investor with a reasonable amount of "dry powder" available. The leveraged investor cannot tolerate major losses: The phone will be ringing off the hook with margin calls from the lenders. (We will return to margin calls in Chapter 9.)

Hedge funds are well suited to provide everyday liquidity. They can take long or short positions, they often have a short time horizon, and they can add volume, or trading activity, to a security. But hedge funds cannot provide heroic liquidity. There are some hedge funds that use little or no leverage, take pride in their long investment horizons and contrarian bias, and have carefully explained to their investors that periods of loss are inevitable. But most hedge funds are not like that. Most hedge funds are leveraged investment vehicles that have sold themselves to their clients as risk-averse funds trying hard to generate consistently positive returns. These funds cannot afford to be heroic.

INVESTMENT BANKING

Investment banking is the business of originating *securities* and originating *transactions*. When a small technology company goes public by issuing stock to the public, it is a job for the investment bankers. The investment bankers put together the block of customers who will buy the stock at the *initial public offering* (IPO), and they play a crucial role in determining the price at which the new company will come public. Once the company is public, the investment bankers will be involved in helping the company to issue new equity, or new debt. So the investment bankers are helping the company gain access to the capital markets. When investors buy a new equity issue or a new debt issue, they are not buying securities from other investors. They are providing capital directly to the company.

Investment bankers also lie at the center of the merger and acquisition (M&A) business. When companies buy, or merge with, other companies, investment bankers are often the people who proposed the transaction in the first place. And even if they did not propose the idea, they almost inevitably get involved in the details of working out the transaction.

Hedge funds are important customers of investment banking departments. For one thing, they are very active investors in the new-issue market. During the peak years of the tech bubble, many hedge funds made handsome profits in the ebullient IPO market. Convertible hedgers are major players in the new-issue market for convertible bonds. And risk arbitrageurs, who invest in companies involved in mergers and acquisitions, are major consumers of the M&A deal flow originated by investment bankers. In all these cases there is a symbiotic relationship between the investment banks and the hedge funds. Neither can survive without the other.

CONFLICTS OF INTEREST (AGAIN)

The major Wall Street firms are financial conglomerates in which many businesses coexist under one roof. These businesses often complement one another, and sometimes compete with one another. The hedge fund community needs all those businesses, and all those businesses need hedge funds as customers. Given the multiple lines of business, it is important to be watchful for situations in which two lines of business may have conflicting interests. For example, after the collapse of the tech bubble in early 2000, it became clear even to the ordinary investing public that the research analysts at the major brokerage firms have conflicting loyalties. On the one hand, the technology analyst owes unbiased research advice to her money management customers. On the other hand, the technology analyst is part of a larger firm that may be trying to win investment banking business from the company being analyzed. Here the potential for conflict is obvious.

We also looked at the example of a firm that has both a prime brokerage business and a private banking business. The prime brokerage business serves hedge funds as customers. The private banking business serves wealthy individuals as customers. The private banking clients may want hedge fund investments, and the private bankers may feel some corporate pressure to favor the hedge funds that are important prime brokerage clients. But the funds that are best for the prime brokerage business may not be the funds that are best for the private clients.

So we come back to the point made at the end of Chapter 2. Virtually every business faces conflict-of-interest issues at some level or another. The object of the game is to seek out firms that face the issues forthrightly, disclose them honestly, and manage them effectively.

CHAPTER 4

The Lure of the Small

Hedge funds tend to be much smaller than mutual funds. The largest mutual funds have almost $100 billion in assets, and there are many funds with assets over $10 billion. In the hedge fund arena, $1 billion in assets is considered very large. Only a few dozen managers have reached that level. Most hedge funds are under $250 million. In the mutual fund business, small funds are often not economically viable, and they may well be shut down unless they are part of a larger mutual fund family that is willing to subsidize the smaller fund. But a hedge fund with less than $250 million in assets can easily be viable if expenses are kept under control and investment performance is good enough to generate meaningful performance fees.

Hedge fund managers will often tell you that smaller is better: Size is the enemy of quality. The guerrilla investor will beat the large bureaucracy, just as David killed Goliath and Sir Francis Drake's nimble warships defeated the Spanish Armada.

We have to admit that being large can be a disadvantage. But it can also be a major advantage. The object of this chapter is to look dispassionately at the idea that smaller is better, separating myth from reality. There are really two issues before us. One issue relates to the advantages of the *small organization*, the other relates to the advantages of the *small portfolio*.

THE GREAT BRAIN DRAIN

The investment business attracts people who are interested in the financial markets and focused on making a lot of money. For these

people, an essential first step is often a job inside a very large organization: a bank, brokerage house, insurance company, or large independent money manager. The first job in the big company can provide
an invaluable platform of knowledge and contacts. But many people
who are genuinely fascinated by the investment business have difficulty functioning well within a large organization. They do not want
to manage people, and they do not want to be managed. They do not
fantasize about having 1000 people reporting to them. They fantasize
about investing in a company everybody hates, and tripling their
investment in two years. Like the naval officer who would rather be
on the bridge of a ship than behind a fancy desk in Washington, there
is a certain kind of investment professional who needs to be directly
linked to the markets and who does not want to be saddled with the
management responsibilities that come with success in a large business organization.

Consequently, large investment organizations almost always
are struggling with some sort of brain drain. Part of the problem is
a "lateral drain": a talented individual at one firm leaves to join
another large firm. Wall Street firms are always poaching each other's
people. But the problem of more relevance to the hedge fund business is the *entrepreneurial drain*: the talented investor who leaves the
large firm to start up her own shop.

The entrepreneurial drain is not unique to the investment business. Law firms, advertising agencies, and technology companies
all face the problem of the highly talented employee who is tired of
dealing with life in the large organization and wants to strike out
on her own. Even rock bands have to deal with the talented band
member who wants to try a solo career. Money is always a part of
the motivation, but it is never the whole story.

For the true entrepreneur, risk is attractive in its own right, and
winning is attractive in its own right, not just because of the financial rewards. There are certain people who love to compete, and
must compete, simply so that they can win, or at least demonstrate
that they can cope with losing. The people who climb mountains,
write novels, and tinker all night in their laboratories are not doing
what they do for financial rewards. And even when the financial
rewards are enormous, those rewards are usually not the key moti-
vator. The investment business, like many other businesses, has
many people who have already earned more money than they could

spend in several lifetimes. As these people gear up to scale the next peak, they are not merely doing it for the money.

The big financial rewards are possible only because the level of risk is high. The fledgling hedge fund manager has to run a portfolio and run a small business at the same time. Running a business means dealing with everything from personnel compensation to the color of the carpet. Many "wannabe" hedge fund managers are not up to the task, so the failure rate is high. In this respect, starting a hedge fund is like any other new business venture. Launching a hedge fund is like buying a lottery ticket: The odds of winning are small, but if you win, you can win big. It's what we will later classify as a long volatility trade.

In the earlier days of the investment management business, the primary brain drain was from the large banks, brokerage firms, and insurance companies to what became the large independent money management firms. And even now, talented individuals leave the big firms to form *investment boutiques*. These boutiques are not hedge funds but small firms that practice "traditional money management": They do not use leverage, sell short, charge performance fees, or engage in the other activities that are distinctive to hedge funds. But, increasingly, when talented individuals leave larger firms, they leave to form hedge funds rather than small firms devoted to traditional money management techniques. They skip the intermediate step and go directly into the hedge fund world. Who are these people, and what is their motivation?

Hedge fund managers come from a broad variety of backgrounds. Some were lawyers, accountants, or just accomplished businesspeople who became fascinated by investing and the financial markets. But most hedge fund managers migrate from other parts of the investment business, either the money management business ("the buy side") or the brokerage/trading/investment banking business ("the sell side").

Hedge fund managers who migrated from the money management business were probably either portfolio managers or research analysts. Research analysts conduct research on individual stocks, or other trading ideas, but they do not "pull the trigger": They do not decide what to buy or sell. Those decisions are made by the portfolio managers, who sift through the analyst's recommendations to look for the best nuggets.

Hedge fund managers who migrated from the brokerage business may have a variety of different backgrounds, reflecting the broad range of activities that takes place under the single roof of a large modern financial services firm. There are four main job categories that have served as a talent pool for the hedge fund business: research analyst, institutional salesperson, trader, and investment banker.

Research Analyst Research analysts in large brokerage firms usually cover a single specialty area and offer their research to institutional buy-side portfolio managers. For example, the banking analyst at Merrill Lynch might prepare a large research report on the regional banking business and use this report as the basis for stock recommendations to institutional portfolio managers. If a portfolio manager accepts the analyst's bullish view on XYZ Bancorp, then the manager might buy large amounts of XYZ through Merrill Lynch, which generates trading commissions for Merrill Lynch. If the volume of commissions is large enough, then some portion of that commission flow will enter into the analyst's year-end bonus. Wall Street research is highly transaction oriented: The object of the game is not high-level academic research but trading ideas that will lead to transactions that will produce commissions.

Institutional Salesperson The institutional sales force markets the firm's research ideas to the institutional portfolio management community. Whereas the individual analyst will often be focused on a single industry, the salesperson will interact with a broad variety of analysts and will pick and choose what ideas will work best for individual clients. The institutional salesperson is thus a generalist who can use other people's research in many areas and may well do some modest amount of research on his own. The skilled salesperson will not be able to match the analyst's detailed knowledge of specific companies, but he may well have a better "feel for what works" than the analyst who is buried in a mass of detail regarding balance sheets, income statements, and so on.

Trader The very large Wall Street firms act as brokers for their customers, but they also take positions for their own accounts. The latter function belongs to the firms' traders, who take long and short positions in stocks, bonds, currencies, and anything else that moves.

Some traders have a very short time horizon and are kept on a very "short leash," with very tight restrictions on the size of the positions that they can take or the amount of risk that they can assume in the name of the firm. Other traders who have compiled a record of intelligent risk taking and profit generation may gradually be given more responsibility and wider position limits. The trader is, in effect, a portfolio manager who has responsibility for a portion of the firm's proprietary capital.

Investment Banker Research analysts, institutional salespeople, and traders are dealing with securities that already have a history of trading in the public marketplace. Investment bankers are focused on originating new securities and new transactions. Although investment bankers do not manage companies or manage portfolios, they often develop a very keen understanding of corporate valuation and the motives that drive corporations to undertake transactions of various sorts. That understanding can provide a useful background in implementing various hedge fund strategies. It is especially useful in managing an equity-oriented hedge fund, a risk arbitrage portfolio (for which the focus is mergers, acquisitions, and other corporate transactions), or a distressed debt portfolio.

The jobs described above all have their own challenges and rewards. For some people, the big challenge is to move higher and higher in the organization of which they are a part. But this means more time spent on general management problems, less time spent on investment problems. For a certain kind of person, that evolution becomes intolerable. That kind of person has to move on, and out.

The brain drain is an important phenomenon, and there has definitely been a migration of investment talent from the large firms into the world of hedge funds. That migratory pattern is bound to continue. This may suggest that ultimately all the smart people will be running hedge funds, while the large firms will be filled with people who lack ambition, or brain power, or both. This is a ridiculous caricature, though one very congenial to those who are selling hedge fund products.

First, there are lots of very talented investors in the large firms. They have their own reasons for not joining the great migration, and they devise positions in the large firms that enable them to stay focused on investment issues, without getting chewed up by management responsibilities. Second, the migration is filled with risk. The investment world is like the biological world: Not all the animals survive the migration. The people who migrate are people who think that they have the talent and want to prove that they have the talent. Whether they in fact have the talent is another question altogether.

SMALL FIRMS VERSUS SMALL PORTFOLIOS

So much for the lure of the small firm. Now let's think about the advantages of a small portfolio. Two obvious advantages stand out: The manager can invest in interesting situations that are too small to be exploited by the larger investor, and the manager can trade more actively without disturbing the markets. The trading advantage is especially important when it comes to risk management: limiting the damage when things start to go wrong. We'll take these points in turn.

You can't drive an aircraft carrier very far up the Mississippi, and you can't invest a very large portfolio in small companies, or small "situations." In the U.S. stock market, companies are available in four sizes: small, medium, large, and extra large. We are measuring size by *market capitalization*: the total number of shares outstanding multiplied by price per share. At the end of 2001, the largest company in the United States was General Electric (GE), which had a market capitalization of $398 billion. The S&P 500 had a total capitalization of $10.4 trillion, so GE represented 3.8 percent of the total S&P 500 portfolio. The full census of the 3000 companies in the Russell 3000 Index is shown in Table 4–1. The U.S. equity market is clearly very "top-heavy": 1 percent of the companies account for 42 percent of the market cap, and 7 percent of the companies account for 71 percent of the market cap.

Suppose you are running an equity mutual fund with $10 billion in assets. You hear about a wonderful company whose market cap is $500 million. You'd like to invest in the company, but you have to limit the size of your investment relative to the size of the company. For example, if you own 5 percent or more of the company, then you are subject to various federal regulations that require certain disclosures and may limit your trading activity. In addition, it's hard to acquire a significant stake in a small company without driving the stock price up, and it's hard to liquidate a significant stake without

TABLE 4-1

Market Capitalization Census

Market Cap Size Range, U.S. Dollars, Billions	Number of Companies	Total Market Cap, U.S. Dollars, Billions	Percent of Total Number of Companies	Percent of Total Market Cap
Extra large >50	39	5,217	1	42
Large 10–50	169	3,613	6	29
Medium 1.5–10	708	2,644	24	21
Small <1.5	1,990	1,040	69	8
Total	**2,906**	**12,514**	**100**	**100**

Analysis based on the Russell 3000 Index holdings as of December 31, 2001. Data provided by Vestek and actual market cap breakpoints established by EACM.

sending the stock price into a tailspin. So most investors prefer to remain "under the radar," which usually translates into owning no more than 2 or 3 percent of a company. But 2 percent of a $500 million company is $10 million, which is 0.1 percent of your $10 billion fund. And the question arises: Is that investment worth your trouble? Clearly, you do not want to run a portfolio that consists of 1000 positions, each one representing 0.1 percent of the total. So, in the real world, somebody running a $10 billion fund can't be bothered looking at $500 million companies.

Managers of large investment funds are forced to confine their attention to investment situations that are large enough to absorb the capital that they have to invest. And this means that they are forced to overlook a vast number of investment opportunities. Hedge funds, and the smaller mutual funds, become the nimble predators who can take advantage of the prey left over by the larger hunters.

This line of thought applies not just to specific companies but to entire markets. As we saw in Table 4–1, the U.S. stock market is very large, with a total market cap of about $12.5 trillion. But even within that very large market, there are submarkets that are quite small. The universe of small U.S. companies (roughly 2000 companies with a market capitalization below $1.5 billion) adds up to a mere $1 trillion, which is only 2.5 times the size of General Electric, which was the largest publicly traded U.S. company at the end of 2001. Moving outside the United States, the developed equity markets (i.e., the stock markets in the developed European countries,

Japan, and elsewhere) are very large, with an aggregate capitalization of roughly $7 trillion. But the emerging equity markets (i.e, the stock markets in the "developing countries") are comparatively small, with a combined market capitalization of about $700 billion.

We see the same phenomenon in the fixed income markets. The government bond markets in the major developed countries are very large, but some of the "niche markets" are very small. The entire U.S. junk bond market is under $1 trillion. The market for defaulted bonds is less than $100 billion, and the market for emerging markets bonds adds up to about $150 billion. Very large institutional investors have a hard time maneuvering in these markets, which are very important for hedge funds.

Some markets expand and contract depending on what is going on in the economy and the business cycle. The chief examples here are risk arbitrage and distressed debt. Risk arbitrage requires *deal flow*: a stream of mergers and acquisitions to provide investment opportunities. Deal flow comes and goes. For example, Figure 4–1 shows that the M&A scene was fairly active in the late 1980s, went quiet in the early 1990s, and then became downright hyperactive in the late 1990s. Similarly, as you will see in Figure 4–2, the size of the bankruptcy market ebbs and flows depending on the state of the economy and the corporate default rate.

So the small portfolio can be invested in companies and situations that are off-limits to the larger portfolio. In addition, the small portfolio can move more nimbly, whether the investments are in large companies or in small companies. Buying or selling 1000 shares of stock moves the price much less than buying or selling 100,000 shares. This fact has very direct implications for risk management.

There are two basic forms of risk management: staying out of trouble and getting out of trouble. The best way to stay out of trouble is to conduct intensive research, hold a highly diversified portfolio, and be preternaturally alert to all the different things that can go wrong. Size does not hurt these efforts and can even help. But getting out of trouble is a different matter altogether. The key step in getting out of trouble is to cut back on the positions that are causing the pain: Sell the long positions that are going down, and cover the short positions that are going up. This is a tough job even under the best of conditions, but it is harder for the big investor than for the small investor. If a stock is caught in a downdraft, then any seller will have a hard time selling

FIGURE 4–1

M&A Activity: Total Announcements and Value in U.S. Dollars

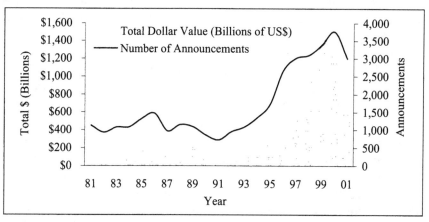

Total dollar value of M&A transactions and total accouncements based only on situations disclosing a purchase price. Total number of merger accouncements in 2001 was 8290, including mergers and acquisitions with undisclosed purchase price information.

Source: *Mergerstat®*.

FIGURE 4–2

Distressed Debt Market
Annual Results for 1971 through 2001

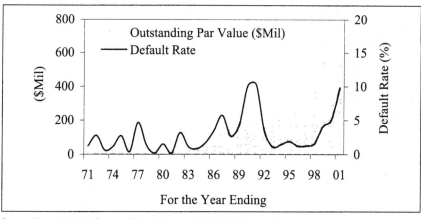

Source: Altman. High Yield Bond and Default Study, April 2002, NYU School of Business.

shares, but sellers with bigger orders will have a tougher time than sellers with smaller orders.

Since hedge funds tend to be small, and exploit the advantages of being small, the question arises whether the hedge fund community can absorb the additional assets that might flow if the level of interest in hedge funds continues to grow. To answer this question, the hedge fund community must be carved up into its distinct segments and strategies. Some hedge fund managers operate in very deep, liquid markets where size is not a major issue. The major markets here are large capitalization stocks (both in the United States and abroad), high-quality bonds, and currencies. Other hedge fund managers operate in markets where size will always be an issue. The main examples here would be small cap stocks and some of the specialized debt markets. In addition, some managers operate in liquid markets, but they invest in a way that requires a lot of in-and-out trading. That kind of trading is best done at smaller sizes. Finally, there are the *variable-capacity strategies*, like risk arbitrage and distressed debt, where capacity comes and goes.

The capacity issue is further complicated by the fact that the hedge fund manager has the ability to be either long or short. Investment bubbles are created when there is too much money chasing too few investment opportunities. At different times we have seen this in real estate, emerging market equities, technology stocks, and so forth. But these situations all emerged when too many people wanted to buy the same thing. Hedge fund managers can buy, or sell, or sell short. They have the ability to take advantage of market distortions created when too much money is chasing too few opportunities. This additional level of flexibility adds to capacity.

Some hedge fund practitioners will tell you that, even within the hedge fund community, "smaller is better." In other words, you should put your money in smaller, younger funds, rather than the larger, more established funds. But this advice is an oversimplification, often designed to support the marketing efforts of those who are trying to gather assets for small hedge funds. And you need to remember that small funds carry special risks, at least in part because their managers are under tremendous pressure to perform well in order to attract additional assets. When investors get too interested in smaller, newer funds, it is often a sign of speculative excess, analogous to what happens in the stock market when investors become excessively focused on initial public offerings of small companies.

Although being large by itself is not necessarily bad, it can become a problem when it results from investment success. As we shall see in detail in Chapter 6, a fundamental feature of the investment business is that past success does not guarantee future success. Indeed, past success can often sow the seeds of future failure, thanks to mechanisms that are by no means unique to the investment business. The critical challenge for the large firm is to preserve the intellectual and organizational virtues that drove the firm's successful evolution from small to large. The key insight here comes from Andy Grove, chairman of Intel: Only the paranoid survive.

PART TWO

Hedge Funds, Active Management, and Efficient Markets

CHAPTER 5

The Hedge Fund Challenge

Hedge funds are a clear example of active investment management. The active manager tries to earn superior returns through a combination of diligent research, insightful analysis, savvy trading, and intelligent risk management. Some people think of hedge fund managers as *hyperactive* managers because hedge funds are even further away from index funds than the more traditional active managers. They trade more actively, they use leverage and short selling, and they are willing to make even bigger bets away from the indexes. It is useful to think in terms of a spectrum of active management such as what you see in Figure 5–1.

As you move from top to bottom, the money manager has a bigger opportunity to "add value" through his specific strategy. And this means, of course, that the money manager has a bigger opportunity to subtract value. As the level of manager-specific opportunity rises, so does the level of manager-specific risk. And so do the fees. At the top of the spectrum are index fund managers who might charge a management fee of 5 basis points (0.05 percent) or less. At the bottom are hedge funds charging 1 percent of the assets (100 basis points) plus 20 percent of the profits.

Passive management became extremely popular during the great bull market of the 1980s and 1990s, both among large institutional investors and among smaller individual investors. The popularity of indexing has both a practical source and a theoretical source. The practical source is the performance record of index funds: It's surprisingly

FIGURE 5–1

Spectrum of Active Management

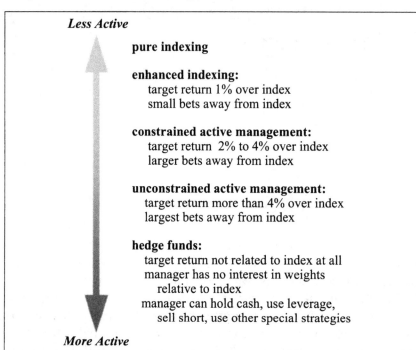

Less Active

pure indexing

enhanced indexing:
    target return 1% over index
    small bets away from index

constrained active management:
    target return 2% to 4% over index
    larger bets away from index

unconstrained active management:
    target return more than 4% over index
    largest bets away from index

hedge funds:
    target return not related to index at all
    manager has no interest in weights
        relative to index
    manager can hold cash, use leverage,
        sell short, use other special strategies

More Active

good. The theoretical source is a body of academic thinking known as *modern portfolio theory*, or the *efficient market theory*.

Both of these labels are misleading. The problem with *modern portfolio theory* is that the theory is no longer very modern. The foundations were laid by Harry Markowitz in the early 1950s, and various architects and builders have been working on the structure ever since. And *efficient market theory* can be misleading because the theory isn't really a theory, or a hypothesis, but rather a way of looking at the markets, or a framework for thinking about the markets. This framework dominates much current thinking and practice in the investment world. The 1990 Nobel Prize in Economic Sciences was awarded to Markowitz, Merton Miller, and William Sharpe to honor their contributions to this body of thought, which we will refer to as the *efficient market viewpoint*.

We will have a closer look at the performance records of active managers versus index funds in Chapter 8. Meanwhile, let's have a look at the three main ideas that drive the efficient market viewpoint. These ideas are often developed with elaborate mathematical structures and highly sophisticated analyses of historical data, but the basic ideas are very simple and can be grasped—and evaluated—without any fancy mathematics.

The first idea is that *markets are efficient*. Modern financial markets are massive information processing mechanisms in which thousands of investors have access to the latest information. Investors compete to gather the information, analyze it, and then place bets that will enable them to beat the other players. Some of these investors run huge portfolios that enable them to get unusually good access to information, analysis, rumors, trading ideas, and so forth. The global financial poker game is arguably the most competitive game in the world.

The general idea of market efficiency manifests itself in four very specific beliefs. First, the theory holds that investors are completely rational calculators of return and risk, unaffected by emotion. What flows in the veins of the idealized investor is ice water, not blood. The second belief is that there are no free lunches in the investment world. You have to take risk to earn return. This idea is crystallized in a joke about two finance professors walking down the hallway of a prestigious business school. One says to the other, "Look, there's a $100 bill lying on the floor." The other says, "That can't be. If there had been a bill there, somebody would have picked it up."

The third idea is that the past performance of a stock, or a money manager, is not a good predictor of future performance. Last year's winners may do well next year, but they may not. Last year's winners are no more likely to win next year than last year's losers. And this leads to the fourth belief, that in the investment business, it is virtually impossible to distinguish skill from luck.

The third and fourth ideas are often expressed with the analogy of a coin-flipping contest. To set the stage, remember that if we put 10,000 monkeys in a room and give each monkey a laptop computer (earlier versions of this fable used typewriters, but typewriters are hard to find these days), they will eventually produce *Hamlet*. Similarly, if we put 10,000 people in a stadium and ask each of them to flip a coin 10 times, a surprisingly large number of people will flip heads 10 times in a row. But those people do not possess any special skill; they were just lucky. And the fact that they have flipped heads 10 times in a row does not make it more likely that they will flip heads the next time.

We shall probe these ideas in Chapter 6. To make a long story short, we will wind up accepting two of the ideas, and rejecting two others. It is true, and important, that there are no free lunches. And it is true, and important, that the past does not predict the future. Indeed, these two ideas are related. If the past did predict the future, then investing would be much easier than it is. But markets are not totally rational; fear and greed are key drivers of market action. And there is such a thing as investment skill. But the link between skill and return is complicated.

The second fundamental idea behind the efficient market viewpoint is that investors should own an efficient portfolio, or, more accurately, an efficiently diversified portfolio. The *theory of efficient diversification* is a sophisticated mathematical elaboration of a familiar idea: Don't put all your eggs in one basket. That was the idea that gripped Markowitz, according to whom investors are constantly trading off return and risk. They want high return with low risk, but in the real world higher return almost always requires higher risk. Markowitz's major contribution was to study risk at the level of the total portfolio, not a single investment. He examined the way in which the risk of a portfolio is related to the risk of its component parts. His key insight was that the risk of the total portfolio depends not just on the risk of the component parts but also depends critically on the way in which the parts relate to one another. In the ideal portfolio the components will have a *low correlation* with one another, or even a *negative correlation*. One part will zig when another part zags. So the risk of the total portfolio will be substantially less than the risk of the component parts.

We will probe these issues further in Chapter 7, where we will also have a look at some of the quantitative tools developed by Markowitz and others to make their theories more concrete and easier to implement. But, as always, we will look at these tools in a way that does not require any sophisticated mathematical knowledge.

The third fundamental idea behind the efficient market viewpoint is that investors should invest in *capitalization-weighted indexes*. The Dow Jones Industrial Average (DJIA) is probably the most widely followed U.S. equity index. But the Dow Industrials is a small group of 30 blue-chip stocks, weighted in a highly complicated scheme. Most investment professionals are more focused on the S&P 500, which includes more stocks and weights those stocks according to their capitalization. *Capitalization*, as noted earlier, is simply the number of shares outstanding times the dollar value of each share. If General Electric has a market capitalization of $400 billion, while Johnson & Johnson has a market cap of $180 billion, then General Electric's position in a cap-weighted index will be 2.2 times bigger than Johnson & Johnson's position.

The cap-weighted index reflects the collective judgment of millions of highly competitive, and well-informed, investors. If you hold a portfolio in which Johnson & Johnson and General Electric have equal weights, then you are implicitly "betting against" General Electric. You are saying that the collective judgment of all those investors is wrong: General Electric shouldn't be worth that much. And the usual question arises: Who are you to say that you are right, and the market is wrong? And then we have to add in the fact that the historical performance record of index funds is surprisingly good.

But cap-weighted indexes have problems of their own, as we shall see in Chapter 8. First, they often look like momentum-driven portfolios: They will have comparatively large positions in stocks, or sectors, whose recent performance has been very strong. This leads to the second problem: Cap-weighted indexes are often surprisingly undiversified. The indexes can contain "big bets," as we saw clearly in the late 1990s when the technology sector became a bigger and bigger component of the S&P 500.

The lack of diversification ties in with the third problem: The very idea of a cap-weighted index tends to conflict with the idea of an efficiently diversified portfolio. There are really two conflicts here. First, the cap-weighted portfolio is a one-size-fits-all portfolio, whereas the theory of efficient diversification presumes that there is no such thing as the right portfolio for everyone. Rather, there is only a right portfolio for a particular level of risk. Second, the cap-weighted portfolio makes no attempt to take into account the correlation relationships among the individual components, so that the total portfolio might have a risk level lower than that of the individual parts.

When the ideal of efficient diversification conflicts with the ideal of the cap-weighted index, it is clear where hedge funds stand. Hedge fund managers struggle hard to build well-diversified portfolios, and they have no interest at all in tracking, or beating, the cap-weighted indexes. The reason that hedge fund managers use short selling and other hedging techniques is that they want to build a portfolio in which the parts do not all zig and zag together. As you devote more effort to building a diversified portfolio, you move further and further away from the world of index funds.

CHAPTER 6

Efficient Markets, Emotion, and Skill

The efficient market viewpoint begins with the premise that the investment business is a highly competitive business in which well-capitalized players struggle against one another for big rewards. The efficient market viewpoint then offers four more specific claims:

1. Markets are completely rational.

2. There is no free lunch: Return requires risk.

3. The past does not predict the future.

4. Investment skill does not exist, or it cannot be shown to exist.

The two middle claims are true and important. Investors ignore these claims at their peril. But the first and last claims are false and misleading. Investors follow them at their peril.

NO FREE LUNCHES

Let's begin with the second claim. If you want to earn a return, you have to take risk. If you don't want risk, buy U.S. Treasury bills. You won't make much money, but at least you won't lose money. If you want to beat the return of Treasury bills, you're going to have to take some risk.

Sometimes markets seem to present opportunities for *riskless arbitrage*. In theory, a riskless arbitrage is an opportunity to "lock in" a return higher than the Treasury bill return. For example, once upon a time you could buy gold in New York at one price, and then sell it immediately in London at a higher price. That opportunity no longer exists. And even when it did exist, the trade was not as riskless as it may have appeared. Suppose the dealer you bought from in New York goes out of business and does not deliver the gold. But the dealer in London still wants his gold. So there is some element of credit risk, or counterparty risk, even in this apparently riskless transaction.

When the futures contract on the S&P 500 Index was introduced in the 1980s, there were intrepid investors who set up "arbitrage trades" between the stock market and the futures market. These trades looked like riskless opportunities to lock in an arbitrage profit. But you couldn't invest a lot of money in these trades, and even then the trades may not have been totally riskless. The equity futures market was still in an early stage of development, and there was still some uncertainty about what might happen in certain very unusual circumstances. The early arbitrageurs were pioneers who were willing to bear the risk of exploring a new investment frontier.

The argument against riskless arbitrage is like those arguments in geometry books that were called "indirect proofs." You prove that something is true by assuming that it is false, and then deriving a contradiction. So, to show that there are no riskless arbitrages, let's suppose for a moment that there were some. In that event, investors would immediately swoop down on the opportunity, and the opportunity would disappear. The riskless arbitrage opportunity is like the mechanical toy that turns itself off: You press a button to turn the machine on, whereupon a hand emerges from the box to turn the machine off. Thus the joke about the $100 bill lying on the floor. If there were a bill there, then somebody would have picked it up, and so there wouldn't be a bill there.

It's safe to say that there aren't many $100 bills lying around on the floor. But it's absurd to argue that there couldn't be a $100 bill lying on the floor. So it makes sense to keep your eyes open. But, if there are $100 bills lying around, they aren't likely to be lying right in the middle of the hallway. And, if you see one, or think you see one, it's prudent to ask yourself whether there might be a catch. Maybe the bill is glued to the floor, and alarm bells will go off if you try to pick it up.

To preserve the spirit of the efficient market viewpoint, it is not necessary to argue that there could not possibly be a free lunch. The more important point, and the more practical point, is this: If you think you've found a free lunch, think again. Look harder. See if there might be some catch that you have overlooked. This has very direct implications for the process of conducting due-diligence on money managers. If a money manager tells you that he is able to make money for you by exploiting a risk-free strategy, run (do not walk) in the opposite direction.

Risk is necessary for return. But risk is not sufficient for return. Sometimes people will tell you that investors are rewarded for taking risk. Investors talk about getting paid for taking risk, as you might get paid for repairing a car engine, or mowing the lawn. But life is not that simple. Sometimes you get paid for taking risk, sometimes you don't. That's why they call it "risk."

FEAR AND GREED

If markets are competitive mechanisms where return requires risk, does this mean that markets are completely rational calculating machines, totally unaffected by human emotion? Absolutely not.

There are two emotions in particular that are critical to the functioning of markets. These "investment emotions" are *fear* and *greed*. Fear is the fear of losing money. Fear is what gripped the U.S. stock market during October 1987, August 1998, and September 2001, as investors raced to sell stock in order to avoid further losses on the stock that they owned. The opposite of fear is greed, the appetite for gain. Greed is what gripped the stock market during the great technology bubble of the late 1990s, as investors decided that they could not stand the idea of not participating in the wealth being created by the new-economy stocks. If fear is mainly the fear of losing money, greed is the fear of not making money. Greed is what you feel when you can't stand not being invested in a tech stock that's going up every day.

Professional portfolio managers try to be rational and dispassionate, but they are not bloodless calculating machines. They get scared, and they get excited. They do not try to banish these emotions; they try to channel them in useful directions. Fear translates into a respect for risk, which means the unending search for ways in which your information might be mistaken, or your analysis might be flawed. Fear is akin to Andy Grove's paranoia, which is essential to survival in a highly competitive game. Greed translates into the competitive instinct to generate good returns for your investors and to beat your competitors. Greed keeps you in the game, while fear keeps you on your toes.

Excessive greed creates bubbles, while excessive fear creates panics. Panics and bubbles create major investment opportunities. But they do not create free lunches. Because markets are very competitive, taking advantage of the markets' irrationalities is not a risk-free undertaking.

Let's look at a recent bubble and a recent panic. Many very intelligent investors thought that the tech bubble in the late 1990s made no sense at all. Outrageous valuations were given to companies that had no profits at all. Some of those companies didn't even have revenues. Some of those companies were nothing more than business plans. Venture capitalists were throwing billions of dollars at *PowerPoint* presentations.

But the tech bubble did not create a free lunch. Many smart investors simply moved to the sidelines. They didn't participate in the bubble, but they didn't bet against it either. Those who did bet against it took a lot of risk, and some of them lost a lot of money. Hedge fund managers who took short positions in overvalued tech stocks sometimes found themselves sitting on big losses as the overvalued became the outrageously overvalued. Alan Greenspan warned about "irrational exuberance" in December 1996, but the tech bubble didn't peak until March 2000. The S&P 500 doubled in the interim. As Lord Keynes famously observed, markets can stay irrational longer than you can stay solvent.

To identify a panic, we need go back only to September 2001, when terrorist attacks on the United States injected a wholly new level of fear into the financial markets. Investors accustomed to worrying about their pocketbooks were suddenly worrying about their survival. There were brave contrarians who smelled the fear in late September and decided that a major investment opportunity was being created. It remains to be seen whether their courage will be rewarded. But the buyers of late September showed real courage. They weren't just leaning over to pick up $100 bills.

THE PAST AND THE FUTURE

The third plank in the efficient market viewpoint is the idea that the past does not predict the future. This point is true, and crucially important. Probably the greatest single mistake that most investors make is to assume that the future will be like the past. They buy stocks that have been going up on the assumption that they will continue to go up. They buy funds that have been doing well on the assumption that they will continue to do well. But, even without a lot of fancy evidence and elaborate research studies, we know that things change. Trends continue until they stop. A strategy works until it stops working. What can't go on forever, won't.

In theory, everybody knows that the past does not predict the future. The investment business is filled with jokes about the generals who keep fighting the last war, and the drivers who look only in the rear view mirror. It's one thing to know that the past does not predict the future, but it's another thing to incorporate that knowledge into your daily investment practices.

Academics and practitioners have established the point in many forms. The past performance of a stock is not a good predictor of its future performance. The past performance of a money manager is not a good predictor of his future performance. A manager with an outstanding historical record may become merely average, or may become a downright disaster. Mutual funds that have outperformed in one period may be terrible laggards in the next period. The past winners are no more likely to be future winners than the past losers.

There is a very strong relationship between the two key insights of the efficient market viewpoint: There is no free lunch, and the past does not predict the future. If the past did predict the future, it might not be enough to create free lunches but it would certainly make life easier. To identify stocks that are likely to do well, find stocks that have done well. To identify money managers that are likely to do well, find managers who have done well. If investing were that simple, then breakfast would get a lot cheaper, even if there were no free lunches. But investing is not that simple. Even after we have dissected the past in excruciating detail, risk remains.

The Securities and Exchange Commission constantly reminds us that past performance does not guarantee future results. That warning has to be prominently displayed on mutual fund prospectuses and other legal documents. Some people consider the warning to be merely formal and legalistic. The message seems to be that past success is a pretty good indicator of future success, but it is not a perfect indicator. Bizarre things sometimes happen. The loyal dog who has been your best friend for 10 years could sink his teeth into your calf tomorrow. The restaurant where you have always enjoyed a good meal could suddenly give you food poisoning. The person who has flipped heads 50 times in a row could flip tails the next time.

But the SEC warning language contains a much stronger and more important point. The point is not merely that past success does not *guarantee* future success. The point is that past success may not even create a *presumption* of future success. Indeed, past success may get in the way of future success. Past success may sow the seeds of future failure. And past trends, after spending a long time reinforcing themselves, are likely to destroy themselves.

THE ROLE OF SKILL

This brings us to the fourth plank in the efficient market viewpoint: There is no such thing as investment skill. Or, there is no way to tell whether a money manager has skill. Every money manager wants to be a skilled manager, and every investor wants to identify skilled managers. But if a golden historical record can turn to lead, and if markets are mercilessly competitive, what room is there for investment skill? What is it, and how can we identify it? How can we distinguish between real skill and mere luck?

Efficient markets do not rule out skill. Rather, investment skill is one of the ingredients that keep markets efficient. But the link between skill and investment returns is complicated. Skill is not the sole driver of returns: It is one of several factors involved in the production of good returns. There can be good returns without skill, and there can be skill without good returns. Moreover, skill is not forever. Skill needs to be constantly sharpened. The skilled manager can lose his edge or can experience difficulty adapting to changing market conditions, or business conditions, or personal conditions.

Let's go back to the coin-flipping contest. Suppose that we put 10,000 people into a football stadium and give them each a coin. Each person flips a coin 10 times. Most people will get some combination of heads and tails. But it may happen that somebody flips heads 10 times in a row. After all, the chance of flipping heads once is 1 out of 2. The chance of flipping heads twice is $\frac{1}{2}$ times $\frac{1}{2}$, or $\frac{1}{4}$. To calculate the probability of flipping heads 10 times out of 10, we multiply $\frac{1}{2}$ by itself 10 times. The answer is $\frac{1}{1024}$. There is 1 chance in

1024 of flipping heads 10 times in a row. If there are 1024 people in the stadium, there is a 63 percent probability that somebody will flip heads 10 times in a row. (I will spare you the details of the calculation.) With 4664 people in the stadium, the probability of a run of 10 heads in a row increases to 99 percent. With 10,000 people in the stadium, the probability is 99.994 percent

If Jennifer flips 10 heads in a row, we would not conclude that she had some special skill. Nor would we necessarily conclude that her coin was imbalanced in such a way as to favor heads over tails. We would just say that Jennifer was lucky. Somebody in the group of 10,000 was very likely to pull off the trick, and Jennifer just happened to be one of the lucky people.

Suppose that we are looking at a money manager with a superb 10-year performance record that stretches over a wide variety of market environments. It's tempting to assume that a record that long reflects real skill, not just luck. And it's tempting to assume that the skill will persist, so that the good record will continue. We are assuming, in effect, that skill is the missing link between the strong historical performance and the strong future performance that we expect.

But this can't be right. We have already agreed that past success does not predict future success. So we can't say to ourselves, "The record is good, so there must be some skill there, so that skill will create good returns in the future." If we can't argue from past success to future success, then we can't argue from past success to future success via skill as an intermediate stop. If you can't walk from New York to London, then you can't stop in Bermuda on the way.

The efficient market viewpoint is right to emphasize that, no matter how long the record is, there is always the theoretical possibility that the record manifests luck, not skill. A roomful of monkeys could eventually produce *Hamlet*. And a roomful of monkeys could, in theory, have typed out the buy and sell decisions that generated the performance record of the Magellan Fund. But, in fact, *Hamlet* was written by William Shakespeare, who had some talent for writing plays. And the Magellan Fund was run by Peter Lynch, who had some talent for managing money.

The "quants," who take a highly statistical approach to the markets, will tell you that many years of performance data are required in order to be able to attach any "statistical significance" to the conclusion that a money manager has genuine skill and is not merely lucky. But this way of thinking misrepresents the problem. As the track record gets longer and longer, thus acquiring more and more *statistical significance*, it may actually have less and less *investment significance*. If you are looking at an exemplary track record covering 30 years of investing in a wide variety of market environments, you are probably looking at a record that is already *too long*! The record begins when the money manager was, let's say, 27. The manager is now 57. His money management business is a stunning success, thanks in part to the great record, which has served as a magnet for additional assets. The manager is wealthy beyond his wildest dreams, has several houses, and is a high-profile mover and shaker in political and charitable circles. It goes without saying that we wish we had invested with him 30 years ago. We kick ourselves for not investing 10 years ago. But should we invest with him *now*?

Maybe, maybe not. It all depends. A long and exceptional record creates special risks, chief among which are the risk of getting *too defensive* and the risk of getting *too aggressive*. The first risk arises because the manager wants to protect what he has built. He has lost some competitive zeal and is starting to "coast," enjoying the fruits of his success. He is playing it safe, trying to safeguard the record that made him famous. Thus the exceptional manager becomes merely average. The second risk arises when the record is so good that the manager becomes too confident in his own abilities, taking risks that he would not have taken in the past. He pushes the envelope until the envelope breaks. Thus the exceptional manager blows up. And then, of course, there are more mundane issues. The manager's health is failing, or his marriage is failing, or some other problem is getting in the way.

In the real world, there are all sorts of reasons for hesitating to invest with a manager whose performance record is good enough, and long enough, to enable a statistician to declare that the manager has investment skill. Exceptional records create exceptional risks. If the object of the game is to wait until the track record is long enough to have maximal statistical significance, then the best policy is to hire money managers only when they are retired, or dead.

The efficient market viewpoint is right to emphasize that good performance results can be the result of luck, not skill. Conversely, a skilled investor may fail to produce superior results, because of bad luck or other factors. If we define *skill* as "the one and only source of exceptional performance," then skill does not exist because there is no such unique source of good performance. Good performance results from the interaction of multiple factors, and these factors interact in different ways with different money managers.

Investment people always say that they'd rather be lucky than smart. This adage draws attention to the very loose linkage between brainpower and results. Sometimes very smart people fail to deliver the goods. And sometimes good results are bestowed upon managers who seem not to deserve them. To form a picture of the factors that combine with skill to produce good results, it is useful to ask why smart people often fail to produce good returns. When this happens, the basic failure is a failure of implementation, or execution. The engine is in superb condition, but for some reason power does not get delivered to the wheels. Implementation can be divided roughly into four different factors: *focus, competitiveness, self-confidence,* and *luck*. This list is not intended to be complete or definitive. The object here is merely to suggest some of the crucial factors that are quite separate from brainpower.

Skill is the element most directly related to brainpower. How smart is the money manager? Does she make a genuine effort to perform independent research, or does she just accept Wall Street research at face value? Does she analyze the information in a unique way? Is she aware of the relevant risk factors in implementing her strategy, and has she taken adequate measures to monitor and manage those risks? Does she have a realistic view of the way in which her market activities relate to the activities of other market players?

But brains are not enough. Sometimes smart people get lazy or distracted. *Focus* is the ability of the money manager to bring his intellectual abilities to bear on the problem at hand. Is the manager willing and able to do the hard work, and is he functioning in a set of circumstances that facilitate that effort? When analyzing a money manager, there is a laundry list of background factors that serve as warning signals to the experienced investor. Is the manager in good health? Is he going through a divorce? Are the children OK? Are there business-related conflicts that might get in the way?

Competitiveness is the willingness to go the extra mile, spend the extra hour, in pursuit of good ideas and good returns. The financial markets are ruthlessly competitive. If a money manager is not straining to compete, then she shouldn't be in the game at all. But there are different kinds of competitiveness. The best money managers have a kind of *controlled* competitiveness. This label is designed to draw attention to the two risks that we mentioned earlier: the risk of becoming too defensive and the risk of becoming too aggressive.

On the one hand, the successful manager may get lazy, rest on her laurels, and start to coast. This is the phenomenon of *regression to the mean*: The above-average manager gradually morphs into an average manager. The manager loses her competitive edge.

On the other hand, the successful manager may become so impressed with his success that he forms a totally inflated idea of his own capabilities. He begins to take bigger risks, in the desire to succeed even more dramatically. He develops the sense that he can do no wrong. And the result is some sort of dramatic blowup. Here the competitive edge gets out of control and leads to disaster. The newspaper accounts will say that "the manager was a victim of his own success." The situation is like that of the test pilot who pushes the envelope until the envelope pushes back, and the plane breaks up. Some of the most conspicuous hedge fund disasters have been the result of a dangerous feedback loop in which success leads to a certain kind of overconfidence, which in turns leads to failure. This pattern is hardly unique to the investment business. Success breeds pride, and pride goeth before a fall. It's what the Greeks called *hubris*.

The ideal money manager will have a kind of controlled competitiveness that is a mean between two extremes. The competitive fires are still burning, but they are not burning so brightly as to create a new risk factor.

Self-confidence is the manager's willingness to pit her judgment against the judgment of other investors, both as individuals and as that immense collection known as the "market." But, as with competitiveness, the challenge is to have the right amount, or right kind, of self-confidence. What works best is an open-minded self-confidence that is liberally laced with humility.

There are two very different syndromes that can prevent smart people from being successful investors. At one extreme lies the smart person who has very strong opinions and has a hard time changing them. At the other extreme lies the smart person who sees two sides to every question and thus has a hard time forming any definite opinions at all. The best investors fall in the middle: They have opinions, but they are willing to revise those opinions in the light of new information. Sometimes the new information is new fundamental information: The company reports negative earnings, or the inflation number is worse than expected. But sometimes the new information is simply information about what the market is doing, which leads the prudent investor to consider the possibility that maybe he is wrong and the market is right.

If an investor has no opinions, she has nothing to do. This category includes the extreme devotees of the efficient market viewpoint, who are so intimidated by the collective wisdom of the market that they no longer feel entitled to any valuation opinions of their own. These people wind up running index funds, or other *information-free strategies*. On the other hand, if an investor becomes too attached to her opinions, then she falls into a kind of intellectual stubbornness where she spends all her time *fighting the tape*. The second problem is much more dangerous than the first. The stubborn investor is an accident waiting to happen. Never invest with anybody who has a hard time admitting that she was wrong.

The final ingredient in success is *luck*. We include luck on the list to remind ourselves that investment success is a complicated matter in which the final results reflect the interaction of a large number of factors, some of which lie totally beyond the control of the money manager. It may seem "unscientific" to include luck as an ingredient of success, but in fact it would be unscientific not to include it. Luck is part of life. The good things that happen to us are not always the result of our virtues, and the bad things that happen do not always flow from our vices. People who eat carefully and exercise regularly sometimes get sick for no reason at all.

When we include luck as an ingredient in success, we are not diminishing the importance of the other factors. Nor are we suggesting that luck is the most important factor, despite the theoretical possibilities suggested by the coin-flipping analogies. Peter Lynch, Warren Buffett, George Soros, and other successful investors are smart, focused, competitive, and open minded. But luck always plays a role. If you have an exceptional 10-year performance record, then you survived the full 10 years without succumbing to a fatal automobile accident or a heart attack. Bad luck could have intervened in many forms. If bad luck didn't intervene, that was good luck.

WHAT'S THE DIFFERENCE BETWEEN A MONEY MANAGER AND A SILVER DOLLAR?

To place the problem of skill in perspective, let's go back to the coin-flipping contest. Suppose that Jennifer has flipped heads 50 times in a row. We are not likely to conclude that she has a special knack for flipping coins. But we might suspect that the coin is not perfectly balanced. And we might perform various physical tests on the coin to see if it is very slightly, or perhaps not so slightly, out of balance.

Looking for a good money manager is like looking for a coin that is slightly out of balance. Let's say that a coin is *heads biased* if it is slightly imbalanced, so that heads are more likely to come up than tails. Given the complexity of the situation, we know that there is no simple link between being heads biased and producing a long run of heads. A heads biased coin could, in theory, produce a long run of tails. And a long run of heads could be produced by a coin that is unbiased, or even tails biased.

Similarly, there is no simple and direct linkage between investment skill and investment results. But there is also a fundamental dissimilarity between coins and money managers. If a coin is heads biased, then repeated flipping of the coin will not alter that characteristic. Maybe we could put the coin in a high-temperature oven to alter the materials in such a way as to make the coin tails biased or make it perfectly balanced. But this procedure is much more radical than mere flipping.

In the investment business, however, repeated success can easily get in the way of future success. The manager with the exceptional record gets too defensive, or too aggressive. Success can pave the way for failure, thanks to familiar processes that operate in all walks of life. There is no analogue to this phenomenon in the coin-flipping business. A long run of heads can turn into a long run of tails. But the long run of heads does not bring into play any natural processes that sow the seeds for a long run of tails.

So here's the difference between a money manager and a silver dollar: When you flip heads 50 times in a row, the coin doesn't get nervous or overconfident. *You* might get nervous or overconfident, but that will have no impact on the next toss of the coin. But managers get nervous or overconfident all the time. And those attitudes can have a major impact on their future performance. That is one reason why exceptional records create exceptional risks.

Investment risk refuses to go away. The process of identifying excellent money managers is fallible. You look for people who are smart, focused, competitive, and self-confident. And, although it may sound strange to say this, you look for people who might get lucky. You're probably looking at people whose historical performance is pretty good, if not very good. But it's also likely that you have eliminated some people whose records look "too good." Even after all this work, the future performance may disappoint. So you have to be diversified across a significant number of managers. And you, like the ideal manager, have to be willing to admit your mistakes.

Will Rogers had a famous piece of investment advice: "Buy a few good stocks and wait for them to go up. If they don't go up, don't buy 'em." The ideal technique for selecting money managers is equally simple: "Hire a few good managers and wait for them to perform well. If they don't perform, don't hire 'em."

HEDGE FUNDS, EFFICIENCY, AND SKILL

So the efficient market viewpoint combines two important truths with some equally important falsehoods. The first truth is that return requires risk: There are no free lunches. Or, it's prudent to assume that there are none. The second truth is that past success does not guarantee future success. Past success can easily obstruct future success. But efficient markets do not rule out emotion, and they do not rule out skill. Fear, greed, and skill are essential parts of the mechanism that keeps markets efficient. And skill, though crucial, is not the sole driver of investment success: There can be success without skill, and there can be skill without success.

The themes of this chapter bear directly on the question, "Where do hedge fund returns come from?" It is sometimes claimed that hedge funds generate their returns from identifying and exploiting market inefficiencies. This is not true. The required inefficiencies are either nonexistent or are too few to support an entire industry. Hedge funds are looking for good investment opportunities, not for free lunches.

Other people will tell you that hedge fund returns are driven entirely by manager skill. Indeed, some people refer to hedge fund managers as "skill-driven managers." So the hedge fund manager is very different from the more traditional equity manager, who takes long positions only, and thus benefits from the fact that equity markets tend, over the long term, to go up. The traditional equity manager has the wind at his back, whereas the hedge fund manager has no such help.

But this idea requires two crucial qualifications. First, there are some hedge fund strategies that are not entirely dependent on manager skill for their return. If a hedge fund manager is working at risk arbitrage investing at a time when risk arbitrage is producing good returns, the return is not due entirely to skill but due to the manager's strategy. A number of hedge fund strategies play a very useful economic function. The hedge fund manager may be providing liquidity to other investors or performing a risk transfer function, assuming a risk-return profile that other investors would prefer not to bear.

Second, and more important, hedge fund managers have no monopoly on investment skill. There are both skilled and unskilled hedge fund managers just as there are both skilled and unskilled traditional money managers. Especially as the hedge fund community has grown in the last five years, it is clear that a reasonable number of new entrants are investment opportunists attracted by the potential for big rewards. Their level of skill may be less than investors anticipate. On the other hand, there are traditional money managers who are highly skilled professionals who have chosen, for one reason or another, not to join the hedge fund migration. There are people in the hedge fund community who will tell you that hedge funds are *smart money*, thus insinuating that the more traditional money managers were out of the room when investment skill was being passed out. This claim is hopelessly naïve and an insult to the community of traditional money managers.

CHAPTER 7

Efficiently Diversified Portfolios

In an ideal world, you could obtain a very high return from an investment with very low risk. But in the real world, such an outcome is highly unlikely. There is no free lunch. If you think you've found a free lunch, check carefully under the plate.

Once you accept the idea that return and risk are related, you begin to focus on a more modest objective. You seek the greatest possible return for a given level of risk. Or, to reverse the process, you seek a given level of return with the minimum amount of risk. Making these ideas more concrete has been the main focus of investment theory and practice ever since Markowitz's pioneering work of the early 1950s.

The key idea here is the difference between an *efficient portfolio* and an *inefficient portfolio*. Let's assume that a portfolio of U.S. stocks will return 12 percent annually over the next 10 years. But to earn that return, we have to take on some amount of risk. We won't worry right now about what risk is, or how to measure it. But we know that we have to take on some risk to get that 12 percent rate of return.

Now suppose that I could show you a portfolio with the same risk level as the U.S. stock portfolio but with a higher expected return. Then, in theory, you should prefer that portfolio to the U.S. stock portfolio. Or suppose I show you a portfolio with the same expected return as the U.S. stock portfolio but with a lower level of risk. Again, you should prefer that portfolio to the U.S. stock portfolio. If there are alternatives to the U.S. stock portfolio that offer the same return with less risk or a higher return with the same risk, then the

U.S. stock portfolio is not an efficient portfolio. An *efficient portfolio* is one that makes the best possible use of the raw materials at hand, extracting the greatest return from the chosen risk level, or delivering the chosen return at the lowest risk level.

So how do we build efficient portfolios? By taking very seriously the idea that we shouldn't put all our eggs in one basket, and by constructing a set of mathematical tools to help us think more clearly about portfolio efficiency and the nature of diversification. Intuitively we know that the way to diversify a portfolio is to construct it so that its individual parts will not all move together at the same time. One part will zig while another part zags.

The most familiar portfolio building blocks are stocks, bonds, and cash. These three components thrive in very different economic environments. Stocks tend to do best in a financial temperate zone, which features low inflation, reasonable economic growth, and reasonable growth in corporate profits. Bonds tend to do best in colder climes, where economic growth is flat or even negative and the inflation rate is falling. Cash does best in warmer regions, where short-term interest rates are rising in response to inflationary pressures, which are often caused by excessive growth. If the economy is Too Hot, cash is king. If the economy is Too Cold, bonds will thrive. If the economy is Just Right, stocks should be the best bet.[*] If a portfolio has exposure to all three assets, there is a decent chance that most of the time some portion of the portfolio will be doing well no matter how well the economy is doing generally.

The main achievement of Harry Markowitz and others was to put some specific mathematical meat on these very intuitive bones. Two mathematical tools are especially important: *standard deviation,* used as a measure of risk, and *correlation,* used as a measure of the degree to which two investments zig and zag together. Markowitz developed a detailed framework for showing how the risk of a

---

[*]Barton Biggs, global portfolio strategist at Morgan Stanley and one of the best writers on Wall Street, often used the story of the three bears in talking about the outlook for the U.S. stock market. One of the chief drivers of the bull market of the 1980s and 1990s was an economic background of steady growth with stable or falling inflation, the so-called *Goldilocks economy.* Biggs is a distinguished alumnus of the hedge fund community. He formed Fairfield Partners in 1965 with Richard Ratcliffe, who had been a partner of A.W. Jones. He ran Fairfield until the early 1970s, when he joined Morgan Stanley.

portfolio depends not just on the risk of the components but on the degree of correlation among those components.

To make these ideas more concrete, let's work through the problem of constructing a well-diversified portfolio of U.S. stocks. For this exercise, we can divide the U.S. stock market into eight industry groups as shown in Table 7–1.[*]

Technology stocks are usually viewed as high-risk, high-return investments, and utility stocks are usually considered to be at the opposite extreme. The question is: What *weights* should we assign to these eight components in building a diversified portfolio that will be *efficient*? Should we have 10 percent in technology stocks, or 20 percent, or more? We want to squeeze the greatest possible return from our chosen risk level. Alternatively, we want to achieve our desired return with the lowest possible amount of risk.

To measure risk, we use the concept of standard deviation. *Standard deviation* is a statistical measure that tells us how much the members of a population differ from the mean, or the average. If we measure the height of all the sixth-grade students in North Dakota,

TABLE 7–1

Economic Sectors of the S&P 500

Industry Group	Representative Industries
Financial	Banks, insurance
Utility	Electric, gas, and telephone
Energy	Exploration, production, energy services
Basic industry	Metals, mining, chemicals, forest products
Industrial and Multi-industrial	Heavy machinery, aerospace
Consumer cyclical	Auto industry, retailing, media, airlines and other travel
Consumer noncyclical	Drugs, food, beverages, and tobacco
Technology	Computers, information technology, biotechnology

The economic sectors were determined by EACM based on the holdings in the S&P 500 Index.
Source: Standard & Poor's and EACM.

---

[*]Our firm, like many others, has recently adopted a 10-group scheme in which the technology sector is replaced by health care, information technology, and telecommunications. The 8-group division is useful for our present purposes because we have historical performance data for these groups going back to 1986.

then we can calculate the average height by adding up all the students' heights and then dividing that sum by the number of students. The standard deviation of the heights will tell us how much variation there is around the mean. When we're dealing with the height of sixth graders, having a wide variation around the mean is not a problem. If we run an assembly line that packs ice cream into 1-quart containers, we would like every container to weigh the same. In this case, we would like the standard deviation to be as low as possible.

In the investment business, historical performance is usually divided into monthly, quarterly, or daily returns. The standard deviation of those returns will tell us how much variation there is around the mean return. Standard deviations are always positive numbers, and they can get as high as we want. In Figure 7–1 we show the range of monthly returns for the eight stock market sectors. We've divided the monthly returns in such a way as to show the top, bottom, median, first quartile, and third quartile. The *median* is the return that divides the distribution in half: Half the returns are above the median, half are below. The *first quartile* is the return that lies above 75 percent of all the returns; the *third quartile* is the return that lies above 25 percent of the returns.

As you can see in Figure 7–1, the returns for some sectors are more widely scattered than others. Compare the technology sector and the utility sector. In the utility sector, the spread between the 75th percentile and the 25th percentile is 4.8 percent; in the technology sector, that spread is 9.8 percent. The spread between the best month for utilities and the worst is 22.2 percent; the comparable number for technology is 43.9 percent.

To calculate the standard deviation of returns, first we calculate the mean, or average, monthly return. Then we calculate the difference between each monthly return and the average. Then we square all those numbers, add them up, and calculate the average value of those squares. Finally, we take the square root of that number. That is the standard deviation. The bigger the standard deviation, the bigger the difference between the various individual returns and the average return.

In Figure 7–2 we show two numbers at the same time: the historical return for each of the eight sectors and the standard deviations. Although the chart is based on monthly data, we are showing the return and the standard deviation in an annualized form. This

FIGURE 7-1

Economic Sectors of the S&P 500 Index
Distribution of Monthly Returns, January 1986 through
December 2001

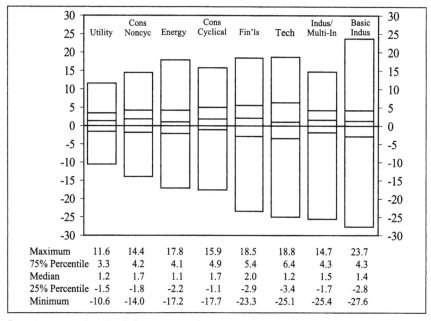

	Utility	Cons Noncyc	Energy	Cons Cyclical	Fin'ls	Tech	Indus/ Multi-In	Basic Indus
Maximum	11.6	14.4	17.8	15.9	18.5	18.8	14.7	23.7
75% Percentile	3.3	4.2	4.1	4.9	5.4	6.4	4.3	4.3
Median	1.2	1.7	1.1	1.7	2.0	1.2	1.5	1.4
25% Percentile	-1.5	-1.8	-2.2	-1.1	-2.9	-3.4	-1.7	-2.8
Minimum	-10.6	-14.0	-17.2	-17.7	-23.3	-25.1	-25.4	-27.6

Economic sectors established by EACM and based on S&P 500 Index historical holdings. Monthly rates of return for each economic sector calculated by EACM.
Source: Standard & Poor's and EACM.

chart illustrates the basic distinction between an efficient and an inefficient portfolio. Notice that the technology sector was extremely inefficient during this period: Many sectors had both higher return and lower volatility than technology. Basic industry, industrial and multi-industrial, and financial were also inefficient. In each case, there is another sector that delivers a better risk-return combination. This leaves four efficient sectors: utilities, energy, consumer cyclicals, and consumer noncyclicals.

There is an important link between standard deviation and probability. Let's suppose that returns are *normally distributed*: They fall within the familiar symmetrical bell-shaped curve. (Although this assumption is often not literally accurate, it provides a helpful starting point.) If returns are normally distributed, then (as shown

FIGURE 7–2

Economic Sectors of the S&P 500 Index
Historical Risk-Return Characteristics,
January 1986 through December 2001

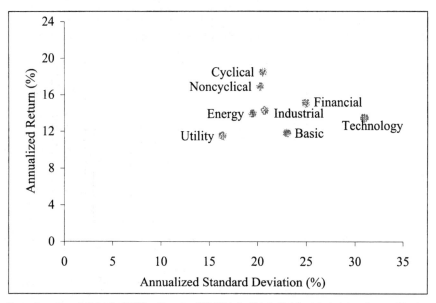

Economic sectors established by EACM and based on S&P 500 Index historical holdings. Analysis based on monthly rates
of return, calculated by EACM.

Source: Standard & Poor's and EACM.

in Figure 7–3) 68 percent of the returns will fall between the mean
plus 1 standard deviation, and the mean minus 1 standard deviation. So 16 percent of the returns will be less than the mean minus 1
standard deviation, and 16 percent of the returns will be greater than
the mean plus 1 standard deviation. This means that there is a 16
percent chance of getting a return less than the mean minus 1 standard deviation. And, given the mathematics of normal distributions,
there is a 2.5 percent chance of earning a return less than the mean
minus 2 standard deviations.

In Table 7–2, we show the "2.5 percent probability returns" for
the various stock sectors. In theory, for each sector there is a 2.5 percent chance of earning a return equal to or less than the number
shown. Again, utility stocks and technology stocks provide a convenient contrast. In utilities, there was a 2.5 percent chance of losing

FIGURE 7–3

Probabilities and Standard Deviation

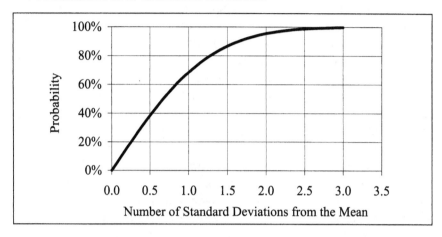

TABLE 7–2

Economic Sectors of the S&P 500
Return Less 2 Standard Deviations

Economic Sectors	Annualized Rate of Return	Annualized Standard Deviation	Return *Less* 2 Standard Deviations
Utility	11.5	16.4	−21.3
Consumer cyclical	18.4	20.5	−22.6
Consumer noncyclical	16.9	20.3	−23.7
Energy	13.9	19.5	−25.1
Industrial and multi-industrial	14.2	20.7	−27.2
Basic industry	11.7	23.0	−34.3
Financial	15.1	25.0	−34.8
Technology	13.4	31.0	−48.5

Economic sectors established by EACM and based on S&P 500 Index historical holdings. Analysis based on monthly rates of return for the period January 1986 to December 2001.
Source: Standard & Poor's and EACM.

more than 21 percent; in technology stocks, there was a 2.5 percent chance of losing more than 48 percent.

Correlation is a number that tells us to what degree two series of returns tend to move up and down together. Correlations always fall in a range between 1 and –1. When the correlation is 1, the two investments move up and down together in lockstep. When the correlation is –1, one is going up when the other is going down. When the correlation is zero, the two investments are completely unrelated: Sometimes they go up and down together, sometimes they do not. The easiest way to picture correlation is to draw a scatter plot showing the monthly returns for the two investments.

In the left side of Figure 7–4, we picture the relationship between basic industry stocks and industrial and multi-industrial stocks. Each dot represents one month. The horizontal position of the dot represents the return of the basic industry sector in that month, while the vertical position represents the return of the industrial and multi-industrial sector. Notice that most of the dots fall either in the upper right-hand quadrant (both sectors were earning a positive return for the month) or the lower left-hand quadrant (both sectors were negative for the month). It turns out that the two sectors are either up together or down together in 85 percent of the months. These two sectors have a correlation coefficient of 0.8. In contrast, in the right-

FIGURE   7–4

Economic Sectors of the S&P 500 Index
High- and Low-Correlation Pairs,
January 1986 through December 2001

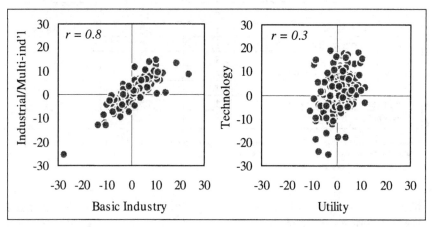

Economic sectors established by EACM and based on S&P 500 Index historical holdings. Monthly rates of return for each economic sector calculated by EACM.

Source: Standard & Poor's and EACM.

hand picture, which shows the utility and technology sectors, we see more dots in the upper left-hand and lower right quadrants: One sector is zigging while the other is zagging. These two sectors have a correlation coefficient of 0.3. They move in the same direction in 64 percent of the months. Finding pairs of assets that have low or negative correlations with one another is the key to building diversified portfolios. We can summarize the correlation statistics in a correlation matrix, as shown in Table 7–3.

Notice that every single pair of sectors shows a positive cross-correlation. Despite the differences among the various sectors, there is still a pronounced tendency for stocks, in general, to move up and down together. Investors who are looking for more complete diversification need to find cases of *negative correlation*, which requires looking outside the sectors that we have been showing or taking short positions in those sectors. This is the course chosen by hedge funds.

The correlation statistic gives us, in theory, a measure of the degree to which changes in one variable explain changes in the other variable. If two assets have a correlation coefficient of 0.7, then the

TABLE 7–3

Economic Sectors of the S&P 500
Historical Correlation Matrix

Economic Sectors	Utility	Consumer Cyclical	Consumer Noncyclical	Energy	Industrial and Multi-industrial	Basic Industry	Financial	Technology
Utility	1.0							
Consumer cyclical	0.6	1.0						
Consumer noncyclical	0.5	0.6	1.0					
Energy	0.4	0.4	0.4	1.0				
Ind and multi-industrial	0.5	0.6	0.8	0.6	1.0			
Basic industry	0.4	0.5	0.7	0.6	0.8	1.0		
Financial	0.6	0.7	0.7	0.5	0.8	0.7	1.0	
Technology	0.3	0.3	0.6	0.4	0.7	0.5	0.5	1.0

Economic sectors established by EACM and based on S&P 500 Index historical holdings. Analysis based on monthly rates of return for the period January 1986 to December 2001.
Source: Standard & Poor's and EACM.

square of that number is 0.49, or 49 percent. This means, in theory, that 49 percent of the change in the one variable is explained by the change in the other variable. So even when the correlation coefficient is 0.7, which sounds pretty high, only half the return of one asset is explainable by the return of the other asset.

Let's focus on the five years ending in December 2001. We first calculate the return for each of the eight sectors, the standard deviation for each sector, and a matrix of cross-correlations. Armed with these inputs, we can calculate the return and the standard deviation of any portfolio built from those eight sectors. Thanks to the miracle of modern computing, small machines can perform this task in less than a second. When we look at the millions of portfolios that can be built from the eight sectors, it turns out that most of those portfolios are *inefficient*. For most portfolios, there will be another portfolio that offers the same return with less volatility, or higher return with the same volatility. If we throw away those *inefficient portfolios*, then what remains is a set of *efficient portfolios* that define the *efficient frontier*. If a portfolio lies on the efficient frontier, then no other portfolio offers a better risk-return combination.

Figure 7–5 shows the efficient frontier based on the inputs calculated from the 60 months ending December 2001. Notice several points. First, the western end of the frontier is defined by a portfolio (A in the table) that has less volatility than any of the individual eight sectors. This is the magic of diversification: The whole is less risky than any of the parts.

Second, some sectors look unattractive when considered in isolation, but they are very attractive as part of a larger portfolio. For example, the energy sector is clearly inefficient when considered in isolation. But energy is a large piece of portfolio A, the lowest risk portfolio because it has a low correlation with several of the other sectors.

Third, although these portfolios are efficiently diversified relative to the set of inputs that drive the calculations, the portfolios certainly do not *look* diversified in any intuitive sense. They may be *efficiently* diversified, but they do not look *intelligently* diversified. For example, portfolio C, the "medium risk portfolio," has 83 percent invested in consumer noncyclical stocks, and no exposure at all to five of the eight market sectors. These portfolios were constructed with the benefit of perfect hindsight. If we knew, in December 1996, that the ensuing five years would deliver exactly the returns, volatilities,

FIGURE 7-5

Economic Sectors of the S&P 500 Index
Efficient Frontier, Five Years Ending December 2001

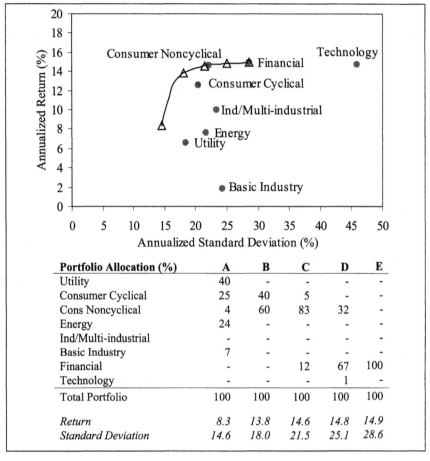

Portfolio Allocation (%)	A	B	C	D	E
Utility	40	-	-	-	-
Consumer Cyclical	25	40	5	-	-
Cons Noncyclical	4	60	83	32	-
Energy	24	-	-	-	-
Ind/Multi-industrial	-	-	-	-	-
Basic Industry	7	-	-	-	-
Financial	-	-	12	67	100
Technology	-	-	-	1	-
Total Portfolio	100	100	100	100	100
Return	8.3	13.8	14.6	14.8	14.9
Standard Deviation	14.6	18.0	21.5	25.1	28.6

Economic sectors established by EACM and based on S&P 500 Index historical holdings. Monthly rates of return for each economic sector calculated by EACM.

Source: Standard & Poor's and EACM.

and correlations that drive all the calculations, then we would have constructed the frontier as shown. But, of course, nobody knew in December 1996 what the next five years would bring. To protect ourselves from the unknown, most people would want more diversification than is reflected in the frontier shown here. If you invest today in one of the portfolios on the frontier shown in Figure 7–5, you are in effect, betting that the inputs driving the analysis will hold over the next five years. Given the difficulty of predicting the course of the financial markets, it's imprudent to bet too much on any particular set of inputs.

Fourth, notice that this analysis offers us a frontier of portfolios from which to choose, but it does not tell us which one is best. Investors with a low tolerance for risk will prefer to stay in the western part of the frontier, while more aggressive investors will be comfortable moving further east. The efficient frontier analysis tells us not to go below the frontier, but it does not tell us how far west or east to go.

The theory of efficient diversification is a remarkable intellectual achievement, and it has had a profound influence both on academic theories of investing and on the real world of investment practice. Indeed, the fundamental insight is the key insight that drives the hedge fund business. Hedge fund managers want to build well-diversified portfolios. Building such portfolios is easier if the manager can identify pairs of investments that have a low, or negative, correlation. Identifying such pairs is easier if the manager can take short positions.

But the theory has to be taken with three major grains of salt. These grains of salt do not diminish the elegance of the theory, but they do affect the way in which the theory is used.

GARBAGE IN, GARBAGE OUT

In the real world of investing, it is extremely difficult to arrive at reliable estimates of future return, volatility, and correlation. The past can be measured to three decimal places, but the future cannot be measured at all. The numbers for the next five years may be totally different from the numbers for the last five years, and those numbers are probably very different from the numbers for the prior five years. When looking at historical data over long time periods, the striking fact that emerges is that *all* the statistics change. Everybody knows that returns change. But volatility changes too: Periods of high volatility alternate with periods of low volatility. And correlations change. For much of the bull market of the 1980s and 1990s, U.S. stocks and bonds were highly correlated: Stocks and bonds would rise together on news of continuing noninflationary growth, and they would fall together on fears of inflation. After the tech bubble burst in early 2000, investors began to worry about the basic health of the economy, and the correlation pattern reversed. If the economic news suggested continuing economic weakness, stocks would fall but bonds would rise. If the economic news suggested that a rebound was approaching, stocks would rise and bonds would fall.

To see how changes in the inputs affect the output, let's repeat the efficient frontier analysis using data for the five years ending March 2000, at the very height of the technology bubble. The picture in Figure 7–6 is totally different from the picture in Figure 7–5. Technology stocks and utility stocks are a prominent part of the frontier shown in Figure 7–6, but they were much less important when we used data from 1997 to 2001.

So the past statistics are a very unreliable basis for making estimates regarding the future. No matter how carefully we sift through the past, no matter how sophisticated our analysis, our predictions of the future are fundamentally uncertain. You can't just extrapolate the past onto the future. To make intelligent estimates, and to use them prudently, requires some skill.

You've probably heard the story about the man who drives to his favorite bar one night, gets drunk, and loses the keys to his car. A passerby comes across the drunk looking for his keys under a street light. The passerby asks the drunk where he lost the keys, and the drunk says, "Over there." The passerby says, "Then why are you looking here?" And the drunk responds, "Because the light's better here." The investment business thrives on vast databases of historical information and massive amounts of computer power for analyzing that information. The light on the historical information is exceptionally bright. But that's not where the keys are.

DOWNSIDE VOLATILITY AND DOWNSIDE CORRELATION

Standard deviation tells us how much a series of returns fluctuates around the mean. Correlation tells us to what degree two series of returns tend to move in the same direction. In the real world, however, investors do not mind returns that are above the mean. What they do mind are returns that are below the mean, or below zero, or below some target rate of return, such as the rate of inflation. Similarly, if two assets tend to have positive returns at the same time,

FIGURE 7–6

Economic Sectors of the S&P 500 Index
Efficient Frontier, Five Years Ending March 2000

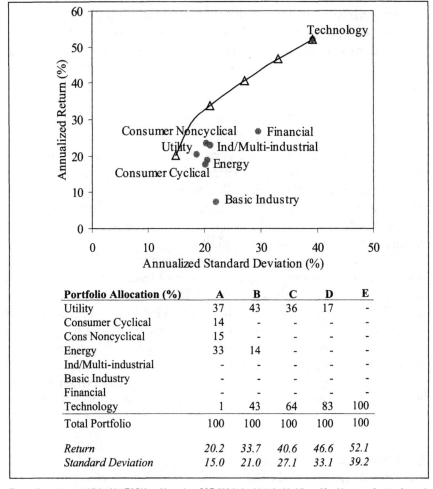

Portfolio Allocation (%)	A	B	C	D	E
Utility	37	43	36	17	-
Consumer Cyclical	14	-	-	-	-
Cons Noncyclical	15	-	-	-	-
Energy	33	14	-	-	-
Ind/Multi-industrial	-	-	-	-	-
Basic Industry	-	-	-	-	-
Financial	-	-	-	-	-
Technology	1	43	64	83	100
Total Portfolio	100	100	100	100	100
Return	*20.2*	*33.7*	*40.6*	*46.6*	*52.1*
Standard Deviation	*15.0*	*21.0*	*27.1*	*33.1*	*39.2*

Economic sectors established by EACM and based on S&P 500 Index historical holdings. Monthly rates of return for each economic sector calculated by EACM.

Source: Standard & Poor's and EACM.

that is not a problem for most investors. The problem arises when both assets tend to lose money at the same time. To achieve diversification we need to identify assets that will be making money when other assets are losing money.

So it is useful to supplement standard deviation with measures that focus more specifically on *downside volatility*. There are two key measures here: the probability of experiencing a loss and the size of the average loss. Think of the difference between AM radio and FM radio. AM radio works by modulating the amplitude of the signal, while FM works by modulating the frequency of the signal. Similarly, money managers attempt to modulate both the amplitude of losses and the frequency of those losses. (We will return to the AM/FM analogy in Chapter 11.) Figure 7–7 shows the average loss, and the loss frequency, for the eight U.S. equity market sectors that we have been talking about. (We have inverted the vertical axis so that the "best sectors" will be in the northwest: low loss frequency and low average loss.) Again, contrast the utility and technology sectors. Both sectors lost money about 40 percent of the time, but the average loss for utilities was much smaller than the average loss for tech stocks.

Similarly, we can focus on *downside correlation* by looking specifically at the performance of one asset when another asset is experiencing negative returns. For example, Figure 7–8 shows the performance of the various U.S. stock sectors when the S&P 500 as a whole is down. Here we look at frequency of making money when the benchmark is down versus the average return in the months when the market is down.

Tech stocks made money in only 15 percent of the months when the market was down, and the average return for tech stocks in all the down-market months was a loss of 5.1 percent. Utility stocks made money in 31 percent of the down-market months, and their average return in all those months was a loss of 2.2 percent. Utility stocks didn't make money in the down-market months, but they held up much better than tech stocks.

The measures just described are convenient measures of downside volatility and downside correlation. There are many other measures available. But all these measures leave one big question hanging: How do measurements of the past help us organize our uncertainty regarding the future?

VOLATILITY VERSUS UNCERTAINTY

Although professional investors often identify risk with volatility, for most people risk is much more closely related to uncertainty than

FIGURE 7-7

Historical Monthly Loss and Frequency
Average Monthly Loss Versus Frequency of Monthly Loss

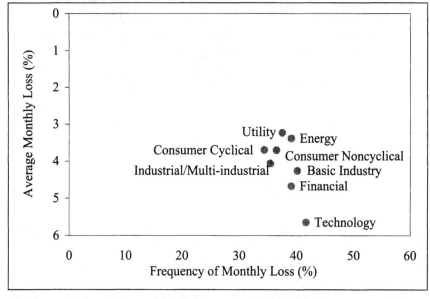

Calculations are based on monthly rates of return for January 1986 to December 2001. Economic sectors established by EACM and based on S&P 500 Index historical holdings. Monthly rates of return for each economic sector calculated by EACM.
Source: Standard & Poor's and EACM.

to volatility. The problem for the investor is not the bounciness of prices and returns *within* the expected holding period. The problem is the uncertainty that attaches to any estimate regarding the return across the full holding period. This point applies even if conventional measures of volatility are replaced with measures of downside volatility. Downside volatility within the holding period is not the same as uncertainty regarding the full holding period.

Suppose that you have a young child who will (you hope) start college in about 15 years. You think that it makes sense to start a program of equity-related investing to finance the expenses that you will start to incur in 15 years. But you aren't sure. How well will equities do over the next 15 years? If economic growth is lackluster, maybe bonds will do better. If inflation becomes a real problem, maybe cash will do better. What you are worrying about is the return of the invest-

FIGURE 7-8

Performance in Down U.S. Equity Markets
Average Monthly Return Versus Frequency of Monthly Gain

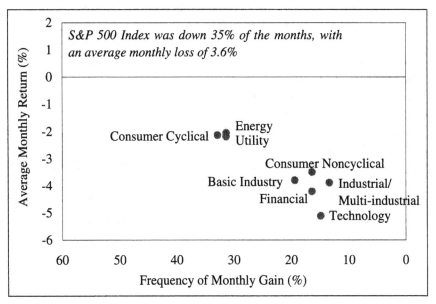

Calculations are based on monthly rates of return for January 1986 to December 2001. Economic sectors established by EACM and based on S&P 500 Index historical holdings. Monthly rates of return for each economic sector calculated by EACM.
Source: Standard & Poor's and EACM.

ment over the full 15-year holding period. Whatever estimate or pre-diction you make is shrouded in uncertainty. That point is totally sep-arate from any worries that you might have about the volatility of the investment within the holding period.

Investing is like flying. When you board a plane in New York for a flight to Los Angeles, there are two very different things to worry about. First, you might worry that the flight will be bumpy and turbulent. Second, you might worry that you won't get to Los Angeles at all. Maybe weather will force you to land in San Francisco, or maybe more dire scenarios will play out. These are totally sepa-rate worries. But the worry about bumpiness can feed the worry about the final destination. When the aircraft starts to bounce around erratically in turbulent air over Kansas, you start to worry more about where you'll finally land.

Investment volatility is like the bumpiness of a flight. But worrying about bumpiness is different from worrying about where the
flight is going to end up. Still, the two worries can get mixed up,
especially when the weather turns nasty. Both flying and investing
have their white-knuckle moments.

You have to separate volatility and uncertainty in order to understand their interrelationship. Uncertainty springs from the fact that
your expectations are very likely to be wrong. And the more precisely you formulate the expectations, the more likely they are to be
wrong. Suppose, for example, that you estimate that the S&P 500 will
return 10 percent, with a standard deviation of 15 percent. We said earlier that in a normal distribution, 68 percent of the returns fall within 1 standard deviation of the mean. Roughly 25 percent of the returns
fall within ⅓ standard deviations of the mean. This means that you
have only 1 chance in 4 of earning a return between 5 percent and 15
percent. Even if you *expect* to earn 10 percent, you are not *likely* to
earn a return close to 10 percent. You should expect the unexpected.

Volatility relates to the bounciness of returns within the holding period. When you make an investment, you will probably have
some expectations regarding the volatility of the investment while
you own it. And those expectations may wind up being pretty close
to the actual volatility, or very far off. But the expected volatility and
the actual volatility are both quite separate from the uncertainty of
your expectations regarding the full investment period. Bouts of
high volatility during the investment period may shake your confidence in your expectations for the full investment period. But you
can't understand the relationship between the two things unless you
keep them separate.

To drive home the difference between volatility and uncertainty,
remember that people worry about risk in all sorts of situations
where price volatility is totally irrelevant. You're trying to decide
whether to cross the street against a red light. You're trying to decide
whether to accept a new job. You're trying to decide whether to start
a new business. All these situations contain risk, and uncertainty,
but no price volatility.

In most real-life situations, we approach the problem of risk
assessment through a process of scenario analysis. On the one hand,
you think about the various good things that might happen if you
cross the street, or take the new job, or start the new business. But the

good things have to be balanced against the various bad things that might happen. With regard to each scenario, there are two crucial questions: (1) What is the likelihood that this scenario will take place? and (2) How desirable, or pleasant, or profitable, is the scenario? The decision is simple when there is a high probability that various good things will happen, balanced against the smaller probability that various bad things will happen. The decision is harder when the good and the bad are more evenly balanced.

In most real-world situations the process of scenario analysis moves along in a very informal, rough and ready way. We cannot assign definite numbers to the probabilities of the various scenarios. Nor can we assign definite numbers to the pleasantness, or desirability, or profitability, of the various scenarios. Finally, we cannot even be sure that we are working with the appropriate list of scenarios. There may be important scenarios that we have overlooked altogether. But, in real life, that is not a problem. Indeed, in the real world, if somebody tried to get very precise about the numbers, it would not be regarded as a sign of intellectual sophistication but as a sign of naivete.

Consider the complexities of space travel. Putting a man on the moon is a technological triumph that requires, among other things, a very subtle and precise understanding of some very complicated physical processes. There are a lot of figures that have to be worked out to three decimal places. But sometimes space travel requires risk assessment. Consider the various crises that beset the Apollo 13 mission. Very smart people had to make some very tough decisions. There was a lot of uncertainty, and not a lot of time. A lot of calculations were made with great precision. But if a bright young engineer had announced, "If we do XYZ, then there is a 4.37 percent probability that the guys will land safely," he would have been laughed out of the room.

So there are all sorts of real-life situations in which risk has nothing at all to do with price volatility. These situations exist even in the financial world, thanks to the universe of nonmarketable investments. *Marketable investments* are financial instruments like stocks, bonds, options, and futures that trade on a regular basis. Willing buyers and willing sellers gather together daily to set a price. The category of *nonmarketable investments* includes real estate and various forms of private equity investing, such as venture capital, buyouts, and related strategies. These investments do not trade on a daily basis. Nonmarketable investments present risk, but their risk has nothing to do with price volatility.

Consider a real estate investor trying to decide whether to buy an office building. She tries to form a realistic picture of the potential risks and the potential rewards. She will probably go through some form of scenario analysis, with each scenario containing different assumptions regarding financing costs, leasing rates, terminal values, and so forth. She might even try to calculate an *expected value* for the building, by taking all the scenarios, multiplying the probability of each scenario's occurring by the value of the building in that scenario, and then adding up all the probability-weighted values. But the various estimates of probabilities and valuations would be pretty rough. And at no point would the exercise have anything at all to do with price volatility. Office buildings don't trade on a regular basis, so they have no price volatility.

Office buildings offer risk without price volatility. There is also price volatility without risk. Consider the difference between a zero-coupon bond and a more conventional bond. A conventional bond makes semiannual interest payments and then a final payment of principal at maturity. The zero-coupon bond pays you nothing until the final maturity date. It turns out, for reasons that I will not inflict on you here, that zero-coupon bonds are much more sensitive than conventional bonds to changes in interest rates. Zero-coupon bonds are more volatile than conventional bonds. Are they more risky? It all depends on what you mean by "risk." Conventional bonds present reinvestment risk. When you own a conventional bond, you will receive a coupon payment every six months, and that payment has to be reinvested. The reinvestment of those coupon payments is an important part of the total return of the bond. But the return that you will earn is very uncertain, since it depends on the future course of interest rates. Zero-coupon bonds do not have reinvestment risk. If you buy a bond today for $174.11, and it matures in 30 years at $1000, then your return for the full period will be exactly 6.00 percent annually compounded. There is no uncertainty at all regarding the return over that period. (We are talking here about nominal return. There is uncertainty about the return after adjusting for inflation, but that is a different story.)

So the zero-coupon bond is more volatile than the conventional bond. But the return of the zero-coupon bond, if you hold it for the full 30 years, is much more certain that the return of the conventional bond. Once again, volatility and uncertainty are totallly different. The bumpiness of the flight is not the same as uncertainty regarding the end point.

The example of the zero-coupon bond illustrates again the importance of the length of the investment period. If you hold the zero-coupon bond for 30 years, you know to the penny what it will be worth. If you have to sell the bond in 20 years, or 2 years, you don't know what the bond will be worth. That depends entirely on the level of interest rates at the time of sale.

The length of the investment period also affects equity investing. The monthly returns for U.S. stocks are very widely scattered. As you extend the investment period, the returns fall within a narrower channel. Figure 7–9 shows the distribution of returns for the various holding periods. This pattern of returns shows that stocks have been a good long-term investment, with a lot of short-term volatility. The investor who has a long time horizon can point to the historical record to defend his confidence that stock prices will be higher in 10 years than they are today. But it's much harder to be confident that stock prices will be higher in 1 year, or 1 month, than they are today.

Of course, even the longer-term investor may turn out to be wrong. The next 20 years might turn out to be radically unlike the last 20, or the last 75. Maybe inflation will reemerge as a major issue, maybe growth will subside to a chronically lower level, or maybe new forms of geopolitical uncertainty will dominate the markets. Perhaps an asteroid will destroy all human life in 2019. But even with all these possibilities, there is still a big difference between investing for the next 20 years and investing for the next 20 months. When you think about longer time periods, you face three questions: (1) How much return will I earn from this investment over the full investment period? (2) How much uncertainty attaches to my estimate of that return? and (3) How volatile will the investment be within the holding period? These questions are all separate. The difference between the second and third questions is the difference between uncertainty and volatility. But they do interact since stomach-churning episodes of short-term volatility will test your confidence in your original expectations.

We have been emphasizing the difference between uncertainty and volatility. Ironically, standard deviation *can* be interpreted

FIGURE 7-9

S&P 500 Index
Distribution of Returns for Varying Holding Periods

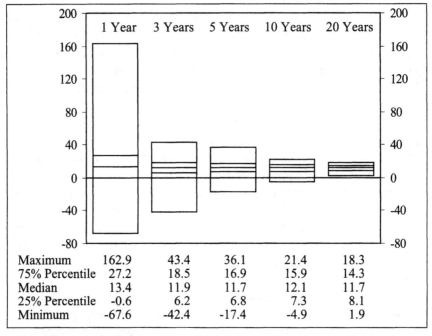

	1 Year	3 Years	5 Years	10 Years	20 Years
Maximum	162.9	43.4	36.1	21.4	18.3
75% Percentile	27.2	18.5	16.9	15.9	14.3
Median	13.4	11.9	11.7	12.1	11.7
25% Percentile	-0.6	6.2	6.8	7.3	8.1
Minimum	-67.6	-42.4	-17.4	-4.9	1.9

Annualized returns for rolling 1-, 3-, 5-, 10-, and 20-year holding periods. Calculations based on monthly returns for January 1926 through December 2001.

Source: Standard & Poor's.

either as a measure of uncertainty *or* as a measure of volatility. But most quantitatively oriented investment professionals use standard deviation as a measure of volatility. Let me explain.

Suppose somebody tells you that the S&P 500 will return 10 percent with a standard deviation of 15 percent. This is usually understood as two predictions: a prediction about return and a prediction about the volatility with which that return will be delivered. The forecaster is crawling out on a limb with the return estimate, and then crawling further out on the same limb with the volatility estimate.

But the standard deviation figure can also be understood as a reminder that the return estimate for the full holding period is very uncertain. If returns are symmetrically distributed, then 68 percent of the returns will fall between a 5 percent loss and a 25 percent gain. The probability of getting a return between 5 and 15 percent is only 25 percent. And so forth. On this interpretation, the forecaster is crawling out on a limb with the return estimate, and then giving you some indication of how shaky that limb is. Instead of getting two predictions, you're getting a prediction and a disclaimer.

The theory of portfolio optimization is a remarkable intellectual achievement. It can help investors organize their thinking about the ways in which the parts of a portfolio interact, with the potential to create a total portfolio that is less risky than the individual parts. Hedge fund managers do not always use sophisticated mathematics to build efficiently diversified portfolios. But they do try hard not to put all their eggs in one basket. They want multiple baskets that are independent of one another, which is one reason that hedge funds use short selling and other hedging techniques.

The sophisticated mathematics of portfolio diversification can also be a powerful distraction when used as a practical tool for portfolio construction. The models invite us to measure historical statistics to several decimal places, and then estimate the future with equal precision. But, as we have seen, the essence of risk is uncertainty, not volatility, nor anything else that can be measured to three decimal places. The precision of the mathematical tools can seduce us into underestimating that uncertainty rather than dealing with it more intelligently.

CHAPTER 8

The Tyranny of the Cap-Weighted Indexes

The third pillar of the efficient market viewpoint is the idea that index funds are the investment vehicle of choice for the rational investor. The belief in index funds is not merely an idea favored by abstract theoreticians of finance. It is an idea that has also moved into the daily lives of investors, both institutional and individual. The popularity of index funds derives not merely from their academic respectability but also from their historical performance.

Passive management became more and more popular as the great bull market of the 1980s and 1990s rolled on. Vanguard's S&P 500 Index fund was launched in 1976 and languished for many years. Its assets are now close to $100 billion. The success of the Vanguard fund inspired many other mutual fund companies to introduce index funds for their retail clients. Indexing has also become an increasingly popular institutional strategy. Reliable statistics are hard to come by, but it is reasonable to estimate that roughly 20 percent of all institutional equity portfolios are in index funds or "closet index funds," that is, funds that hug the standard indexes very closely.

Indexing is popular partly because it is academically respectable—a natural outgrowth of the efficient market theory. If markets are efficient, then investment skill is an illusion, and active management is no better than astrology. So index funds have a sound intellectual basis, while hedge funds are just advanced astrology.

Indexing also has a decent performance record, especially in the realm of large capitalization U.S. stocks. In Figure 8–1 we show the performance record of active U.S. equity managers against the

U.S. Large Cap Equity Manager Universe Versus
S&P 500 Index

Distribution of Annual Returns,
January 1980 through December 2001

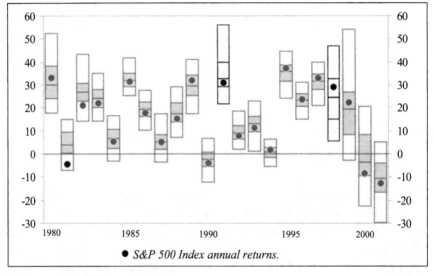

● *S&P 500 Index annual returns.*

Based on a universe of U.S. large cap equity managers.

Source: Effron PSN Database, Standard & Poor's, and Evaluation Associates.

S&P 500. Figure 8–1 reveals definite cycles in the relationship between active managers and the passive benchmark. The index return was below the median manager return from 1990 through 1993, then the situation reversed in the 1995 to 1999 period. The pattern reversed again in 2000 and 2001, as the tech wreck hurt the index more than it hurt the average manager.

The passive benchmark is, in a sense, "just another portfolio." That portfolio has some special characteristics that help explain why active managers sometimes tend to beat the index, and then tend to lag behind the index. Two characteristics of the S&P 500 are especially important. First, as the bull market rolled on, the technology sector became a larger and larger part of the index portfolio. Second, the technology sector became increasingly dominated by a small number of mega cap technology companies. The "Big Five" were Microsoft Corp, Intel Corp, Cisco Systems Inc, Dell Computer Corp, and

Lucent Technologies Inc. Table 8–1 shows how the extraordinary returns in the tech sector made that sector a bigger and bigger piece of the S&P 500. Most active managers were unwilling to make such a big bet on technology, and they were especially unwilling to make such a big bet on the mega cap tech stocks. So their portfolios lagged the index as technology surged and then began to beat the index after the tech bubble burst.

The easiest way to grasp the importance of the capitalization-weighting scheme is to contrast cap weighting with equal weighting. In the cap-weighted S&P 500, at the end of 2001 the largest position was General Electric, with a 3.8 percent weight. The 10 largest names in the index collectively accounted for 24.9 percent of the total index. The 100 largest companies accounted for 72 percent of the index, while the 200 largest companies accounted for 86 percent of the index. In the equal-weighted S&P 500, every stock is 1/500th of the portfolio: 0.2 percent. Figure 8–2 shows the difference in return between the two indexes for the period 1987 through 2001. Notice that cap weighting outperformed equal weighting from 1995 through 1999, which is when

TABLE 8–1

S&P 500, Technology Sector Versus the Big Five
Annual Returns and Percentage Allocation,
1994 through 2001

	Percentage Allocation		Percentage Annual Return	
	Technology Sector	The Big Five	Technology Sector	The Big Five
1994	10	2	14.5	2.4
1995	11	3	40.8	65.6
1996	14	5	39.8	81.9
1997	14	6	29.5	42.7
1998	20	10	75.7	124.8
1999	32	13	78.4	63.6
2000	23	7	−38.0	−52.2
2001	20	8	−21.2	−1.7

Percentage allocation data reflect year-end allocations for the technology sector and the top five mega cap technology stocks, within the technology sector. The top five mega cap stocks (Microsoft Corp, Intel Corp, Cisco Systems Inc, Dell Computer Corp, and Lucent Technologies Inc) were selected by EACM based on December 31, 1998, holdings in the S&P 500 Index. The technology economic sector allocation was established by EACM and based on S&P 500 Index holdings.
Source: Standard & Poor's and EACM.

FIGURE 8–2

S&P 500, Cap-Weighted Versus Equal-Weighted Index
Annual Returns, 1987 through 2001

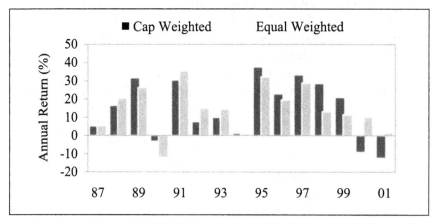

Analysis based on monthly returns for the S&P 500 Index and an equal-weighted index based on S&P 500 Index holdings
and calculated by EACM.

Source: Standard & Poor's and EACM.

active managers lagged behind the index. Then the cap-weighted
index lagged behind the equal-weighted index in 2000 and 2001, which
is when active managers outperformed the index.

The historical data do not show that index funds are universally superior to actively managed funds. The data suggest that the
index is a portfolio with peculiarities of its own, which will lead to
cycles of underperformance and outperformance. To place the point
in a larger context, it is helpful to look at the record of active managers in asset classes other than large cap U.S. equity. Figure 8–3
shows the performance record of U.S. small cap equity managers
against the Russell 2000 Index, the most widely followed U.S. small
cap index. And Figure 8–4 shows the record of international managers (that is, managers who invest in non-U.S. stocks) against the
EAFE (Europe, Australia, and the Far East) Index, the most widely
followed benchmark for international investing.

The small cap managers have been able to beat their benchmark with reasonable consistency. The international case shows more
variability, due almost entirely to Japan. In the late 1960s Japan was
about 15 percent of the main international index. As the Japanese

FIGURE 8-3

U.S. Small Cap Equity Manager Universe Versus
Russell 2000 Index
Distribution of Annual Returns, January 1980 through
December 2001

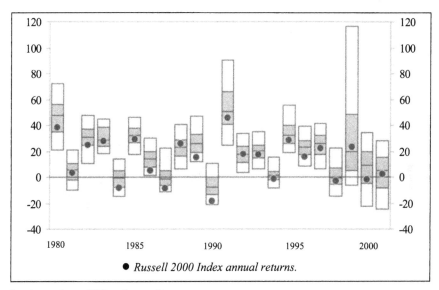

● *Russell 2000 Index annual returns.*

Based on a universe of U.S. small cap equity managers.
Source: Effron PSN Database, Frank Russell Company, and Evaluation Associates.

stock market moved upward through the 1980s, the Japan weight
increased to 65 percent. (Yes, 65 percent.) Then the Japanese bubble
burst, and the Japan weight drifted steadily downward. Japan now
accounts for 20 percent of the main international index. Most active
managers were underweight in Japan during the bubble years: Their
exposure to Japan was less than the index exposure. And so they
lagged as Japan kept moving up. Once the Japanese bubble burst,
active managers started to beat the index again.

There is a perfect analogy between Japanese stocks and technology stocks. In each case what developed was an *index bubble*. In
fact, there was a *double bubble*: a bubble inside a bubble. Each index
rose to an unsustainable level, driven in large part by an unsustainable advance within a particular portion of the index. Active managers tend to lag as the bubble is expanding, and then outperform
in the postbubble period.

FIGURE 8–4

Non-U.S. Equity Manager Universe Versus
MSCI EAFE Index, U.S. Dollars
Distribution of Annual Returns, January 1980 through
December 2001

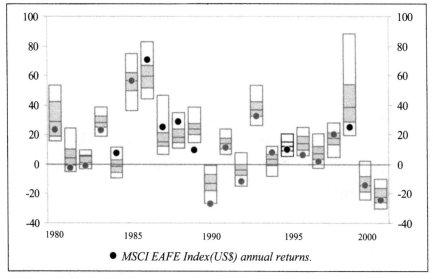

● *MSCI EAFE Index(US$) annual returns.*

Based on a universe of non-U.S. equity managers.
Source: Effron PSN Database, Morgan Stanley Capital International Inc., and Evaluation Associates.

Index funds have many advantages. Investment management
fees are low, and the low-turnover trading style leads to very low
trading costs and high tax efficiency. Moreover, the cap-weighting
scheme offers the very large investor a way to "buy a slice" of the
market without moving prices as much as other investment approaches. Imagine that you are responsible for a $20 billion U.S. equi-
ty portfolio invested in 100 stocks. If you run an equally weighted
portfolio, you will have $200 million invested in each company,
whether the company is a $500 billion market cap company or a $5
billion market cap company. In the former case, your position represents 0.04 percent of the market cap of the company; in the latter case,
your position represents 4 percent of the company. Accumulating a
4 percent position in a small company is much tougher than accumulating a 0.04 percent position in a big company. You move the
price up as you buy, and you are likely to destroy the price if you try

to sell. When a large institution assembles a cap-weighted portfolio, every position represents the same percentage interest in the underlying company. For extremely large investors, cap weighting, or something close to it, can seem almost inevitable.

Despite these advantages, index funds also have some definite disadvantages, most of which are a direct consequence of capitalization weighting. Cap weighting means that the index fund investor often behaves like a momentum-driven investor. Once momentum takes hold, the index can then develop a big bet, or a bubble, inside the index. The index begins to look highly *un*diversified, in the familiar, intuitive, nontechnical sense of *diversified*. Moreover, the index even begins to look highly undiversified in the more technical sense associated with efficient frontiers and portfolio optimizers. The fundamental irony of the efficient market viewpoint is that the realities of the cap-weighted portfolio come into conflict with the ideal of the efficiently diversified portfolio.

MOMENTUM AND CONCENTRATION

Investors tend to sort themselves out into three basic groups. The *buy-and-hold investor* trades very little, showing little or no response to changes in price. The *momentum investor* likes to buy when prices are going up and sells when prices are going down. If he buys a stock at $20, he is likely to buy more if the price rises, because the market is confirming his judgment and may be about to enter a longer-term upward trend. If the price moves down, the momentum investor moves quickly to reduce, or eliminate, the position. The *contrarian investor* has the opposite behavior: She likes to buy when prices are going down and is inclined to sell when prices are going up. If she buys a stock at $20 that moves down to $17, she may well buy more, averaging down as the initial bargain becomes a better bargain. If the price moves up, she will be tempted to take some profits.

The index fund itself is a buy-and-hold portfolio, but those who invest in index funds are momentum investors. The fund does not respond at all to changes in price. But those who invest systematically in index funds are making bigger and bigger allocations to the "hot sectors" of the index. For example, if you put money into an S&P 500 Index fund at regular intervals throughout the 1990s, each investment had a bigger and bigger exposure to technology, largely (but not entirely, as we shall see) because tech stocks were doing so well. At some point the active money manager begins to worry that the great tech uptrend might soon be coming to an end. But the index investor simply accepted the results of the great uptrend and accepted the technology weight created by that uptrend.

CAP WEIGHTING VERSUS EFFICIENT DIVERSIFICATION

The great technology expansion created a situation in which the S&P 500 did not pass the most elementary "smell test" for diversification. There was a bubble inside the bubble. Now let's ask whether the index was diversified in the highly technical sense associated with sophisticated portfolio optimization. This brings us face to face with the basic challenge for the optimizer: estimating the inputs. To simplify, let's consider, once again, the five years ending December 2001. Suppose we had perfect foresight in December 1996. Then we would construct the efficient frontier shown in Figure 8–5. And if we plot the position of the cap-weighted index for the same five years, we see that the index falls below the frontier.

The cap-weighted index has a technology weight that begins at 14 percent and ends at 20 percent. But the efficient frontier offers us a higher-return, same-risk portfolio that begins with a tech weight of zero. And it also offers us a same-return, lower-risk portfolio that begins with a tech weight of zero. So, given this particular set of optimizer inputs, the cap-weighted portfolio is not efficiently diversified.

Now let's suppose that we are running the optimizer in February 1995, with perfect foresight for the five years ending March 2000, the peak of the tech bubble. Figure 8–6 shows the efficient frontier for that period, and it again shows the cap-weighted index falling below the frontier. In this case the lower risk portfolio and the higher return portfolio have higher technology weights than the S&P 500.

Now let's come back to the real world, where perfect foresight does not exist. You run the optimizer with a set of imperfect inputs, and you arrive at a set of portfolio weights. It would be a cosmic coincidence of the first magnitude if the optimizer weights were the same as the capitalization weights.

So the efficient market viewpoint gives us two completely separate and independent ideas. On the one hand, there is the idea of

FIGURE 8—5

Economic Sectors of the S&P 500 Index
Efficient Frontier, Five Years Ending December 2001

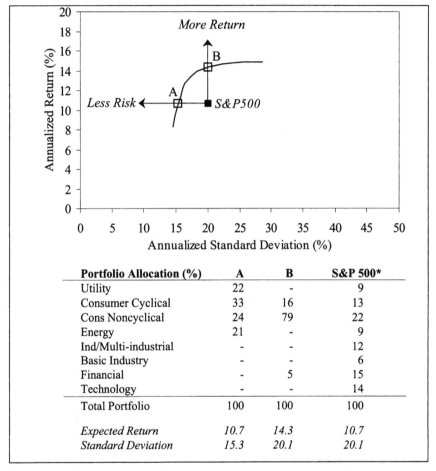

Portfolio Allocation (%)	A	B	S&P 500*
Utility	22	-	9
Consumer Cyclical	33	16	13
Cons Noncyclical	24	79	22
Energy	21	-	9
Ind/Multi-industrial	-	-	12
Basic Industry	-	-	6
Financial	-	5	15
Technology	-	-	14
Total Portfolio	100	100	100
Expected Return	*10.7*	*14.3*	*10.7*
Standard Deviation	*15.3*	*20.1*	*20.1*

*Economic sector allocation as of December 31, 1996, based on EACM calculations. Economic sectors established by EACM and based on S&P 500 Index historical holdings. Monthly rates of return for each economic sector calculated by EACM.
Source: Standard & Poor's and EACM.

the efficiently diversified portfolio, which is the sophisticated mathematical embodiment of two very intuitive ideas. First, don't put all your eggs in one basket. Second, when you assemble a multibasket portfolio, pay attention to the interactions among the baskets. On

FIGURE 8-6

Economic Sectors of the S&P 500
Efficient Frontier, Five Years Ending March 2000

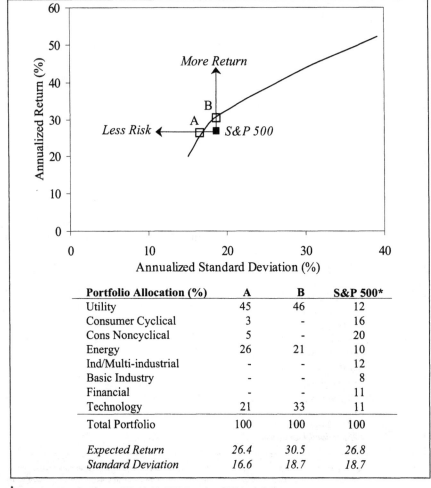

Portfolio Allocation (%)	A	B	S&P 500*
Utility	45	46	12
Consumer Cyclical	3	-	16
Cons Noncyclical	5	-	20
Energy	26	21	10
Ind/Multi-industrial	-	-	12
Basic Industry	-	-	8
Financial	-	-	11
Technology	21	33	11
Total Portfolio	100	100	100
Expected Return	*26.4*	*30.5*	*26.8*
Standard Deviation	*16.6*	*18.7*	*18.7*

*Economic sector allocation as of March 31, 1995, based on EACM calculations.

Economic sectors established by EACM and based on S&P 500 Index historical holdings. Monthly rates of return for each economic sector calculated by EACM.

Source: Standard & Poor's and EACM.

the other hand, there is the idea of the capitalization-weighted index, the portfolio whose returns are completely independent of investment management skill.

In the crunch, these two ideas come into conflict. The cap-weighted portfolio is not likely to be efficiently diversified, and vice versa. And there is a deeper conflict related to two views of investment skill. The crucial advantage of the cap-weighted portfolio is that it does not require skill. The index fund pursues the George Mallory approach to investing. Mallory climbed Mount Everest because it was there, and the index fund buys securities because they are there.

But the construction of a diversified portfolio does require skill. If you are taking a Markowitz-style approach, then you have to estimate a complicated set of inputs, and you know from the start that history is a fallible guide. Even if you don't explicitly use a sophisticated portfolio optimizer, you know that building a well-diversified investment portfolio requires skill, judgment, experience, prudence, and related virtues. No such virtues are required to run an index fund. When cap weighting conflicts with diversification, hedge funds fall clearly on the side of diversification. The mission of the hedge fund manager is simple: Ignore the index, and do your best to build a well-diversified portfolio that will produce decent positive returns in a wide variety of market environments.

OTHER PROBLEMS WITH CAP WEIGHTING

In addition to the larger issues raised above, the following three smaller issues should help remove index funds from their pedestal.

Bond Indexes Special ironies arise when the cap-weighting approach is transferred from the world of stocks to the world of bonds. For example, if you think of the U.S. bond market as one giant portfolio of bonds, then that portfolio has a shorter maturity now than it did 10 or more years ago. The U.S. Treasury has shortened the average maturity of its borrowings, and the bond market now includes the mortgage-related market as an important component. Mortgage-related bonds tend to have shorter "effective maturities" than more traditional bonds. Since investors often assemble bond portfolios with specific investment purposes in mind, it may easily turn out that those purposes are not well served by a portfolio that tracks the overall bond market.

The issue arises in a different form when you think about global bond portfolios. As the United States government got its financial house in order, the total amount of U.S. government debt gradually shrank, and so U.S. debt became a smaller and smaller piece of the global bond pie. As Japan's financial condition deteriorated, the Japanese government issued more and more debt, and so Japanese debt became a bigger and bigger piece of the global bond pie. If you invested in a global bond index at regular intervals, you were putting less and less money in the United States as the United States was improving, and putting more and more money in Japan as Japan was deteriorating.

Market Cap Versus Float The composition of the cap-weighted index is driven by the market cap of the underlying companies, which is simply the number of shares outstanding multiplied by the price per share. But in many cases the number of shares available for purchase in the marketplace—*the float*—is much less than the number of shares outstanding. This can produce major distortions. Consider Yahoo, whose total market capitalization was $114 billion at the end of 1999, thus representing 0.9 percent of the S&P 500 Index. But Yahoo's float was only 48 percent of its market cap: Only 48 percent of Yahoo's shares were available for purchase in the marketplace. As index funds bought Yahoo to bring its weight up to 0.9 percent, their buying interest was focused on half the outstanding shares, thus they exerted artificial upward pressure on the price. This price pressure increased Yahoo's position in the index, thus requiring new buying, and so on. So the index funds wound up chasing their tails as they tried to invest a disproportionately large amount of money into an artificially small number of shares outstanding.

Qualitative Selection Criteria To the pure efficient market theorist, the best index is a pure cap-weighted index, with no qualitative stock selection criteria applied at all. But the best-known U.S. equity index, the S&P 500, relies heavily on qualitative criteria. The S&P 500 is not a cap-weighted index of the 500 largest stocks in the U.S. stock market. Rather, the index is a cap-weighted index of the 500 stocks that the Standard & Poor's selection committee has decided to include in the index. Generally speaking, the committee prefers stocks that are liquid and that represent leaders in their various industries. Berkshire Hathaway, for example, is a very large company, but the stock is not very liquid. Berkshire Hathaway had a market cap of $115 billion at the end of 2001, which would place it outside the top 10 (number 10, Johnson & Johnson, is at $181 billion) but well within the top 100 (which begins at $20.8 billion). But Berkshire has (so far) been excluded from the index because of concerns about liquidity.

As the new economy began to overshadow the old economy in the late 1990s, the S&P 500 selection committee added more and more technology stocks to the index as other companies dropped out of the index. Index attrition is inevitable: Companies drop out due to mergers, acquisitions, bankruptcy, or other developments. When Venator Group, the parent of Woolworth & Co., dropped out of the index, the replacement was America Online. When Mobil and Exxon merged, the new vacancy was taken by Citrix Systems. JDS Uniphase, one of the hottest tech stocks, entered the index to replace Rite Aid, the discount drug chain that filed for bankruptcy. The new stocks had some claim to being leaders in their respective industries, even if they were very young companies or trading at very high valuations. So the steadily increasing weight of the tech sector had two separate sources: the number of tech stocks increased steadily, and the newly added tech stocks outperformed their nontech competition.

CONGRATULATIONS!

You've just finished the hardest part of this book. And you may be asking: Why did I have to go through all this when I just wanted to learn about hedge funds? Who really cares about efficient markets, efficient portfolios, and capitalization-weighted indexes? The answer is: a lot of people. It is difficult to convey to somebody outside the investment business how much that business has been transformed by the ideas that we have been discussing in the last four chapters. Every investment professional has to deal with the challenges of market efficiency, passive benchmarks, and the ideal of the optimally diversified portfolio. And the world of professional money management sometimes seems to be divided into two worlds, or two cultures: the world of passive management and the world of active management. The first world is the world of the Ph.D. quants, financial engineers, and rocket scientists. The second world is the world of skill, judgment, experience, gray hair, and a lot of other "soft stuff." At the extremes, it's a pitched battle between the physicists and the poets.

Hedge funds represent active management par excellence. The hedge fund manager has no interest at all in tracking, or even beating, the cap-weighted indexes. But she does have an interest in building an intelligently diversified portfolio. And she acknowledges from the start that skill is an essential part of the game. But skill is partly a matter of maintaining a proper respect for the efficiency and the competitiveness of markets.

The orthodox theology of market efficiency boils down to six main ideas. Here's where hedge funds stand:

1. Markets are highly competitive and totally rational. *False.* Markets are highly competitive but not totally rational. Fear and greed are essential elements of markets. So panics and bubbles are inevitable.

2. There is no free lunch. *True.* Return requires risk. Even if there are a few free lunches, there aren't very many, and it's always prudent to assume that what looks free isn't. If you think you've found a free lunch, think again.

3. The past does not predict the future. *True.* Past success does not guarantee future success, and it may even obstruct future success. If the past did predict the future, investing would be much simpler than it is.

4. Investment skill does not exist. *False.* Skill does exist, but there is no simple and direct linkage between skill and performance. Sometimes good returns are produced by sheer luck, not skill. And sometimes there are failures of implementation. So skill does not guarantee good returns.

5. The capitalization-weighted market index is the best investment for the rational investor. *False.* Although the capitalization-weighted index presents itself as a buy-and-hold portfolio, in fact the portfolio is momentum oriented and thus becomes perilously undiversified.

6. Mean/variance optimization is the ideal tool for constructing an efficiently diversified portfolio. *False.* An elegant theory is not the same as a practical tool. Efficient portfolios are only efficient relative to a set of inputs, and those inputs are difficult to estimate. So the *efficiently* diversified portfolio is not always *intelligently* diversified. Moreover, the theory of efficient diversification generally assumes that volatility is the key proxy for risk. But risk is uncertainty, not volatility.

Given the view of financial markets suggested above, what is the role of hedge funds? For starters, it's misleading to insinuate that hedge funds are in the business of "exploiting market inefficiencies." If such inefficiencies exist, there aren't enough to go around. Hedge funds, like other active managers, are in the business of mobilizing their skill to join the competitive fray. And remember, the efficient market theorist needs competition in order to keep the markets efficient. So the moral to the efficient market story is not that it makes no sense to compete. The moral is that if you're going to compete, never forget how tough the game is.

The current interest in hedge funds reflects disenchantment with index-tracking strategies. Every investor now knows, viscerally, that index tracking is not a strategy for all seasons. But hedge funds represent the opposite end of the spectrum. There are many styles of active management that lie between pure indexing and hedge funds. If equity markets remain challenging in the aftermath of the tech wreck, the terrorist attacks of September 2001, and the corporate scandals of 2002, then investors will become more interested in many different forms of investment management that are not totally benchmark driven. Hedge funds are an important part of that world, but hardly the only part, or the most important part.

PART THREE

The Tools of the Trade

CHAPTER 9

Leverage, Short Selling, and Hedging

Hedge funds try to deliver an attractive rate of return that has a low correlation with the standard investment markets. In pursuit of this objective, most hedge funds use leverage or short selling or both. But there are some hedge funds that do not take advantage of this freedom. Conversely, most "traditional managers" do not use either leverage or short selling. But some traditional managers do use these strategies sparingly, and even mutual funds may use these strategies within defined limits.

Leverage and short selling both require borrowing. In the case of leverage, you want to buy something, but you don't have enough money. So you borrow the money. In the case of short selling, you want to sell something that you don't own. So you borrow it. Then you sell the asset that you borrowed, in the hope that you will be able to buy it back at a lower price and then return it to the person who loaned you the asset. (If this quick description of short selling has left you totally mystified, don't worry. All will become clear before too long.)

Since leverage and short selling both require borrowing, these strategies can be used only in margin accounts held at a brokerage firm. Unlike a conventional brokerage account, which contains only assets, a margin account has both assets and liabilities. The assets serve as collateral for the liabilities.

LEVERAGE

Buying on margin is like taking out a mortgage to buy a house. Mortgage lenders are typically willing to lend 80 percent or more of the value of the house. In the securities business, brokers will typically lend 50 percent of the value of stock to be purchased. But some stocks, viewed as especially risky, may not be eligible for margin purchase; that is, the broker will not lend funds against those securities. Conversely, if the securities to be purchased are government bonds, the required down payment may be as little as 5 percent or less. In the securities business, the down payment is called the *haircut*.

Buying on margin creates an interest expense and magnifies both gains and losses. Suppose that you have $100,000 in a broker-age account, and you want to buy $200,000 worth of IBM stock. Suppose further that IBM trades at $100 per share, so $200,000 is 2000 shares. So you borrow $100,000 from the broker, pledging the 2000 shares of stock as collateral, and the full account, including both assets and liabilities, is as shown in Table 9–1. Here the value of the asset fluctuates, but the value of the liability is fairly stable. The liability may increase slightly as you begin to incur interest expenses on the borrowed $100,000. If you want, you can add those charges to the liability. So you begin with assets worth $200,000 and a liability of $100,000, which results in a *net equity* (assets less liabilities) of $100,000. You begin 200 percent invested; that is, the ratio of assets to net equity is 2:1.

Suppose that the broker charges you 5 percent interest (annually) on the borrowed funds. If IBM goes up by 20 percent in the course of the year, then you earn $20 per share on 2000 shares, for a profit of $40,000. But you owe $5000 in interest on the borrowed $100,000. So the net profit is $35,000, on a net investment of $100,000. Thanks to leverage, you earned 35 percent in the account, even though IBM only went up by 20 percent.

Now suppose that IBM goes down by 20 percent. Then the $40,000 gain becomes a $40,000 loss, but you still owe $5000 in interest. So the combined loss is $45,000, on a net investment of $100,000,

TABLE 9–1

Structure of a Leveraged Long Position

Assets		Liabilities	
2000 shares of IBM	$200,000	Margin debt	$100,000
Net equity	**$100,000**		

for a percentage loss of 45 percent. In other words, if you are 200 percent invested in IBM, then the return to the leveraged position is twice the unleveraged return, minus the interest rate on the borrowed money. If IBM goes up by 47.5 percent, then the return to the leveraged position is two times 47.5 percent, minus 5 percent, which equals 90 percent. If IBM goes down by 47.5 percent, then the loss on the leveraged position is two times 47.5 percent, less 5 percent. You are down 100 percent. You are wiped out.

Leverage makes it possible to lose more than you have invested. If IBM declines by 60 percent, then the shares are worth $80,000 and the account has a loss of $120,000. But you still owe the broker $100,000 (plus interest), even though the stock is worth only $80,000. You need to come up with an additional $20,000 to satisfy your obligations. The $120,000 loss is greater than the original equity of $100,000.

The use of leverage is absolutely guaranteed to increase the *risk* of a position. It is *not* guaranteed to increase the *return*. The key question is whether the unleveraged return is greater than the borrowing cost. If it is, then leverage increases return. If it isn't, then leverage hurts return.

To understand the impact of leverage on risk, we can mobilize our old friend, the concept of *standard deviation*. When returns have a low standard deviation, they are constrained within a fairly narrow channel. When returns have a high standard deviation, the channel of returns is wider. We observed earlier that, in a normal distribution, 68 percent of the returns fall in a channel between the mean plus 1 standard deviation and the mean minus 1 standard deviation.

Suppose that the S&P 500 has a return of 12 percent, with a standard deviation of 15 percent. Then 68 percent of the returns will fall between the mean plus 1 standard deviation, which is 27 percent, and the mean minus 1 standard deviation, which is –3 percent. So we have a channel of returns with 27 percent at the top, 12 percent in the middle, and –3 percent at the bottom. If we invest in the S&P 500 with 2:1 leverage, we create a new channel of returns that is both higher and wider. Suppose the cost of borrowing is 5 percent. To define the new channel, we take each point in the old channel, multiply by 2, and subtract 5 percent. The new mean is 19 percent, the new upper point is 49 percent, and the new lower point is –11 percent. The width of the new channel is the distance between 49 and –11 percent, which is 60 percent. The width of the old channel was 30 percent. In each case, the width of the channel is 2 standard deviations. So 2:1 leverage increased the standard deviation from 15 to 30 percent. Using 3:1 leverage would triple the standard deviation, and so forth.

You may remember that, in a normal distribution, there is a 2.5 percent probability of earning the mean return less 2 standard deviations. If the S&P 500 returns 12 percent with a standard deviation of 15 percent, then the mean less 2 standard deviations is –18 percent. So there is a 2.5 percent chance of losing more than 18 percent. At 2:1 leverage, the new mean is 19 percent, the new standard deviation is 30 percent, and there is a 2.5 percent chance of losing more than 41 percent. At the 3:1 leverage, the new mean is 26 percent, the new standard deviation is 45 percent, and there is a 2.5 percent chance of losing more than 64 percent. The numbers get very scary very fast.

Leverage increases risk, and reduces the investor's staying power. Both the lender and the borrower want the loan to be repaid, so both sides begin to worry when the equity in the account gets close to the value of the loan. When this happens, the broker will notify the investor that he needs to add to the equity in the account by depositing cash or other securities. This notification is a *margin call*. If the investor does not meet the margin call, the broker will sell the stock, pay himself back the amount of the loan, and return any excess to the investor. So the leveraged investor may be forced to transact: He must sell the stock, even though he does not want to, and the margin call may come at a time when the stock is artificially depressed, poised to come back.

The leveraged investor is automatically very focused on cutting losses. If you buy a stock without leverage, and the stock goes from $50 to $35, you can always persuade yourself that the stock will come back. You may even buy more at $35. It may be a mistake to hold onto the stock, but at least you can afford to live with the mistake. The leveraged investor cannot afford such mistakes. The leveraged investor is always living in fear of the margin call, and the first rule of investing is to sell before the broker makes you sell. So the leveraged investor has weak hands and may be forced to sell when he doesn't want to. The leveraged investor is at the other end of the spectrum from the well-capitalized investor who has a reserve of *dry powder*. Dry powder helps an investor through the hard times and enables the investor to take advantage of other people's distress when times get tough.

A *margin loan* is a demand loan; the lender of the money can, in theory, ask for her money back at any time. In addition, the terms of the loan are subject to change. For example, the interest rate on margin debt is generally tied to a short-term interest rate benchmark. If short-term rates go up, then margin rates will go up. In addition, the lender may have the ability to alter the *haircut*, or down payment.

Suppose you buy a house for $400,000. You use $100,000 of your own money, and you borrow $300,000 from the bank. Your initial equity is $100,000, since you own an asset worth $400,000, and you have a $300,000 liability. Now suppose that the value of the house declines to $300,000. Your equity is zero, and the lender faces the risk of not recovering the value of the loan. To address this risk, the bank might ask you for more money. If the bank were still willing to lend 75 percent of the value of the house, then the bank would be willing to lend $225,000, which is $75,000 less than the current loan. So the bank would ask you for $75,000.

But now suppose that, in this new environment, the bank is no longer willing to lend 75 percent of the value. The new number is 50 percent. So the bank is willing to lend only $150,000, which is $150,000 less than the current loan. This means that you have to come up with $150,000. And that $150,000 is on top of the original down payment of $100,000. That money is gone; it went to the seller of the house.

This very unfortunate scenario could not arise with houses. When banks lend against houses, they take the risk that the house value will decline below the loan value. In these circumstances, the owner of the house may "walk away from the mortgage." The bank then assumes ownership of the house and sells the house to recover as much value as it can. There are no margin calls in the home lending business. But there are margin calls in the investment business. When the underlying investments are stocks, government bonds, or other familiar instruments, the percentage down payment requirements are fixed in advance and do not change. When the investments are more exotic, the broker has wide latitude in setting the haircut. And the percentage requirement may go up just as prices are going down. So the leveraged investor faces the possibility of a devastating double whammy: The price of the investment declines, *and* the percentage haircut is raised. Some of the major hedge fund disasters have resulted directly from this combination of events.

To avoid these nasty surprises, hedge fund managers try as hard as possible to *lock in* the terms of the financing. In particular, they will try to lock in a financing rate that will apply over the next three to six months, or perhaps longer. And they will try to lock in the percentage haircut requirement. Locking in these arrangements requires complicated negotiations between the hedge fund manager and the broker. And, by the way, this is an area where the larger fund may have a real negotiating advantage.

Before we leave the topic of haircuts and margin requirements, it is important to observe that the margin requirement set by the broker is a very fallible guide to the risk of the investment. If a broker requires a 50 percent down payment on a stock and a 5 percent down payment on a government bond, then the broker regards the stock investment as more risky than the bond investment. But down payment requirements can get unrealistically low when there is a lot of speculation going on and brokers are competing against each other to lend money. In situations like this, the probability of a double whammy (lower prices plus higher haircuts) gets very high. So the prudent hedge fund manager will take the broker's margin requirements with a grain of salt and will form an independent, and more conservative, opinion of the real risk of the investment.

There is a broader lesson here. The relationship between a hedge fund and its lenders is like the relationship between any other business and its lenders. When times are good, borrowing is easy and the lenders compete to make it still easier. Borrowers who take full advantage of those easy conditions, who "borrow to the hilt," are bound to experience distress when conditions change—as they invariably will. And that distress will affect both the borrower and the lender.

That, in a nutshell, is what happened to Long Term Capital Management. Thanks to the size of the assets and the reputation of its principals, the firm had extraordinary market clout. LTCM was able to borrow at remarkably favorable terms, sometimes avoiding collateral requirements altogether. So, when conditions changed, the distress was extreme, for borrower and lender alike.

One final note on leverage: There is often a lot of hand wringing in the financial press about "the level of leverage in the system." The New York Stock Exchange compiles statistics on the total amount of margin debt outstanding. At the end of 2001, this figure was $150 billion. That's a lot of money. But the total capitalization of the stocks that trade on the New York Stock Exchange is $16 trillion. So the total margin debt was only 1 percent of the total market capitalization. To be fair, there are types of leverage not captured in this statistic. And major changes in the level of margin debt can be very important. But when you're looking at very big numbers, it's important to view them in the context of other numbers that are even bigger.

SHORT SELLING

Short selling is the mirror image of buying on margin. When you buy on margin, you buy stock that you can't afford. So you make some sort of down payment, then borrow the cash that you need to make the purchase. When you sell short, you sell a stock that you don't own. So you borrow the stock, pledging cash or some other asset as collateral for the loan. Then you sell the stock, in the hope that you will be able to buy the stock back in the open market at a lower price, at which point you can return the borrowed stock to the lender. The long investor hopes to buy low and then sell high; the short seller hopes to sell high and then buy low.

(If your eyes are starting to glaze over, don't worry. Short selling does that to people. Just relax. It will all be over in a few paragraphs.)

Short selling breaks down into three steps: You *borrow* the stock, you *sell it short*, and then you *cover* the short. Suppose that, during the height of the Internet bubble in late 1999, you begin to feel that Amazon.com is overvalued. You short Amazon at $100; then you cover your short at $50 in the middle of 2000. You've made $50 per share without ever owning the stock. How did this happen?

First you deposit money (or securities) into a margin account. Then you use that money as collateral to borrow the Amazon shares. This requires that somebody who owns Amazon be willing to lend you his shares. This is usually not a problem since anybody who owns stock in a margin account has consented to having his stock lent to other investors. The prime broker arranges the borrowing. This means, incidentally, that when a hedge fund manager chooses a prime broker, he will want, among other things, a broker who has excellent access to stock available for borrowing.

Then you sell the borrowed shares, and that sale produces real money, which is called *the proceeds of the short sale*. The proceeds of the short sale go into an account at the prime broker, where they earn interest. The interest is split three ways: the lender of the Amazon shares earns a lending fee, the broker earns a fee for arranging the transaction, and the short seller earns the remainder of the interest.

Let's assume that you open the account with $100,000, and you sell short 1000 shares of Amazon.com at $100 each. Then the assets and liabilities in the account are as shown in Table 9–2. The account has total assets of $200,000 and a liability that is originally valued at $100,000. So the net equity in the account is exactly $100,000, which was the starting amount. We added a new liability, and a new asset, but the net equity did not change.

When you buy on margin, the asset value fluctuates while the liability value remains stable. The object of the game is to increase the net equity by increasing the value of the asset. When you sell short, the asset value remains stable while the liability fluctuates. The object of the game is to increase the net equity by decreasing the value of the liability.

Both the margin buyer and the short seller have borrowed something that they must return. The margin buyer has to pay back a definite number of dollars, even if the asset that he bought becomes worthless. Similarly, the short seller has to return a definite number of shares of stock, even if those shares at the time have an astronomically high value.

Let's suppose that Amazon.com goes from $100 to $50, so the value of the liability goes from $100,000 to $50,000. This $50,000 decline in the value of the liability boosts the net equity in the account by $50,000. Now you can *cover the short* by taking $50,000 from the original deposit, buying Amazon in the open market, and then using

TABLE 9–2

Structure of a Short Position

Assets		Liabilities	
Original deposit	$100,000	1,000 shares of Amazon.com	$100,000
Proceeds of short sale	$100,000		
Net equity	**$100,000**		

the newly purchased shares to pay back the original borrowing of stock. At the end of the day there is $150,000 in the account, and no liabilities. You sold high and bought low. Or, more accurately, you shorted high and covered low.

The function of the original $100,000 deposit is to serve as collateral for the borrowing of the stock. If Amazon goes from $100 to $120, then the value of the liability goes to $120,000, the assets are still at $200,000, so the net equity is only $80,000. As the price of the shorted stock goes up, the broker begins to worry about getting paid back, and at some point he will make a margin call. At that time you can put more money into the account. If you do not, the broker will force you to cover the short at current prices. Like the leveraged long investor, the short seller may be forced to transact.

Notice that short selling creates a new interest-bearing asset. If you open the account with $100,000, and then short stock worth $100,000, there would then be $200,000 in the account that is earning interest. So even if the shorted stock appreciates modestly, you can make money if the appreciation in the stock does not cancel out the interest on double the account equity.

Short selling was an extraordinarily profitable strategy during the 1970s, when short-term interest rates were high and stock prices were weak. Suppose that short-term interest rates are at 10 percent, and you short a stock that goes down 5 percent. You earn 10 percent interest on the original deposit, 10 percent interest on the cash proceeds of the short sale, and a 5 percent gain on the short sale. Total return is 25 percent. Not bad, considering that the stock went down only 5 percent.

When you short a stock, you have to make sure that the lender of the stock continues to get any dividends to which she is entitled. So you have to make those up out of your own pocket. The borrowing fee that you pay is on top of any other income that the lender would ordinarily receive. This fact, by the way, sheds light on more familiar forms of borrowing. When you take out a home mortgage at 8 percent, you may think that you are paying an 8 percent borrowing fee. That is not exactly right. The person who lends you the money could invest that money in bonds to earn, let's say, 6 percent. When you pay 8 percent, you are paying out 6 percent to make sure that the lender gets what she would have earned otherwise, and then you are paying a borrowing fee of 2 percent or so. This phenomenon applies also to U.S. Treasury bills, which are often regarded as risk-free investments. Those who invest in Treasury bills *earn* "the risk-free rate." But nobody can *borrow* at the risk-free rate. If you borrow Treasury bills, you owe the lender the risk-free rate and *then* you owe a borrowing charge.

Borrowing rates are set by supply and demand. If a stock is hard to borrow, then the lender of the stock will demand a higher interest rate, so the short seller will earn a correspondingly lower rate on the proceeds of the short sale. It is also worth noting that when small retail investors engage in short selling, they often receive no interest at all on the proceeds of the short sale. What would have gone to the short seller is simply retained by the broker who arranges the stock borrowing.

There are two aspects of short selling that make it more troublesome than long investing. First, the short seller has limited upside potential but unlimited downside risk. This is opposite to long investing, in which the investor faces limited downside risk and unlimited upside potential. If you buy a stock at $100 per share, the worst that can happen is that it goes to zero. But it could go to $500, or $1000. If you short a stock at $100, the best that can happen is that it goes to zero. But there is no worst case: The stock could go to $500, or $1000, or higher. Of course, the short seller may decide to cover the short before this happens, or he may be forced to cover by a margin call. But if the short seller is willing to put additional equity into the account, then the losses can go up without limit. This is the nightmare scenario of the *runaway short*. So the short seller needs to be even more vigilant about cutting losses than the leveraged long investor.

The second troublesome feature of short selling is that losing positions become a *bigger* piece of the portfolio, so the total portfolio becomes increasingly sensitive to your mistakes. To see this, consider an unleveraged $1,000,000 portfolio that consists of nine long positions, at $100,000 each, and one short position, initially valued at $100,000. Now suppose that one of the long positions goes down by 50 percent, while everything else remains the same. The losing position is now worth $50,000, while the total portfolio is worth $950,000. So the losing position, which started out at as a 10 percent position, becomes a 5.3 percent position. The total portfolio is then less responsive to further declines in the price of your mistake.

But now suppose that the short position goes from $100,000 to $150,000, while everything else remains the same. Then the total

portfolio is again worth $950,000 (the appreciation in the short posi-
tion counts as a loss), while the losing position is $150,000, or 15.8 per-
cent of the total. What began as a 10 percent position is now a 15.8
percent position. So the total portfolio is now more responsive to
further appreciation in the stock you were wrong about.

In a well-diversified long portfolio, you can afford to make a few
mistakes. The mistakes get smaller and smaller until you can almost
forget about them. In a well-diversified short portfolio, your mistakes
get bigger and bigger, and eventually they can put you out of business.

The short seller operates from a doubly vulnerable position.
He accepts unlimited downside in the pursuit of limited upside and
pursues a strategy in which mistakes become more and more visible. Experienced hedge fund managers treat their short positions
with a vigilance that borders on paranoia. In particular, diversification is even more important on the short side of the portfolio than
on the long side. Many managers have position limits designed to
enforce a certain degree of diversification on the long side. For example, a manager might have a rule that he will not place more than 5
percent of the portfolio in a single long position. If the upper limit
on the long side is 5 percent, then the upper limit on the short side
may well be 2 or 3 percent, in order to allow for the fact that short
positions become bigger when they move against you.

Short selling involves borrowing, which creates the risk of the
margin call. Just as the leveraged long investor may be forced to sell
in a falling market, so the short seller may be forced to buy in a rising market. This forced buying can lead to a *short squeeze*, in which
short sellers are forced to cover their positions at disadvantageous
prices. In addition, a short squeeze can result if the owners of a stock
decide to make their stock unavailable for borrowing. When the
short seller borrows stock, the loan is a demand loan. If the lender
wants the stock back, the borrower must either borrow stock from
somebody else or buy the stock in the open market.

Some investors feel that a large short position in a stock can be
a bullish sign. The reasoning here is that if the stock does start to move
up, then short sellers will experience margin calls, and hence there
will be forced buying in the stock. The forced buying will accentuate
the upward move already in place. All this is certainly true. But bear
in mind that the upward move may never develop, in which case the
shorts will make money and escape the pain of forced covering.

The analogy between shorting and leverage is helpful here. If a large short interest can be a bullish sign, then a large leveraged long position can be a bearish sign. If a stock is owned mainly by investors who have borrowed money to buy the stock, then any meaningful decline in the stock will trigger margin calls, which will trigger further declines. But if the stock keeps moving up, then the leveraged long investor will make money and escape the pain of forced selling.

The stock exchanges have imposed various rules to limit the activities of short sellers. For example, there is the *uptick rule*, which means that a stock can't be sold short when the price is going down. This rule is designed to prevent *bear raids* in which short sellers gang up on a stock already in free fall, thus exacerbating an already difficult situation. Notice that there is no analogous rule on the long side. If prices are going up, investors are welcome to buy, even if they are buying on margin. This is one of the ways in which the stock market favors the longs over the shorts. The futures markets offer a more level playing field, as we shall see in Chapter 10.

Short selling is a relatively minor activity when compared to the total size of the U.S. equity market. For example, at the end of 2001 the New York Stock Exchange reported that there were approximately 6.5 billion shares sold short. Remember, the obligation of the short seller is to return a fixed number of shares no matter what their price is. So short interest is always reported in shares, not dollars. If we assume an average share price of $50, this works out to $325 billion in short positions. This sounds like a lot of money, but it's smaller than the market cap of General Electric (roughly $400 billion) and represents only about 3 percent of the market cap of the S&P 500.

When short sellers put on their positions, they are usually very careful to size their positions in such a way as to avoid liquidity problems. They want to be sure that they can cover their short in the event that the stock rises sharply, so they want their position to be manageable relative to the size of the company, and relative to the trading volume in the stock. The *short interest ratio* (sometimes called *days to cover*) is an important statistic for the short seller. Suppose that XYZ is a small company for which the average daily trading volume is only 20,000 shares. And suppose that the total short interest is 1 million shares: Short sellers, in aggregate, are short 1 million shares of the company. This short interest represents 50 days of average trading volume, which means that covering the shorts would be a long and tricky proposition. In a situation like this, the potential for a *short squeeze* is high, so hedge fund managers are wary of stocks that already have a large short interest.

Despite all the perils mentioned above, short selling can be an extremely useful strategy when intelligently applied within a broader portfolio context. As we have noted before, the ability to take short positions makes it easier to build well-diversified portfolios. In addition, most investors focus their research efforts and their analytical capabilities on identifying stocks to buy. In particular, most of the research generated by the large Wall Street brokerage houses focuses on buy recommendations, not sell recommendations. So the short seller is following the time-honored strategy of devoting her efforts to an area that most people are not covering. This has the opportunity to create incremental return.

SHORT SELLERS

The hedge fund community includes a small group of managers whose mission in life is to take short positions in overvalued stocks. The short seller is not merely *net* short. She is *only* short.

And now we must immediately make two qualifications. First, the short seller may have a very limited number of long positions that arise from the research effort that drives the short portfolio. But the long portion of the portfolio will always be insignificant compared to the short portion.

Second, there is a subtle but important distinction between *covering* a short position and *boxing* the position. (This terminology leads to bad jokes about boxing your shorts, but we will not go down that road.) When you *cover* a short position, you buy stock and deliver the newly purchased stock to close out the stock borrowing. When you *box* a short position, you buy stock, but you do not use the new stock to close out the borrowing. When you box the short position, you wind up with two positions that cancel each other out. When you cover the short, you wind up with no position at all.

Boxing a short position used to have tax advantages over covering a short position. All gains from short sales are treated as short-term gains, so delaying those gains is a worthwhile exercise. Boxing a profitable short position was a technique for protecting the profits without creating a tax liability. But tax laws were changed to treat boxing a short as economically equivalent to covering a short, and hence subject to the same tax treatment.

Boxing may be preferable to covering when a stock is hard to borrow. Suppose that the manager wants to trim back a short position temporarily, with a view to reestablishing the full short position sometime in the future. If she boxes the short position, she leaves the stock borrowing intact rather than returning the stock to the lender.

Some short sellers think of themselves as absolute-return investors who just happen to focus on short selling opportunities. Others think of themselves as a hedge against major stock market declines. The absolute-return-oriented short seller has the more ambitious objective: She is trying to make money from short positions whether the market is up or down. In particular, she is trying to guard against major losses in a generally rising market.

If you are a short seller who is focused on absolute return, you face a major problem. When you are trying to deliver positive returns, you have to reduce your short positions in a rising market in order to avoid big losses. On the other hand, you have to increase your short positions in a falling market since your investors expect big gains in bad markets. This means that you wind up looking just like a momentum-driven investor: You buy in a rising market and sell in a falling market. And this produces a major irony. Short sellers often present themselves as taking advantage of opportunities created by the irrational behavior of momentum-driven investors. The short seller is a contrarian investor who tries to make money from the "irrational exuberance" of the momentum crowd. But when the short seller focuses too hard on absolute return, she becomes a momentum investor too.

HEDGING VERSUS SPECULATION

Sometimes hedge funds take short positions simply to make money. They buy stocks that they think are going to go up and short stocks that they think are going to go down. This is officially classified as "speculation," since the object of the short selling is to increase return. But sometimes hedge funds take short positions in order to hedge. The object here is not to increase return but to reduce the risk that is already present in the portfolio.

To understand how hedging works, it's helpful to start with the case of the perfect hedge. We saw an example of this at the end of the last section: boxing a short position. The opposite of this is *shorting against the box*. If you own 100 shares of Microsoft, then one way to reduce your risk is to sell the shares you own. Alternatively, you can short against the box, which means you sell shares you don't own. Instead, you borrow shares and sell them short, and the new short position cancels the risk of the long position. The proceeds of the short sale earn interest, just as the cash proceeds earn interest when you sell the stock you own.

Shorting against the box was once a popular tax-reduction strategy. If you had a big unrealized gain in a stock position, you could short against the box, thus reducing your risk without taking a taxable gain. This tax strategy is no longer available since shorting against the box is now viewed as a *constructive sale*. That is, the tax code now says that the short against the box is economically equivalent to a more conventional sale, so the tax consequences should be the same.

When you box a short position, or short against the box, you wind up with two positions that cancel each other out exactly. The net result is a risk-free position whose return will be equal to some risk-free interest rate. The situation is analogous to the "riskless arbitrage" that we discussed earlier: buying gold in New York at one price, simultaneously selling gold in London at a higher price. But, as we saw earlier, in some of these allegedly risk-free trades, there may be some element of risk. If you are long Microsoft in an account at Merrill Lynch and short Microsoft at a small brokerage firm that goes bankrupt, you will soon wish that you had simply sold the long position.

In most forms of hedging, the long position and the short position are not identical. So there is some element of basis risk in the trade. *Basis risk* is the risk that the long and the short may not exactly cancel each other out. When hedge fund managers put on hedged trades, they do so in the hope that the long position will do better than the short position.

To illustrate the contrast between hedging and speculation, take yourself back to the height of the technology bubble: New-economy stocks are soaring, while old-economy stocks are diving. You decide that this trend will continue so you buy Cisco Systems and short General Motors. Your view is that Cisco Systems will go up and General Motors will go down, and you expect to make money on both sides of the trade. Here the object of the short sale is clearly to increase return.

Now let's change the situation. You like Cisco Systems, but you worry about stocks in general and technology stocks in particular. You regard Cisco Systems as an excellent technology stock, but you want to address the risk of a general stock decline, or a tech-centered decline. Let's say that you focus on Microsoft as a more vulnerable technology stock because of its legal entanglements and its many rivals in the computer business. So you buy Cisco Systems and short Microsoft. In this case, the underlying view is not that Cisco Systems will go up *and* Microsoft will go down. Rather, the view is that Cisco Systems will do better than Microsoft. In this case, the short Microsoft position is being used to hedge the long Cisco Systems position.

Let's work through the arithmetic. You have $100,000 in a margin account, and you buy $100,000 worth of Cisco Systems. You then use your Cisco Systems position as collateral to borrow $100,000 worth of Microsoft, which you then sell short. In the ideal world, Cisco Systems will go up and Microsoft will go down. Then you will make money on both the long position and the short position. But even if this does not happen, there are plenty of opportunities for profit. If Cisco Systems rises by 20 percent while Microsoft rises by 18 percent, then you make $20,000 on the Cisco Systems position, but you lose $18,000 on the Microsoft. So your net profit is $2000. If Cisco Systems goes down 18 percent and Microsoft goes down 20 percent, then you lose $18,000 on the Cisco Systems, but you make $20,000 on the Microsoft. Again, your net profit is $2000. In both cases, Cisco Systems performed better than Microsoft, so your total portfolio is profitable. Notice too that these figures include only trading profits, not interest income. In this example, the short sale of Microsoft produces $100,000 of short sale proceeds, which will bear interest.

Needless to say, hedging doesn't always work out. When you bet that Cisco Systems will outperform Microsoft, you might be wrong. In particular, there is always the possibility that the long position will go down while the short goes up. So both sides of the trade lose money. But this is just a special case of the long side doing worse than the short side. If Cisco Systems loses 10 percent while Microsoft gains 10 percent, you will be down 20 percent. But if Cisco Systems gains 10 percent while Microsoft gains 30 percent, you will also be down 20 percent.

When people think about the difference between hedging and speculation, they think of speculation as *directional trading*. The speculator on the long side is betting that the price will go up, and the speculator on the short side is betting that the price will go down. Hedging seems nondirectional since you are simultaneously long and short. But the hedger is implicitly assuming, or betting, that the long side of the trade will do better than the short side. If you think that Cisco Systems will do better than Microsoft, then you are taking a position on the relationship between the two stocks. In the jargon of the trade, the hedger is *speculating on the basis*. And that speculation can be wrong.

We have been talking about hedging one stock with another stock. Let's take a quick look at some other examples.

Suppose you are an active equity portfolio manager. You own a portfolio that you think will outperform the S&P 500 Index. But you become very worried about the level of the market in general. You like your stocks, but you don't like the market. So you take a short position in the S&P 500 to hedge the market-related risk of your portfolio. This is a hedge, but it is also a bet that your portfolio will beat the index. And that bet doesn't always work out. In fact, the actively managed portfolio could lose money while the S&P 500 makes money. In this case, both sides of the hedge would be unprofitable.

Here's an example from the world of bonds. You own a large portfolio of investment-grade corporate bonds, but you are worried about a rise in the general level of interest rates. If rates go up, bond prices go down so you hedge your risk by taking a short position in U.S. Treasury bonds, or Treasury bond futures. Putting on this hedge reduces the risk related to a general rise in interest rates, but the combined position still has risk. The hedge is a bet that the long portfolio will do better than the short portfolio. But the long portfolio might lag the short portfolio. There are even circumstances where the corporate bond portfolio would lose value as the Treasury bond gained value. Suppose that there were general anxieties about recession, disinflation, and declining corporate profits. Then investors would be likely to sell corporate bonds and buy U.S. Treasuries, in which case the long corporate–short Treasury hedge would come under pressure.

Here is another example, which played an important role in the crisis of August 1998. In the early part of 1998, many hedge funds were invested in emerging markets debt that had a very high yield. But these managers worried that emerging markets debt was vulnerable to a rise in U.S. interest rates: If the price of U.S. Treasury bonds went down, then emerging markets debt would go down too. So managers took short positions in U.S. Treasury debt to address that risk.

That "hedge" led to trouble in the fall of 1998. Russia defaulted on its debt and devalued its currency. This caused losses in many investment portfolios, including massive losses at Long Term Capital Management. Emerging markets debt fell sharply because of anxieties specific to the emerging markets. Meanwhile, the price of U.S. Treasuries rose sharply on a "flight to quality." So the "hedged" position—long emerging markets debt versus short U.S. Treasury debt—lost on both sides. The managers who attempted to reduce their risk by shorting U.S. Treasury debt wound up increasing their losses.

Since hedges can go wrong, it is important to be careful when thinking about the "gross exposure" and the "net exposure" of a hedge fund manager. Suppose a hedge fund has $10 million in net assets, $8 million in long positions, and $5 million in short positions. So the manager is 80 percent gross long and 50 percent gross short. If you add the two numbers, you would say that the manager has 130 percent of *gross* exposure. If you subtract the 50 percent from the 80 percent, you would say that the manager is 30 percent *net* long. The latter calculation is correct as far as it goes, but it can be misleading. The 30 percent figure may suggest that only 30 percent of the portfolio is really at risk. But this assumes that the 50 percent short position cancels out a 50 percent piece of the 80 percent long position. And that may not be the case. Under extreme pressure, the longs can go down while the shorts go up. In that case, what is driving the risk profile of the portfolio is the 130 percent gross exposure.

When evaluating hedge fund managers and strategies, it is essential to separate the purpose of hedging from the realities of hedging. The purpose of hedging is to reduce risk. But hedging does not eliminate risk and sometimes does not even reduce risk. The hedger is betting that the longs will outperform the shorts. Sometimes this bet works out, sometimes it doesn't. In particular, sometimes the longs go down while the shorts go up. Whenever a manager describes a hedging strategy, it is useful to force yourself, and force the manager, to consider situations in which both sides of the hedge will lose money.

CHAPTER 10

Futures and Options

As a general rule, hedge funds use futures and options more than traditional active managers do. This is not universally true; some hedge funds do not use futures or options at all, and some traditional managers have become very active participants in the futures and options markets. Still, to understand hedge funds, it is important to understand something about futures and options: what they are and how they are used.

Options and futures are *derivative instruments,* whose value and usefulness depend on their relationship to the underlying stocks, bonds, or other assets. Derivatives have a bad reputation in some quarters, and there are investment circles where people hesitate to use "the *D* word." But without derivatives the world would be a much poorer place. Derivatives can be misused, sometimes with catastrophic consequences. But any tool can be misused, sometimes disastrously. No matter what you think about the details of gun control, you can't quarrel with the familiar bumper sticker: Guns don't kill people, people do. Similarly, derivatives don't kill portfolios, people do.

SOME BASIC STRATEGIES

Before we get into the nitty-gritty of futures and options, let's look at some simple strategies. Options and futures can be used either to hedge or to speculate. If you think that the S&P 500 Index is going to go up, then you can buy futures, or buy call options, to make money if you are right. If you think the market is headed down, you can sell futures, or buy put options. These are speculative strategies: You are increasing your risk position in order to make a profit. But derivatives can also be used to hedge. If you own a large stock portfolio and start worrying about the health of the market, you can hedge your risk by selling S&P 500 futures, or buying S&P 500 puts. Similarly, if you have a large short position, you can hedge your risk by buying futures, or buying calls. In these cases you are trying to reduce your risk: You are protecting the value of a position that you already have.

Futures offer *symmetrical risk exposure*; options offer *asymmetrical risk exposure*. Buying a futures contract on the S&P 500 is economically equivalent to buying the S&P 500. As we shall explain later on, buying a futures contract is like buying the underlying asset but delaying the settlement of the transaction into the more distant future. If the market goes up 20 percent, you make 20 percent; if the market goes down 20 percent, you lose 20 percent. Options are different. When you buy an option, you buy a *right* to do something. When you buy a *call* option on the S&P 500, you have the right to *buy* the index at a predetermined price, which is the *strike price* of the option. If the market goes up a lot, you get to buy stocks at a discount since the strike price of the option will be much less than the market price of the index. If the market goes down a lot, your option will expire worthless since the option gives you the right to buy stocks at what turns out to be an above-market price. The worst case for the call buyer is that he loses the cost of the call; the best case is that he multiplies his money many times.

Puts are the opposite of calls. The buyer of a *put* acquires the right to sell the asset at a predetermined price, which is the strike price of the option. And the potential profit if the price of the underlying asset falls will be much bigger than the potential loss if the price rises.

Buyers of options acquire rights but not obligations. Sellers of options acquire obligations. Futures contracts involve obligations, whether the investor is buying or selling the contract. Later on we will uncover a simple linkage between futures and options. Buying a futures contract is equivalent to buying a call *and* selling a put, while selling a futures contract is equivalent to buying a put *and* selling a call. The buyer of the futures contract gets to make money from rising prices, but, since she has "implicitly" sold a put, she will lose real money from falling prices. Similarly, the seller of the futures contract will make money from falling prices, but, since he has "implicitly" sold a call, he will lose money from rising prices. A futures position combines a long option position with a short option position. Each of the underlying options positions offers asymmetrical risk, but the combination of the two delivers symmetrical risk.

FUTURES MARKETS

When people think about futures markets, they tend to think about commodity traders screaming at each other in the trading pits of Chicago, buying and selling truckloads of soybeans and pork bellies on a highly leveraged basis. Then they think about the soybean speculator, long 1000 soybean contracts, who wakes up one morning to find large trucks dumping soybeans all over his lawn. In fact, the futures markets are now much more focused on the financial markets than they are on the traditional markets for physical commodities. Futures contracts on interest rates, equity indexes, and currencies are much more actively traded than futures contract on soybeans and pork bellies. These instruments do permit some people to engage in recklessly leveraged speculation. But they also permit other people to engage in prudent forms of investing, hedging, and risk management.

A *futures contract* is a *forward contract* that trades on an exchange. A *forward contract* is a binding agreement to buy or sell a fixed amount of some underlying asset at a fixed price at some fixed date in the future. The buyer or seller of a forward contract is buying or selling an asset today but delaying the settlement of the transaction to some point in the future.

The distinction between the *trade date* and the *settlement date* is common in many markets. When you buy a house, the closing date might be several months after you and the seller agree on the price and other terms. In the stock market, trades used to settle five business days after the transaction date, but the five-day delay was recently reduced to three days. In the government bond market, trades settle the day after the transaction date. You can think of the futures market as a market in which the delay between transaction and settlement can be as long as several months, or even several years. The gold market, for example, is an extremely liquid market in which people can buy or sell gold for settlement in two months or two years.

Given the substantial delay between the transaction date and the settlement date, the seller of the asset might worry about the ability of the buyer to come up with the required amount of money on the settlement date. And the buyer of the asset might worry about the ability of the seller to come up with the required amount of the underlying asset. In particular, if the price of the asset goes down, the seller needs to be confident that the buyer will follow through on her promise to buy the asset at the agreed upon price. And if the price goes up, the buyer needs to be confident that the seller will be able to deliver the required amount of the asset. To address these worries, the futures markets have developed a very sophisticated *margin* mechanism. There are two key forms of margin: initial margin and variation margin.

Initial margin is a deposit whose basic function is to assure that the investor will be able to withstand some reasonable level of loss. For example, one gold futures contract covers 100 troy ounces of gold, so, if gold is trading at $300 per ounce, then one contract has a *notional value* of $30,000. Each $1 move in the price of gold causes a change of $100 in the value of the contract. If gold moves up $1, then the investor who is long the contract makes $100, while the investor who is short loses $100. The required margin deposit for gold is $1350 per contract, which represents the exchange's judgment that the investor needs to demonstrate that he can tolerate a $13.50 adverse price move. (This margin requirement is for a speculator. The margin requirement for a hedger is slightly smaller.)

Variation margin is an arrangement in which positions are marked to market daily, and cash flows from the accounts of those with losses into the accounts of those with gains. If you put on a position this morning that is showing a modest loss as of today's close, then tomorrow morning you will be required to place additional money in the account. Similarly, if you put on a position this morning that has a modest profit by the end of the day, then cash will enter your account tomorrow morning. So gains and losses are realized every day, and cash moves among accounts accordingly. This means that those with winning positions don't have to worry whether the losers have enough capital to withstand their losses. The losers have *already* withstood the losses. If the losing investor is not willing to put up additional variation margin, then the futures broker will close out the position, use the initial margin deposit to settle up any final losses that might occur, and return any remaining amount to the investor.

Futures markets can be used for hedging or for speculation. The hedger is trying to reduce his risk, the speculator is trying to increase his return. Consider the corn farmer and the cereal manufacturer. The corn farmer faces the risk of falling corn prices; the cereal manufacturer faces the risk of rising corn prices. The corn farmer can reduce his risk by selling, or shorting, corn futures, while the cereal manufacturer can reduce his risk by buying corn futures. If the price of corn goes down, the farmer will have profits on his short futures position that will help to offset the decline in value of his crop. And if the price of corn goes up, the losses on the futures position will offset the increase in value of the crop. As for the cereal manufacturer, if prices go up, then he will have profits on his long futures position that will help to offset the higher cost of raw materials. And if prices go down, futures losses will offset lower operating costs. So the farmer and the cereal manufacturer are both happy to use the futures market to reduce their risk.

When a farmer enters the market to hedge his risk, the other side of the trade might be taken by a cereal manufacturer, or by a speculator. Speculators are very useful to hedgers. If hedgers could transfer their risk only to other hedgers, markets would be less liquid, and hedging would be more expensive. The hedger just wants somebody to take the other side of the trade, and she wants to be sure that whoever is on the other side of the trade has the financial ability to perform his obligations under the contract. Hence the elaborate mechanism of initial margin and variation margin.

The futures market is a zero-sum game: For every long position there is a short, and for every short position there is a long. For every winner there is a loser, and vice versa. This is fundamentally different from the stock and bond markets, where long positions do not require corresponding short positions. When you buy 100 shares of IBM, you are probably buying it from an investor who owned the stock, not an investor who is shorting the stock. And the stock you buy is ultimately traceable back to IBM, which issued the stock to the public many years ago. At any given point, there is a fixed amount of IBM stock in the marketplace. To create new equity, there would have to be some sort of corporate action on the part of IBM. In the futures markets, there is no fixed supply of contracts. As long as there are willing buyers and willing sellers, the number of contracts can rise without limit.

When we discussed short selling, we pointed out that the stock exchanges are friendlier to the longs than to the shorts. The uptick rule prevents short sellers from shorting a stock that is already moving down, but there is nothing to prevent momentum-driven investors from buying a stock that is moving up. Longs and shorts do not play on a level field. The futures markets do offer a level playing field. A short position can be either a hedge or a speculation. The same goes for a long position. There is no special stigma attached to being short.

Since the futures markets are based on delayed settlement, the buyer has the use of the money between the transaction date and the settlement date, while the seller does not yet have any money in his pocket. This provides an important clue to the pricing of many futures contracts. There are two kinds of futures markets: *cost-of-carry markets* and *price discovery markets*. In a price discovery market, the price of the futures contract reflects the market's collective judgment about what the price of the commodity will be at a predetermined time in the future. The crude oil market is a good example. The contract for delivery next winter will be priced in a way that reflects expectations about weather, supply and demand, and related factors. The contract for delivery in the following summer may be priced above or below the winter level, depending on expectations about conditions that summer. So, in a price discovery market, the futures price is the *expected spot price*. The *spot price* is the price at which the commodity changes hands for immediate delivery.

A *cost-of-carry market* is a market in which the futures price is today's price, adjusted to reflect an interest charge over the life of the contract. Cost-of-carry markets are markets in which there is an easy arbitrage mechanism that connects today's price with the price for future delivery.

The gold market provides a good example. If you look at gold futures contracts, you will see that the price of the contract moves up as the settlement date moves further out. Does this mean that the futures markets believe that the price of gold will gradually trend upward? No. It means that, in the gold market, the futures price is the spot price adjusted for an interest rate.

Suppose that gold is priced at $280 per ounce today, and you are buying gold for settlement in one year. What price should you pay?

Since you can earn interest on the $280 during the year between purchase and settlement, you should be willing to pay $280 plus whatever interest you would earn on $280. If the interest rate on a one-year deposit in 5 percent, then one year's interest is $14. So the fair price for a gold futures contract that settles in one year would be $294.

Here is another way to look at it. Suppose you buy an ounce of gold today for $280 and sell it for delivery in one year. You are now in a riskless position, having locked in a selling price for the gold. So the return to this position should be essentially the same as the return to a riskless one-year investment. If we assume that the riskless return is 5 percent, then $294 would be a fair price for gold for delivery in one year.

The gold market and many financial markets are cost-of-carry markets. There are easily available arbitrage mechanisms that link current prices with prices for future delivery. There are ample supplies of the asset available for purchase and sale today, and in a year. There are no storage or insurance costs, and no risk of spoilage. Price discovery markets are not as simple. If you buy soybeans today and sell soybeans for delivery in one year, you face storage costs, insurance costs, the risk of spoilage, and all sorts of other uncertainties. There is no riskless arbitrage to link today's prices with prices for future delivery. In these markets, the futures price reflects the market's judgment about what the price will be in the future.

OPTIONS

When you buy or sell a futures contract, your economic position, and your risk, is the same as if you had bought or sold the underlying commodity. Both the buyer and the seller of the futures contract assume specific obligations. An option is a *right*, but not an obligation, to buy or sell an asset at a predetermined price. That predetermined price is the strike price of the option. The buyer of the option acquires the right; the seller of the option takes on the corresponding obligation. There are two basic kinds of options: a *call option*, which is the right to buy the underlying asset, and a *put option*, which is the right to sell the asset.

There are three reasons that the knowledgeable hedge fund investor needs to know about options. First, many hedge funds use options *explicitly*, either to control risk, or to enhance return, or to deliver some combination of the two results. Second, many hedge funds trade securities that involve options *implicitly*. For example, a *convertible bond* is a straight corporate bond plus a call option on the underlying stock. A *mortgage-backed bond* is a bond whose buyer has sold a call option to the underlying homeowner since the homeowner has the right to refinance her mortgage without penalty. Third, many of the trading strategies employed by hedge funds are related to strategies that try to duplicate the pattern of returns that options generate. For example, the broad distinction between *contrarian strategies* (buy low, sell high) and *momentum strategies* (buy high, sell higher) is related to the difference between two different option simulation strategies. The contrarian approach is similar to strategies that simulate the effect of being short an option, while the momentum approach is similar to strategies that simulate the effect of being long an option.

To understand puts and calls, it's useful to think about the natural buyers and sellers of puts and calls. Let's start by asking who sells calls. Suppose you own 100 shares of Microsoft, trading at a price of $55 per share. You think Microsoft has the potential to reach $60 over the next few months, but it is not likely to get beyond $60. You want to hold onto Microsoft for the long term, but you are looking for a way to take advantage of the near-term tepid outlook. In this situation, you might sell a Microsoft call option with a strike price of $60 and a maturity of three months. If Microsoft stays below $60, as you anticipate, then the option expires worthless and you keep the premium you collected. If Microsoft rises above $60, you will be forced to deliver your Microsoft shares at the predetermined price of $60 per share, even if Microsoft is then trading at $70 per share. So you are giving up any appreciation potential beyond $60. In exchange for that, you have the opportunity to earn the option premium as incremental income.

Selling calls is often recommended as a strategy for generating incremental income from a long position. But that incremental income comes with strings attached. The new asset comes with a new liability: the obligation to deliver Microsoft at a price of $60, even if Microsoft is trading at a higher price at the time. If Microsoft ends the period below $60, then the option expires worthless, the liability disappears, and the option premium you collected remains free and clear. If Microsoft ends the period above $60 per share, then the seller of the option is still obliged to deliver the stock at $60.

Who buys calls? The buyer of the call has a view of the situation opposite to that of the call seller. He thinks there is a real possibility that Microsoft will rise above $60, and he wants to participate in any move above $60. But he also doesn't want to risk large losses if Microsoft goes well below the current price of $55. The call buyer wants to participate in the upside, while protecting the downside. So the buyer and the seller have opposite views about volatility. The seller of the call expects price movements to be fairly quiet, constrained within a narrow range. The buyer of the call expects prices to break out of any such range. The seller of the call is *short volatility*, the buyer is *long volatility*.

Who buys puts? Buying puts is like buying an insurance policy to protect the value of what you own. The put owner has the right to sell the underlying asset at a predetermined price. Let's say you hold Microsoft at $55, but you are worried that Microsoft may decline sharply over the next three months. In this situation, you might buy a three-month put option with a strike price of $45. The put option gives you the right to sell your Microsoft at $45, even if Microsoft is then trading at a much lower price. Buying the put places a hard floor under the price of the stock. If Microsoft rises sharply, the put will eventually become worthless, but the loss on the put will be much less than the Microsoft gain. So you retain a good deal of upside participation. Notice that buying puts is very different from selling calls. Selling the call generates a modest amount of incremental cash, but it does not cushion against large losses.

The seller of the put has the opposite view. Suppose, for example, you want to buy Microsoft shares, but you think the current price of $55 is too expensive. Perhaps you think that $45 is a fair price for the shares. If you sell a put with a $45 strike price, then you are obligating yourself to buy Microsoft at $45, even if the stock is trading at a lower price at the time. But this may seem a fair deal since $45 is cheaper than $55 and the price is further reduced by the "insurance premium" that you collected when you sold the put. Suppose that the put cost $5. If you wind up having to buy the shares at $45, your effective cost is really $40 per share since you collected an additional $5 from the sale of the put.

The buyer of the put expects prices to be volatile. He wants protection from a big down move but doesn't want to miss out completely if there is a big up move. The seller of the put expects prices to be more stable. If the stock gets weak, he gets to buy at a lower price; if the stock strengthens, he gets to keep the put premium. Once again, the buyer of the option is long volatility, and the seller is short volatility.

Selling a call against stock that you own places a ceiling on your appreciation. Buying a put to protect stock that you own places a floor under the value of your holdings. Combining the two transactions places a ceiling and a floor on your returns. This transaction is often called a *collar*. Part of the attraction of the collar is that the money received in the sale of the call can be used to help pay for the put. In the jargon of the business, you sell off the upside to pay for protection on the downside. Indeed, many institutional investors have shown a great deal of interest in *zero-cost collars*, in which the money received from selling the call is exactly equal to the amount required to purchase the put.

In the zero-cost collar, the strike prices of the call and the put are adjusted in such a way that the market price of the call is exactly equal to the market price of the put. Another important option transaction is the *forward conversion*, in which the put and the call have exactly the same strike price but may have different market prices. The forward conversion is essentially a collar in which the floor and the ceiling are exactly the same, so there is no longer any risk left in the trade. For example, suppose that you own Microsoft stock, currently trading at $55, then you buy a three-month put, with a strike price of $50, and you sell a three-month call, also with a strike price of $50. You have just "locked in" a $50 selling price. If Microsoft is trading below $50 at expiration, then you can exercise the put; if Microsoft is trading above $50 at expiration, then the call will be exercised against you.

The forward conversion is the basis of numerous options arbitrage strategies. A trader on the floor of the options exchange might look for "mispricings" that would make it possible to set up forward conversions at an implied rate of return higher than the risk free rate. To execute this strategy, it is absolutely essential to keep transaction costs as low as possible. The ordinary retail investor is not in a position to take advantage of any such opportunities. In other words: Do not try this at home.

The forward conversion gives us a basic equation:

- Long stock + long put + short call = cash

In other words, the three positions on the left add up to produce a riskless investment that is economically equivalent to cash. (Remember that we are assuming that the put and the call have the same expiration date and the same strike price.) Once we have the above equation, we can rearrange the various terms to produce other equations:

- Long stock + long put = cash + long call
- Long stock + short call = cash + short put
- Long stock = cash + long call + short put
- Short stock = cash + short call + long put

The first equation tells us that buying puts to protect a stock portfolio is equivalent to holding cash and then placing a small amount of money in call options. In each case you gain participation in a rising market and protection from losses in a falling market.

The second equation tells us that selling covered calls is economically equivalent to selling *cash-secured puts*. In each case, the investor earns an incremental return if the stock trades in a narrow range. If the stock goes up a lot, the gains are limited. If the stock goes down a lot, the investor loses money, but the amount of the loss is slightly reduced by the amount of the option premium that was received.

The third equation tells us that we can create *synthetic stock* by combining cash, a long call position, and a short put position. Buying a call while selling a put (assuming, again, that the strike prices and expiration dates are identical) is a synthetic long position, equivalent to buying the asset. Selling a call while buying a put is a synthetic short position, equivalent to being short the asset.

The third and fourth equations take us back to the fundamental difference between options and futures. Buying a futures contract is financially equivalent to buying the underlying asset, which is financially equivalent to buying a call *and* selling a put. Conversely, selling a futures contract is equivalent to buying a put *and* selling a call. (We assume throughout that the two options have the same strike price and expiration date.) The buyer of the futures contract acquires the right to benefit from rising prices but assumes the obligation to suffer from falling prices. The seller of the futures contract acquires the right to benefit from falling prices but assumes the obligation to suffer from rising prices.

The theory of option pricing has received a great deal of attention both from the academic community and the community of investment practitioners. The pioneering work was done by Fischer Black and Myron Scholes, whose Black-Scholes formula is still widely used. Other formulas have also been developed, but their common theme is that the price of an option is determined by the following variables:

- The strike price of the option
- The maturity of the option (time until expiration)
- The current price of the underlying asset
- The risk-free rate over the life of the option
- The yield of the underlying asset
- The volatility of the underlying asset

Every item on this list is important, but time and volatility deserve special attention. The buyer of an option hopes that her option will be in the money at expiration. A call is *in the money* if the strike price of the call is below the value of the asset; a put is *in the money* if the strike price of the put is above the value of the asset. Other things being equal, options with longer maturities are more expensive. If an option expires in six months, then the underlying asset has six months to perform as expected. If the option expires in six days, the asset has to deliver the goods much faster, and the odds of success are lower. So time favors the option seller, and acts against the option buyer. Each passing day chips away at the value of the option, whether the option is a call or a put. This phenomenon is referred to as *time decay*. Time decay is a headwind for the buyer and a tailwind for the seller.

Higher volatility makes for higher prices, other things being equal. Higher volatility means that the price of the asset moves in a wider range and thus is more likely to perform as required by the time the option expires. Generally speaking, the best time to buy an option is when the underlying asset has been trading in a narrow range. This leads investors to expect continued range-bound trading, which can easily lead to cheap options prices, which creates an opportunity for positive surprises for options buyers. For options sellers, the best time to sell is typically during periods of high volatility and major uncertainty, when options are very expensive. If volatility then declines, as often happens, a profit opportunity is created for those who have sold options.

CHAPTER 11

AM/FM Investing: The Modulation of Returns

WINNING OFTEN VERSUS WINNING BIG

Here is a seriously boring game for a rainy day. You need a friend and a coin, and each of you needs a small stack of $10 bills. You take turns flipping the coin. Whoever flips heads wins $10. Whoever flips tails loses $10. You should be able to make it through the whole day with the two stacks of ten $10 bills. The odds of winning are exactly the same as the odds of losing. The size of the potential win is exactly the same as the size of the potential loss. Boring.

There are two ways to make the game more interesting. One strategy is to try to modulate the *frequency* of winning. Try to flip heads more often than you flip tails. The other strategy is to try to modulate the *amplitude* of the wins. Try to alter the terms so that you win $15 when you flip heads but lose only $10 when you flip tails.

In the ideal world, we would look for investments that offer a very high probability of large gains, combined with a small probability of small losses. But that sounds like a free lunch. If we are looking for situations in which the *probability* of winning is high, then we should assume that the *size* of the win will not be large. Moreover, if the probability of loss is small, then it is prudent to assume that the size of that loss might be large, at least compared to the size of the potential gain. So we wind up looking for situations in which the large probability of a small gain is balanced against the small probability of a larger loss.

But the opposite situation is also very relevant to investors. Instead of looking for situations in which the probability of winning is high, we look for situations in which there is a potential for a big win. Here it is prudent to assume that the probability of winning is small. This means there is a larger probability of losing, but we hope that those losses will not be large. So we look for situations in which the small probability of a large gain is balanced against the large probability of smaller losses.

To illustrate this difference, consider the difference between buying lottery tickets and selling insurance. When you buy a lottery ticket, the probability of winning is low, but if you do win, you win big. Selling insurance is exactly the opposite. Lloyd's of London thrived for many years because individual investors, called *names*, were willing to collect premium checks in exchange for promising to make big payments in the event of large insurance claims. The names enjoyed cashing the checks for many years; then a series of large claims forced many of them into bankruptcy. Similarly, in the mid-1980s many small investors made money by selling puts on the U.S. stock market. As the market kept moving up, the puts expired worthless, and the put sellers were happy. Then the crash of 1987 came, and the put sellers faced losses vastly larger than any gains that they had experienced. The insurance seller is weighing the high probability of small gains against the small probability of large losses.

Investors like to have the odds in their favor. They like the idea that there is a high probability of winning. They like money managers who say that they are only trying for singles and doubles, not home runs. But whenever the probability of winning is very high, it is prudent to assume that the low-probability loss will turn out to be a big loss. Sometimes investors underestimate the downside when they are attracted by the large probability of winning. Conversely, investors sometimes look down their noses at strategies that offer a low probability of winning. These strategies are sometimes dismissed as gambling, or speculation—like buying lottery tickets. But seeking the small chance of a big win can be a very prudent strategy, as long as the high-probability losses are small in comparison.

The contrast between buying lottery tickets and selling insurance is useful but artificial. Think for a moment about the difference between stocks and bonds. Bond investors are looking for steady income and have no interest in making big gains. In contrast, stock investors are looking for bigger returns and do not expect (or should not expect) those returns to be steady. Table 11–1 shows the pattern

TABLE 11-1

Stocks Versus Bonds
Monthly Returns, January 1926 through December 2001

	Average Gain	Average Loss	Frequency of Gains, %	Frequency of Losses, %
Stocks	4.0	-3.9	62	38
Bonds	0.9	-0.8	72	28

Analysis based on monthly total returns for the S&P 500 Index and U.S. Intermediate-Term Government Bonds.
Source: Ibbotson Associates.

of monthly returns for stocks and bonds from 1926 through 2001. Buying stocks is quite different from buying lottery tickets. The stock investor is more likely to win than to lose, and the average gain is roughly the same as the average loss. And buying bonds is very different from selling insurance. The average loss is roughly the same as the average gain, not dramatically higher. But the basic contrast remains: The bond investor wins more often than the stock investor, but the stock investor wins bigger.

The above results apply to "plain-vanilla" stock and bond portfolios. But there are styles of equity investing that are closer to buying lottery tickets, and there are styles of bond investing that are closer to selling insurance.

Venture capital investing is probably the most aggressive form of equity investing. The venture capitalist invests in very young privately held companies, long before they are publicly traded. These are high-risk investments in which the failure rate is high. Some venture capitalists assume that about one third of their investments will turn out to be worthless. And another third will be essentially flat: no big losses, but no big gains either. But if there are enough home runs in the remaining third of the portfolio, then the returns to the total portfolio can be very handsome. The venture capitalist is willing to assume a large number of losses in the expectation that these will be more than offset by a small number of impressive gains.

Aggressive growth managers who invest in public companies have a similar view of risk. They are investing in risky situations in which it is naïve to expect to win frequently. But they expect to win big when they do win. This attitude toward risk is also seen outside the investment business. Corporate executives sometimes say that they expect more than half of their decisions to be wrong. But if the good news that flows from the good decisions more than offsets the bad news that flows from the bad decisions, nobody will care that the bad decisions outnumbered the good decisions. Many corporations go out of their way to encourage this attitude toward risk taking, thus trying to fight the natural risk aversion of many employees.

Now let's move to the bond side of the business. The bond investor wants a steady return, and has no interest in big gains. There is no upside, or a very limited upside, in bonds. If you lend somebody $10,000, the best that can happen is that you get your money back. Of course, you can try to increase the yield on your bonds—increase the interest rate that you are charging on the loans. But "reaching for yield" presents genuine risks that are easy to underestimate.

Suppose that government bonds yield 5 percent and that a portfolio of high-yield "junk bonds" yields 9 percent. The incremental yield of 4 percent looks very attractive. But let's think about risk. The junk bond portfolio does not have a lot of upside. If the bonds are trading close to their *face value* (that is, the value that the bonds will have at maturity), then the potential for capital appreciation is essentially zero. As for the downside, junk bonds sometimes default, and when they default the price can easily plunge to $50 per $100 of face value.

During times of recession and economic difficulty, the default rate can easily rise to 5 percent or more. That is, 5 percent of a junk bond portfolio might default. Let's assume that 5 percent of the portfolio defaults and thus experiences a loss of 50 percent. The expected return calculation looks like this: 95 percent of the portfolio will earn 9 percent, while 5 percent will lose 50 percent. This means that the expected gain is 8.55 percent (95 percent times 9 percent), while the expected loss is 2.50 percent (50 percent times 5 percent). The expected total return is 6.05 percent. This is still a premium over the 5 percent available from government bonds, but a much smaller premium than we assumed before. A risk-averse investor might conclude that 1.05 percent of incremental return is not worth the risk.

Now let's make things more interesting. Maybe our estimate of the downside is wrong. Maybe 6 percent of the portfolio will default, and maybe the defaulted bonds will decline by 60 percent. This means that the expected return is 8.46 percent (94 percent times 9 percent) less 3.60 percent (6 percent times 60 percent), which is 4.86 percent. The expected return is now less than the expected return of the government portfolio.

The trouble is that in the real world, where things are messy and imprecise, it will be virtually impossible to say which is the better estimate of the downside. Is there a 5 percent chance of a 50 percent loss, a 6 percent chance of a 60 percent loss, or something in between, or something outside the range? The calculation of expected return is very sensitive to those small differences.

This point applies not just to the search for higher yields but also to various forms of "value equity investing." Value investors often say that they are looking for consistent returns. Their mission is to deliver singles and doubles, not home runs. They seek investments that offer a high probability of a reasonable gain, thus giving up the search for the big win. But if the probability of losing is small, then it is prudent to assume that those occasional losses might be larger than the more frequent gains.

The buyer of lottery tickets, the venture capitalist, and the aggressive growth investor are more interested in winning big than in winning often. Their attitude is like the attitude of the person who is launching a new software company, forming a new rock band, or opening a new restaurant. Sales jobs have a similar profile: You talk to 100 people to set up 10 meetings to close one sale.

The insurance company, the bond investor seeking to maximize yield, and various kinds of value equity investors are more interested in winning often than in winning big. Their attitude is like the attitude of the person who would rather have a secure job with a steady income. The risk in these situations is that you wind up like a professional airline pilot, whose career involves a massive amount of boring routine punctuated by a few brief episodes of white-knuckle fear.

Think again about the difference between FM radio and AM radio. FM stations modulate the frequency of the signal, while AM stations modulate the amplitude. Some investors like to win *often*, while others like to win *big*. You can't do both. Or you can't reasonably expect to do both. And neither attitude is intrinsically smarter than the other.

LONG VOLATILITY VERSUS
SHORT VOLATILITY

The contrast between winning often and winning big can be connected with our discussions of options. In general, buyers of options are seeking big gains but not consistent gains. They expect to lose more often than they win, but they hope that the total winnings will outweigh the total losses. Sellers of options are in the opposite situation: They want to win often, they expect to win small, and they face the low-probability risk of losing big. Buyers of options, who are *long volatility*, are looking for the low probability of the big win. Sellers of options, who are *short volatility*, are looking for the high probability of the small win.

To make the contrast clearer, imagine a simple game involving 10 envelopes in a drawer. Nine of the envelopes are empty, and the tenth has a $100 bill in it. I am willing to sell you a ticket that gives you the right to pick one envelope out of the drawer. How much would you be willing to pay for that ticket? This takes us back to the concept of *expected value*. You have a 90 percent chance of picking an empty envelope, and a 10 percent chance of getting $100. If you multiply 90 percent times zero, and add 10 percent of $100, the result is $10. In theory, the "fair value" of the ticket is $10. If you can buy the ticket for $9, jump at the chance. If you have to pay $11, you should pass.

Now consider the opposite situation. There are 10 envelopes in the drawer, 9 of which contain $22.22. The tenth envelope is the killer. If you pick that envelope, you have to fork over $100. So you have a 90 percent chance of making $22.22, which makes an expected gain of $20. And you have a 10 percent chance of losing $100, for an expected loss of $10. The combination has an expected value of $10. So, again, $10 is a fair price for a ticket to pick 1 envelope.

The first drawer is the long volatility drawer: a high probability of losing money but a small probability of a meaningful win. The second drawer is the short volatility drawer: a high probability of a small win combined with the small probability of a much larger loss. Theoretically, $10 is the fair price for a ticket to either drawer. So, in theory, if you have a $10 ticket, you shouldn't care which drawer you open. In practice, however, most people will prefer one drawer to the other. Some people really like the idea of winning often:

consistent returns, lots of singles and doubles. These people will prefer the short volatility drawer. Other people like to win big, and they are turned off by the small probability of drawing the $100 IOU. They will prefer the long volatility drawer.

Now let's make things more interesting. This time there are 1000 envelopes in the drawer. The long volatility drawer has 999 empty envelopes and 1 envelope with a $10,000 bill in it. So the fair price for a ticket is still $10 since you have 1 chance in 1000 of getting the prize. The short volatility drawer has 999 envelopes, each of which contains $20.02. And there is one envelope that requires you to fork over $10,000. Here too the fair price for a ticket is $10. In this example, the short volatility drawer looks a lot less appealing than the long volatility drawer. After all, $10,000 is a lot of money. And even though there's only 1 chance in 1000 that you will wind up owing $10,000, you may conclude that you just can't afford to take the risk.

Then again, maybe $10,000 isn't all that much money to you. Maybe you're willing to take the risk. So we'll just make up new games, with more envelopes. Suppose the drawer has 10,000 envelopes, and the killer envelope requires that you fork over $100,000. Or there are 100,000 envelopes, and the killer envelope requires that you fork over $1 million. At some point, you just can't afford to play the game. (Think of Russian roulette, using a revolver with thousands of chambers.)

We have been considering some extreme examples just to sharpen our thinking. Real-life situations are usually less extreme. Let's go back to the contrast between stocks and bonds. If we round off the numbers shown in Table 11–1, then bond investing is a game in which you win 75 percent of the time. When you win, you win about 1 percent; when you lose, you lose about 1 percent. The expected gain is 0.75 percent, the expected loss is 0.25 percent, so the expected total return is 0.5 percent. That monthly return works out to an annual return of roughly 6 percent. When you play the stock game, 60 percent of the time you win 4 percent, and 40 percent of the time you lose 4 percent. The expected return here is 0.8 percent monthly, or about 10 percent annually.

The striking thing about this situation is how close the numbers are. Stocks have a higher expected return and a higher average gain. On the other hand, they have a higher average loss, and they lose money more often. But the contrast is not the contrast between buying lottery tickets and selling insurance. It's not even the contrast between aggressive growth stocks and high-yield bonds. If you believe that these numbers will hold in the future, then it seems crazy not to put all your money in stocks. If you're agonizing about whether your equity allocation should be 60 percent or 70 percent, it's likely that you don't fully believe the numbers. You don't want to make too big a bet on the accuracy of your estimates.

Most people like the idea of consistent returns. They like money managers who just try for singles and doubles, and they wouldn't think of buying a lottery ticket. They may like option selling as a strategy since time is on their side. But the basic position in all these cases is a short volatility position. The investor is seeking the high probability of a modest return, which means that the low-probability loss may be large in relation to the potential gain. At the extremes, short volatility strategies are often compared to picking up nickels in front of a bulldozer. If that's what you're doing, then you better know how far away the bulldozer is, how fast it's moving, and how fast you can run.

When you buy lottery tickets, or make venture capital investments, or engage in other aggressive growth strategies, or buy options, you know in advance what the worst case is. These are long volatility strategies, in which you explicitly accept that there may be many small losses, which you hope will be swamped by some large gains. The major challenge here is to make sure that the many small losses do not turn into death by a thousand cuts.

Some hedge fund strategies tend to be long volatility; others tend to be short volatility. Convertible hedging and trend-following futures trading tend to be long volatility strategies. Risk arbitrage and bond hedging tend to be short volatility strategies. And some strategies, or managers, combine elements of both. The contrast between "long volatility" and "short volatility" sounds clear and absolute, but the difference is really a difference of degree. At the extremes, there is a clear contrast between a 99 percent chance of a small win and a 1 percent chance of a big win. But when the probabilities are less extreme, the distinction gets blurred. And in the real world, where the probabilities are hard to measure in the first place, the situation becomes even more blurred.

Which is better—being long volatility, or being short? There is no general answer to this question, despite the claims of some people that "the smart money" is always long volatility, or always short. Each strategy has its own risks, and the well-diversified portfolio will include exposure to both types of strategies. In particular, the well-diversified investor can afford to have some exposure to extreme long volatility strategies: situations that offer a very small chance of a major win. But even the well-diversified investor needs to be very careful about extreme short volatility strategies. As you're bending over looking for nickels, you may lose track of the bulldozer.

MOMENTUM AND CONTRARIAN INVESTING

The contrast between long volatility strategies and short volatility strategies is connected with the contrast between contrarian strategies and momentum-driven strategies. The contrarian investor buys on weakness and sells on strength, while the momentum investor buys on strength and sells on weakness. The trading pattern of the contrarian investor has important similarities to short volatility strategies, while the trading pattern of the momentum investor has important similarities to long volatility strategies. The key link is the concept of option *delta*.

Delta, the fourth letter of the Greek alphabet, is often used by mathematicians to signify a *change* in some quantity: change in time, speed, location, and so forth. In physics, velocity is change in distance divided by change in time. In the world of options, delta is the change in the price of the option divided by the change in the price of the underlying asset. Delta tells us how sensitive the option is to changes in the price of the asset.

Call options have positive deltas that range from zero to 1. If the price of the asset goes up, then, other things being equal, the price of the call will go up. For simplicity, let's divide call options into three groups: in the money, at the money, and out of the money. A call is *at the money* when the strike price of the option is roughly equal to the market price of the asset. A call is *in the money* when the strike price is below the market price of the asset, so the call gives the holder the right to buy at a below-market price. A call is *out of the money* when the strike price of the option is above the market price of the asset. At-the-money calls often have a delta of about 0.5: If the stock moves up or down $1, then the option will move up or down about $0.50. As the call moves into the money, the delta increases. A call that is deep in the money will have a delta close to 1: The option will move dollar for dollar with the stock. A call that is out of the money will have a delta less than 0.5, and a deep out of the money option will have a delta close to zero.

Puts work in reverse. They have negative deltas: The price of the put goes up when the price of the asset goes down, and vice versa. At-the-money puts often have deltas close to –0.5. In-the-money puts have a strike price *above* the market price of the asset: The put allows the holder to sell at an above-market price. As the price of the asset declines, the put becomes deeper and deeper in the money, and the delta gets closer to –1. As the stock rises above the strike price of the put, the put moves out of the money, and the delta moves closer and closer to zero.

The concept of delta leads immediately to the idea of a stock portfolio that replicates the price behavior of an option. Suppose that you own an at-the-money call on 100 shares of Microsoft. If the option has a delta of 0.5, then the option gains or loses $50 when the 100-share portfolio gains or loses $100. The option has the same price sensitivity as 50 shares of Microsoft. If Microsoft moves up, then the delta of the option increases to 0.6, so the option behaves like 60 shares of Microsoft. If Microsoft moves down, then the delta decreases and behaves like a 40-share portfolio. In other words, if you want to build a stock portfolio that behaves like an at-the-money call, you start out with 50 shares of Microsoft, buy more if the price goes up, and sell if the price goes down. To replicate the price action of a put, you begin with a short position in Microsoft, increase the short position as the price goes down, and reduce the short position as the price goes up.

The net result is a family of *dynamic trading strategies* that are designed to simulate, or replicate, the effect of an option position. A dynamic trading strategy is a strategy that buys or sells in response to specific changes in the price of the stock. To implement a dynamic trading strategy that replicates an option position, you calculate the delta of the option that you are trying to replicate, then let the delta tell you how much stock to own or to short. If you are replicating a long option position (either in a put or a call), the basic strategy is to buy as prices go up and sell as prices go down. If you are replicating a short option position (either in a put or a call), the basic strategy is to sell as prices go up and buy as prices go down. When you replicate a long option position, you look like a momentum investor; when you replicate a short option position, you look like a contrarian investor.

Why should you care about any of this? Because many investors like the pattern of returns associated with buying an option, but they don't like to pay the option premium. If you buy a call, you can make a lot of money, but your downside is strictly limited. If you buy a put on a portfolio, you protect the value but leave room for appreciation. These are appealing goals. But nobody likes to pay for insurance. So people engage in dynamic trading strategies that give them the benefit of the option without the upfront cost.

That, in a nutshell, is why portfolio insurance was such a popular strategy among big institutional investors in the early and middle 1980s. Institutions wanted protection, but they didn't want to pay for it. So they engaged in dynamic trading strategies that were designed to replicate the effect of owning a put on a portfolio. As we saw earlier, an at-the-money put is likely to have a delta of roughly -0.5. To replicate an at-the-money put on 100 shares of stock, you sell short 50 shares of stock. If stocks go down, you short more stock. If stocks go up, you cover some of your short position. In the mid-1980s, billions of dollars of institutional assets were committed to portfolio insurance programs whose basic strategy was to buy in a rising market and sell in a falling market.

Portfolio insurance played an important role in the market crash of October 1987. There are three critical lessons that emerged from that episode. First, portfolio insurance encouraged many large institutions to have higher equity allocations than they would have had without the insurance. This is normal human behavior: If you are driving a four-wheel-drive vehicle on a snowy road, you are likely to drive faster than the other drivers. So the "safer" vehicle may turn out to be less safe when driven by the freshly emboldened driver.

Second, the popularity of portfolio insurance created various *positive feedback loops*, accentuating whatever market trend was generating the trading signal. Buying caused further buying, and selling caused further selling. In October 1987, the initial selling was unusually severe, which caused further selling, and then still more selling. The net result was disastrous.

Third, the crash of 1987 demonstrated that dynamic trading strategies require smooth and continuous market prices. To replicate an option, you need to change the size of your stock position as you try to track the changing delta of the option that you are trying to replicate. But markets are not always so obliging. Sometimes prices *gap up* or *gap down* in such a way as to make option replication difficult, if not impossible. This is exactly what happened in October 1987. Prices moved down so fast that the dynamic strategies could not adjust their positions in time, hence many people found that they had less protection than they thought they had.

Viewed from a distance, portfolio insurance looks like a trend-following, momentum-driven strategy. But what drives the trading is not the belief that trends will persist, or that "the trend is your friend." What drives the strategy is the theory of option pricing and the desire of investors for a pattern of returns that will resemble the returns of a portfolio protected by a put. In 1987 the desire for "protection with the potential for appreciation" led to a trading strategy that looks like pure momentum investing, with all the disadvantages thereof.

Many hedge funds try to deliver substantial capital appreciation while keeping the losses under control. This pattern of returns is very similar to the pattern of returns associated with owning an option. And to replicate that pattern of returns, the manager winds up buying on strength and selling on weakness. Thus the manager behaves like a momentum-driven investor. This does not mean that hedge fund managers are adhering slavishly to some sort of option replication program. It just means that some of their trading strategies, when viewed from a distance, look like options-inspired strategies.

Short option strategies, which are short volatility, have the opposite behavior: The investor buys on weakness and sells on strength. This is the official creed of the contrarian, value-oriented investor, who is attracted by falling prices and gets nervous when prices rise. The value investor winds up betting that trends will reverse and prices will regress toward the mean. The contrarian investor trades against the crowd and provides liquidity to the crowd; the momentum investor trades with the crowd and demands liquidity along with the rest of the crowd.

MOMENTUM AND RISK MANAGEMENT

"Real investors" often make fun of momentum investing, dismissing it as mindless trend following that ultimately destabilizes markets by setting up a dangerous positive feedback loop. The feedback loop accentuates whatever trend is already in place until it becomes unsustainable, at which point the trend collapses dramatically. What markets need is real investors who know a bargain when they see one. They buy when prices are going down, and sell as prices move up. This adds stability to markets and provides a decent investment return.

This characterization is unfair to momentum investors. Buying on strength and selling on weakness sounds like mindless trend following. But this trading pattern is exactly the trading pattern that you would expect if somebody were trying to replicate the effect of owning a call or a put. And that is not a crazy strategy since people like the pattern of returns associated with owning options. The potential gains are much greater than the potential losses. The fly in the ointment, of course, is that winning is less likely than losing. But if the amplitude advantage is big enough to make up for the frequency disadvantage, you'll do fine in the long run.

Although people think of momentum investors as ultra-aggressive investors who buy more and more stock at higher and higher prices, the fact is that the momentum investor may be a more prudent risk manager than the contrarian investor. Momentum investing has two rules: Buy on strength, and sell on weakness. The first rule is the aggressive rule. It tells you to increase your position to take advantage of a continuation in the trend. The second rule is a defensive rule. It tells you to reduce your positions when they are moving against you.

If you're a momentum investor and a position moves against you, your first instinct is to reduce or eliminate the position. If you're a contrarian investor, and a position moves against you, your first instinct is to add to the position. The momentum investor is very focused on cutting losses. His motto is, "The first loss is the best loss." The contrarian investor is more likely to average down when a position moves against her. If the stock was cheap at $50, it's even cheaper at $45, so why not buy more?

Mindless momentum investing and mindless contrarianism are both untenable strategies. At the extremes, the momentum investor becomes so averse to loss that he has no staying power. The contrarian investor averages down so mindlessly that she winds up accumulating bigger and bigger positions in stocks that eventually go to zero. The extreme momentum investor is too quick to acknowledge that he was wrong. The extreme contrarian never admits that she was wrong: Every decline in price presents a better buying opportunity. But, as Keynes observed, a bargain that remains a bargain is not a bargain.

Selling on weakness may sound cowardly, but it can be the height of prudence. Buying on weakness may sound brave, but it may be merely foolhardy. So every money manager faces a struggle between two opposing instincts. Some managers fall pretty clearly on the momentum side: They are quick to take losses. Others fall more clearly on the contrarian side: They are more patient about enduring losses and more willing to think about averaging down. The challenge for the investor in hedge funds is to try to figure out where on the spectrum the manager is located. Since skilled managers are reasonable people who try to avoid the extremes, this can be a formidable task.

The willingness to take losses early is especially critical for the leveraged investor. It is better to take the loss early, and voluntarily, than to take the loss later, and involuntarily, in response to a margin call. Not surprisingly, the "cut-your-losses-early" principle is widely followed by major banks, brokers, and other institutions that have large trading positions in the markets. These are leveraged institutions that all follow strict risk control disciplines that force them to exit losing positions. This behavior, needless to say, contributes to market volatility since it means that large positions are held in weak hands. And it means that there are major positive feedback loops in the markets: Initial selling triggers further selling, which in turn triggers still more selling.

PULLING IT ALL TOGETHER

So now we have another angle on the question of whether it makes more sense to be long or short volatility. That question translates into the question of whether it is smarter to be a momentum-oriented trend follower or a contrarian "countertrend" investor, who is suspicious of trends and is much more comfortable betting on reversion to the mean. And the answer is clear: There is no answer. Sometimes prices do trend, and trend longer than anybody would have expected. But all trends come to an end. Trends reinforce themselves until they destroy themselves. Sometimes the old trend gives way to a new trend in the opposite direction. Sometimes there is simply a long period of aimless range-bound prices. The doctrinaire momentum investor will make lots of money as long as the trend persists, but he risks losing lots of money when conditions change. The doctrinaire contrarian will make lots of money when prices are range bound but will lose money when strong trends develop. In each case, the true test of a manager's skill is how well the manager deals with the market environment to which he is temperamentally unsuited. We return again to George Soros's observation: "It's not whether you're right or wrong, but how much money you make when you're right and how much you lose when you're wrong."

Although both approaches have advantages and disadvantages, it is worth noting again that the long volatility approach does have some special advantages in the risk management area. The momentum investor is quick to take losses, while the contrarian investor sometimes gets stubborn and fights the tape. The buyer of options always knows in advance what her worst-case loss is, whereas the seller of options faces potential losses that dwarf the potential gain.

Table 11–2 summarizes the major contrasts that we have been dealing with. Some of the entries in this table are meant to be sug-

TABLE 11–2

AM Investing Versus FM Investing

	AM Investing	FM Investing
Objective	Win big	Win often
Tradeoff	Small probability of large gain versus large probability of small loss	Large probability of small gain versus small probability of large loss
Examples	• Buying lottery tickets • Venture capital investing • Aggressive growth equity investing	• Selling insurance • Bond investing, especially "reaching for yield" • Value equity investing
Options strategy	Buy options: Long volatility	Sell options: Short volatility
Trading strategy	Momentum: Buy on strength, sell on weakness	Contrarian: Buy on weakness, sell on strength
Role in system	Positive feedback mechanism	Negative feedback mechanism

gestive, not definitive. And remember the proviso mentioned earlier: The contrast between winning often and winning big is very clear at the extremes but less clear in the middle, which is where many real-life situations are located.

The contrast between growth and value is especially interesting when viewed in the light of the contrasts set out above. Growth investing tends to be a long volatility strategy: The investor is hoping that a small number of large gains will swamp a larger number of small losses. But the situation with value investing is more complicated.

Some value strategies are clearly in the short volatility category. Reaching for yield is an obvious example. Speaking more broadly, the value manager often presents himself as explicitly *not* seeking big gains: He is seeking more modest gains, but with greater frequency or consistency—hence the objective of singles and doubles, not home runs. But some value investors are more aggressive: They look for "bombed-out" situations where the news has been extremely bad and investor expectations are extremely low. The bet here is that expectations are so low that the potential for positive surprise is very high. But you have to be careful in forming your expectations here. If you are looking for situations in which there is a very high probability of a very high return, then you might as well look for the Holy Grail and the Easter Bunny too. The more realistic view is that many of the bombed-out situations will never recover, but some of them will offer outsized returns that will make the whole enterprise profitable. So this particular form of value investing becomes a long volatility strategy: The small probability of some major winners is balanced against the larger probability of a lot of disappointments. The aggressive value investor and the aggressive growth investor wind up having a lot in common.

PART FOUR

Some Operational Issues

CHAPTER 12

Legal and Regulatory Issues

We have spent a lot of time looking at investment issues related to hedge funds: investment objectives, strategies, techniques, and so forth. The next few chapters take a brief look at some of the business and operational issues that arise in the hedge fund world. This chapter focuses on the regulatory framework within which hedge funds operate. Then we move on to performance fees, and then to tax issues.

Hedge fund managers use a number of different legal structures to make their strategies available to clients. The "delivery system" can be a limited partnership, a limited liability company, an offshore fund, a commodity pool, or even a specialized separate account. We will begin with the contrast between mutual funds and limited partnerships and then move on to the contrasts between limited partnerships and the other vehicles.

MUTUAL FUNDS VERSUS LIMITED PARTNERSHIPS

Mutual funds and hedge funds both conduct their operations within a highly complicated regulatory framework. Although the popular press often refers to hedge funds as "unregulated investment vehicles," in fact, hedge funds are designed to take advantage of various exemptions, exclusions, and "safe harbors" that are explicitly provided within the regulatory framework.

The underlying regulatory framework is a combination of securities and tax laws. On the tax side, mutual funds and hedge funds both try to conduct their businesses in such a way as to avoid taxation at the fund level. Hedge funds and mutual funds strive to be *pass-through entities*—those on which taxes are paid by the fund investors, not by the funds.

On the securities side, there are three crucial laws: the Securities Act of 1933, the Investment Company Act of 1940, and the Investment Advisers Act of 1940. The Securities Act regulates the process by which securities are offered to the general public. Both hedge funds and mutual funds are securities, but hedge funds do not offer their interests to the general public; they are "private placements" offered only to "accredited investors." The private placement process is defined within Regulation D of the 1933 act, so private placements are sometimes called *Reg D offerings*.

The Investment Company Act of 1940 governs the operation of mutual funds, and the Investment Advisers Act of 1940 governs the operations of the firms that manage mutual funds. Mutual funds are managed by *registered investment advisers*, which are money management firms that offer their services to the general public. Most (but not all) hedge fund managers are *unregistered advisers*, who cannot offer their services to the general public.

The primary purpose of all these laws is to protect the ordinary investor, "the little guy." But the laws specifically allow for a kind of investment operation that is oriented mainly to large and sophisticated investors. Thus the world of hedge funds.

Mutual funds are companies that offer shares. A private investment partnership is not a company but a business arrangement based on the distinction between a general partner and a limited partner. The partners do not own shares in a company; they own a fractional interest (determined by the *partnership percentage*) in the affairs of the partnership. The *general partner* runs the business and bears unlimited liability for anything that might go wrong. Since most individuals are unwilling to accept unlimited liability, the general partner is usually a corporation, or a *limited liability company*. The *limited partner* is a passive investor in the business and bears a limited liability. The investor can lose everything that she has invested in the partnership: all contributed capital plus any accumulated gains. But she cannot lose more than that.

Liquidity A mutual fund is a company that invests in securities instead of making automobiles or selling computers. Like other companies, it offers stock to the public. Unlike other companies, it offers stock on a continuous basis. (We are talking here about the familiar *open-end mutual fund*, which offers shares on a daily basis. *Closed-end funds* do not offer shares on a daily basis.) Individual investors can buy shares of the fund on a daily basis and can sell shares back to the fund on a daily basis. So the mutual fund investor has daily access to his capital. This means that the fund must be managed in such a way that it will be able to handle frequent inflows and outflows of capital. So the SEC imposes specific restrictions that limit the portion of a fund that can be invested in illiquid securities.

A limited partnership is explicitly structured so as *not* to allow daily liquidity. Most hedge funds offer quarterly liquidity or annual liquidity, but some funds require longer-term commitments of capital. As hedge fund managers become successful, they often require a three-year (or longer) lockup of capital to give themselves a more stable asset base.

Number of Investors Most mutual funds are designed to serve a large number of small investors. The SEC does not limit how many investors a fund might have, nor does it limit how small the individual investment might be. But mutual fund companies often place limits on the number of investors or the size of the investments. Many funds have minimum investments of $1000, or $3000, or more. Some institutional funds have much higher minimums, perhaps as high as $10 million or more. Similarly, mutual fund companies sometimes close their funds to new investors. For example, they will do this if they feel that accepting new investors will harm the interests of the existing investors by diluting their investment in a market environment that presents few buying opportunities. But these decisions are all based on business and investment judgments of the fund manager. As far as the SEC is concerned, there are no limits on the number of investors or the size of the fund.

Limited partnerships are designed to serve a small number of large investors. There are two main types of private investment partnerships, defined by two different sections of the Investment Company Act of 1940: Section 3(c)(1) and Section 3(c)(7). A 3(c)(1) fund can accept no more than 100 limited partners, and it cannot conduct a public offering of its interests. As a practical matter, this means that a 3(c)(1) fund may offer its interests only to "accredited investors" as defined in Regulation D of the Securities Act of 1933. An individual accredited investor generally must have at least $1 million in liquid net worth, or an annual income of at least $200,000 for the past two years. An institution must have $5 million in assets. A 3(c)(7) fund can accept up to 500 investors, each of whom must be a "qualified purchaser." Becoming a qualified purchaser is tougher than becoming an accredited investor. The individual investor must have at least $5 million in investable assets, and the institutional investor must have at least $25 million in investable assets.

Marketing Mutual funds are free to advertise and market to the general public, as long as they conform to the rules laid out by the SEC. They can publicize their investment results, their investment philosophy and strategy, and so forth. Sometimes the mutual fund markets itself directly to the public, as in the case of no load funds that advertise in newspapers and other media. Or the mutual fund may rely on stockbrokers or financial planners to sell shares in exchange for a commission.

In contrast, private investment funds are not allowed to advertise or market to the general public. And the managers of those funds, if they are unregistered advisers, are not allowed to market to the general public. So hedge funds and their managers generally keep a low public profile. But some hedge fund managers are more aggressive in raising their public profile while still staying within the SEC limits. For example, *Barron's* frequently interviews hedge fund managers and publishes (on a quarterly basis) the performance results of a large group of hedge fund managers. And many hedge fund managers now have Web sites where interested investors can get general information about the manager and the fund (including fund performance). The hedge fund manager will typically use a password mechanism to limit access to any information whose broad distribution would create regulatory problems.

Investment Restrictions Since mutual funds are designed for a broad audience of investors who may not be knowledgeable about investments and who may not be able to accept a high degree of risk, the SEC limits the amount of risk that a mutual fund can take. Some of the most important limitations relate to leverage, short selling, and diversification.

The basic rule regarding leverage and short selling is that investments meet an assets-to-liabilities test. In particular, the liabilities may not exceed one third of the assets. *Liabilities* include both borrowed money to fund leveraged long positions and borrowed stock to fund short sales. If a fund is 150 percent invested on the long side, with no short exposure, then it will satisfy this test since it will have $150 in assets for $50 of debt. Similarly, if a fund is 100 percent gross long and 50 percent gross short, then it will have $150 in assets for each $50 of liabilities. And if a fund is 125 percent long and 25 percent short, the test would also be satisfied. So the SEC rule means that a fund's *gross exposure* (gross long plus gross short) cannot exceed 150 percent of net assets.

As for diversification, there are two kinds of rules. The rules in the first group are designed to make sure that the fund does not put too much of its assets in a single stock or industry. The rules in the second group are designed to make sure that the fund's position in a company is not too big relative to the size of the company. If a mutual fund does not follow all of these rules, it must explicitly label itself a *nondiversified fund*.

Limited partnerships do not face the same restrictions that govern mutual funds. But hedge funds still face other restrictions. For example, there are limitations on leverage that are imposed not by SEC mutual fund regulations but by Federal Reserve regulations. Under ordinary circumstances, margin purchases require a down payment of at least 50 percent. A hedge fund manager can't put down $100,000 to buy $1 million worth of IBM. (Some hedge fund managers register their funds as "broker-dealers" in order to gain access to higher levels of leverage. But this creates an additional regulatory burden that many funds would prefer to avoid.)

Turnover Regulators used to take the position that a mutual fund should be a long-term investor in securities, not a short-term trader. To this end, mutual funds had to conform to the *short short rule*, which stated that no more than 90 percent of a fund's realized profits could come from positions held less than 90 days. If this rule was violated, then the fund itself would be vulnerable to a tax. This rule was repealed in 1998, so there are now no restrictions on the level of short-term trading.

Hedge fund limited partnerships face no restrictions regarding short-term trading profits, and never have. The freedom now available to mutual fund managers has always been available to limited partnerships.

Distributions Mutual fund companies try to manage their funds in such a way that all taxes are paid by the investors, not the funds. So the mutual fund needs to avoid being classified as "an association taxable as a corporation." And that means, according to the Internal Revenue Service, that the fund must distribute to its investors at least 95 percent of its income and realized capital gains. Investors then have a choice: They can keep the distribution, or they can reinvest the distribution in the fund. Many investors elect to have their distributions reinvested automatically. But even if the distribution is reinvested, the fund must make the distribution to the investor, and the investor (assuming that the investor is taxable) will owe taxes on the distribution whether or not it is reinvested.

Hedge fund limited partnerships are not required to make any distributions at all in order to preserve their pass-through tax status. Some partnerships choose to make regular distributions, but most do not. So the hedge fund investor who needs income will need to make periodic partial redemptions.

Custody Mutual funds are required to hold their assets in a segregated account at a bank. Hedge fund assets may be held in a brokerage account. Since broker custody is required for leverage and short selling, most hedge funds could not conduct their business if they were forced to have their assets held at a bank.

Investment Management Fees Mutual funds sold to the general public cannot charge a *percent-of-profits fee*. The SEC does, however, permit a so-called *fulcrum fee*. Under this arrangement, the investment manager charges a fixed fee and then adjusts the fixed fee depending on the manager's performance relative to an established index. For example, the manager might charge a fixed fee of 50 basis points but then take a *performance bonus* of 10 basis points if she exceeds the performance of the S&P 500 by more than 2 percent over a three-year period. But this bonus is permitted only if the manager adjusts her fee downward by 10 basis points if she underperforms the index by more than 2 percent. The SEC is willing to reward good performance only if there is also a penalty for bad performance.

Private investment funds managed by unregistered advisers are not subject to any such restrictions. Although "1-and-20" is a common fee arrangement, fees can be higher or lower, and even the simple "1 and 20" arrangement is available in many versions, depending on hurdle rates, high-water marks, and other variables. Hedge fund fees are whatever the market will bear.

Governance Mutual funds must have a board of directors whose responsibility is to oversee the fund manager and look after the interests of the fund shareholders. SEC regulations require that a certain number of these directors be totally independent of the fund manager.

Limited partnerships are not subject to that type of governance rule. In a typical domestic partnership, the general partner exercises total control over the management of the fund. Some hedge funds have advisory boards, but such boards are not required, and advisory boards do not have the specific fiduciary responsibilities of a board of directors.

OFFSHORE FUNDS

Many hedge fund managers offer both a U.S. limited partnership for taxable U.S. investors and an offshore fund for nontaxable U.S. investors and non-U.S. investors. So, for example, a hedge fund manager based in New York might offer an offshore fund whose investors might include a wealthy German industrialist as well as a U.S. corporate pension plan. Both of these investors are already exempt from U.S. taxes.

Offshore funds are generally based in "tax haven" countries such as Bermuda, the British Virgin Islands, or the Cayman Islands. In recent years, Ireland has also become increasingly important as a domicile for offshore funds. These offshore funds are not to be confused with funds that are offered to retail investors in the European Union, Japan, or elsewhere. The countries in which these funds are sold all have regulatory schemes very similar to the SEC scheme that governs mutual funds in the United States. The basic message to the fund manager is the same as in the United States: If you want to sell to the general public, then you have to follow investment restrictions designed to protect the general public.

The tax haven countries mentioned above do not restrict the investment activity of the funds, nor do they impose taxes on the funds. But they do impose various administrative fees, so that an offshore fund business is often a significant source of revenue for its host country.

As we have emphasized several times before, an offshore fund is not designed to help investors avoid taxation. It is designed for assets that are already exempt from taxation in the relevant country. Because they are handling tax-exempt assets, managers of offshore funds typically do not collect or distribute the kind of information that an investor would require for a tax filing. A taxable U.S. investor could, in theory, invest in an offshore fund, but he would have to report any taxable income to the U.S. tax authorities. Since the investor would not have access to the relevant information, U.S. taxable investors are effectively locked out of offshore funds.

The world of offshore funds has attracted increased scrutiny since the terrorist attacks of September 2001. There are new levels of concern about money laundering and tax avoidance. Managers of offshore funds are under increased pressure to follow various "know-your-customer" rules.

FUTURES POOLS

Mutual funds are permitted to use futures contracts to a limited degree to hedge portfolio risk, but they are not allowed to do substantial amounts of speculating in the futures markets. *Futures pools* are investment vehicles designed to allow the small investor to participate in the futures markets. Futures pools are essentially mutual funds for the futures markets. Futures pools are regulated by the Commodity Futures Trading Commission (CFTC), which was established in the mid-1970s to regulate the futures markets. Just as mutual funds do not speculate in futures, futures pools generally do not invest in stocks. CFTC rules do not prevent futures pools from buying stocks, but a futures pool that invests in stocks then becomes subject to SEC regulation. Most futures pools prefer to avoid that additional burden.

The CFTC and the SEC have somewhat different approaches to regulation. The SEC imposes definite rules and regulations regarding what must be done and what cannot be done. The CFTC is less concerned with specific dos and don'ts but more concerned with full and fair disclosure. A futures pool can do whatever it wants to, but it must disclose everything relevant to the transaction to the prospective investor. The CFTC disclosure requirements are very high, and the disclosure document for a futures pool can easily be several hundred pages long.

Like a mutual fund, a futures pool can accept any number of investors, and there are no specific net worth requirements or investment minimums. Unlike a mutual fund, there are no specific liquidity requirements. A futures pool can offer daily liquidity, annual liquidity, or anything in between.

SEPARATE ACCOUNTS

Mutual funds, offshore funds, and commodity pools are all commingled vehicles. Hedge fund strategies can also be offered in a separate account format. Needless to say, this format is available only to very large investors, who like separate accounts because the investor then has more liquidity and greater access to information. The separate account has greater *transparency*: The investor can look inside the account on a daily basis if she wants to. If the investor is a large institution whose assets are normally held in segregated accounts at a large bank, then the hedge fund separate account will require special arrangements to permit leverage and short selling. There are some very successful hedge fund managers who have been willing to accept separate account assignments from large institutions, but other successful managers prefer to keep their businesses simpler by turning down such opportunities.

THE OUTLOOK FOR FUTURE REGULATION

Regulations are not static. They change in response to changes in the financial environment, in response to crises, and in response to the activities of special interest groups. The Long Term Capital Management debacle was an especially important crisis. In the immediate aftermath of that crisis, there was a widespread sense that "something should be done." And there was widespread fear within the hedge fund community that "overzealous regulators" would implement new rules that would create huge administrative burdens, destroy returns, and turn an excellent business into a terrible business. These fears turned out to be, by and large, unjustified.

Regulators quickly realized that the hedge fund community is very difficult to police on a regular basis. There are thousands of funds, many of them very small, and many of them located offshore, well beyond the regulatory jurisdiction of U.S. authorities. So attention shifted quickly from the hedge funds themselves to the small number of large financial institutions that lend to the hedge funds. These are the large commercial banks, investment banks, and stock brokerages. These institutions constitute the main "choke points" of the global financial system. This is the group that gathered in the Fed's large paneled room to resolve the LTCM crisis.

As the crisis atmosphere eased, it become clear that the LTCM crisis was largely caused by excessive leverage. But leverage is an activity that takes place between two consenting adults. LTCM was able to borrow too much money only because the banks and brokers were willing to lend too much money. In the aftermath of the crisis, the major institutions have tightened up their own lending practices and procedures, and the regulators have increased the level of surveillance.

In the post-LTCM period there was much discussion about vastly increased reporting requirements. Perhaps every hedge fund should submit a quarterly report detailing its positions, activities, and so on. But people quickly realized that this was a pointless, and potentially damaging, exercise. Millions of documents would descend upon Washington, and then what would happen? Who would review them and would they understand them? If the documents contained information that was already stale, what difference would the reporting make?

Regulators are also aware that they face a *moral-hazard issue*. Prudent investors know that investing is a risky business. If investors begin to think that the regulators have reduced the level of investment risk, then they will become overconfident and misjudge the level of risk. The result is bound to be some sort of blowup down the road. The basic syndrome here is the same as what we observed with portfolio insurance in the mid-1980s. If you think your equity portfolio is protected against loss, then you will have a higher exposure to equities than you would otherwise. (If you're wearing a seatbelt in a four-wheel drive car, then you'll drive down the icy road faster than you would otherwise.) The late stages of the recent bull market presented a similar moral-hazard issue as some investors developed too much confidence in the wizardry of Alan Greenspan. Some people thought that equity investing had become totally safe, thanks to the magic of the Federal Reserve. And that faith led to patterns of behavior that guaranteed that the boom would become a bust.

The regulator walks a fine line. Regulation is designed to protect the financial system at large and to protect the small investor, the "little guy." At the same time, it is very important that investors be reminded that investing is risky. Some companies need to go bankrupt, and some investors need to experience large losses. Failure keeps the sense of risk alive, and the sense of risk is what ultimately keeps the system sound. It's when people stop worrying that things go really wrong.

If the general level of interest in hedge funds continues to rise, then it is likely that regulators will become increasingly interested in the basic tradeoff between investment freedom and marketing freedom. Hedge fund managers are already becoming more aggressive in raising their public profiles, and mutual fund companies are becoming more aggressive in using the mutual fund format to deliver hedge fund strategies to a broader audience. So far, these efforts involve the use of closed-end funds, which are not as liquid as the more common open-end funds. But, if the market environment is one in which mutual fund managers could improve their performance by having access to a bigger toolkit, then the mutual fund industry will inevitably press for broader freedom.

Before leaving the topic of regulation, let us just note, one more time, that "more regulated" does not mean "less risky." The mutual fund business is much more highly regulated than the hedge fund business. But there are many high-risk mutual funds and a good number of risk-averse hedge funds.

CHAPTER 13

Performance Fees

Hedge funds typically charge a fixed asset-based fee plus a performance-based fee. Let's look briefly at how performance fees would work in a hypothetical case. Suppose a hedge fund manager charges 1 percent on the assets under management plus 20 percent of the total return. And suppose the manager's fund is up 20 percent for the calendar year, before any management fees but after brokerage commissions and any other expenses directly related to trading the portfolio. The 20 percent return combines all the elements of total return: interest income, interest expense, realized gains and losses, and changes in unrealized appreciation or depreciation. Interest income includes stock dividends, bond interest, interest on cash balances, and interest earned on the proceeds of short sales. Interest expense includes financing charges related to leverage and dividends or interest owed on short positions. Importantly, the total return that we are talking about is not just total realized return or total taxable return. Total return includes unrealized appreciation. The performance fee is based on total return, even if some of that return evaporates after the fee is paid.

In many hedge funds, the 20 percent performance fee is calculated after deducting the 1 percent asset-based fee. If the return before fees is 20 percent, then we subtract the 1 percent management fee from the 20 percent total return to get a 19 percent return before the performance fee. We then take 20 percent of 19 percent, which is 3.8 percent, which is the performance fee. Subtracting 3.8 percent from 19 percent gives us a net return, after all fees, of 15.2 percent. In other hedge funds, the 20 percent performance fee would be calculated before deducting the 1 percent management fee. In this scheme, the net return, after both fees, would be 15 percent.

Some managers take a performance fee only on returns that exceed some hurdle rate of return. The *hurdle rate* is usually defined in terms of some short-term interest rate benchmark such as the rate on Treasury bills or the London Interbank Offered Rate (LIBOR), which is the rate at which major global banks lend to one another. For example, if the hurdle rate is 5 percent and the performance fee is calculated after deducting the asset-based fee, then a 20 percent return becomes 19 percent after the management fee, which is 14 percent above the hurdle rate. So the performance fee is 2.8 percent and the net return is 16.2 percent. Needless to say, investors would rather have a hurdle rate than not have one. Notice, however, that the hurdle rate will almost invariably be linked to some short-term interest rate, so the hurdle rate will always be a positive number. The hurdle rate will not, for example, be the rate of return on the S&P 500 Index or some other equity index. An equity-related hurdle rate would create an incentive for the hedge fund manager to orient his portfolio around some equity benchmark, which would defeat the purpose of hedge fund investing.

Some managers offer a *high-water mark* in calculating their performance fees, which means that the performance fee is triggered only when the investor has profits that exceed the level of profits that existed the last time a performance fee was charged. This is sometimes referred to as a *loss carry-forward account*. Suppose that a hedge fund is up 20 percent gross in year 1, so the net return is 15.2 percent. (We are assuming that a 20 percent performance fee is charged after a 1 percent managment fee.) If an investor began year 1 with an investment of $1 million, then that investment is worth $1,152,000 at the end of year 1. Now suppose that year 2 is a bad year: The return is negative, so the manager takes his 1 percent management fee but no performance fee. Let's assume that, at the end of year 2, the investor's account has declined so that the net value is once again $1 million. But year 3 is a good year, and the return is positive. If the manager uses a high-water mark, then there will be no performance fee in year 3 unless the investor's account value exceeds $1,152,000. (We assume, for simplicity, that there is no hurdle rate of return.) If the investor's account balance exceeds the high-water mark amount, then the hedge fund manager will take 20 percent of the excess. Otherwise, there is no performance fee.

Ideally, investors would like to see both a hurdle rate and a high-water mark. In practice, fee arrangements can be extremely varied. Sometimes the management fee is more than 1 percent, sometimes less. The performance fee might be more than 20 percent, or less. Sometimes there is a hurdle rate, sometimes not. Sometimes there is a high-water mark, sometimes not. In addition, investors can sometimes negotiate fees, within limits. For example, if a very large institutional investor is willing to leave her investment untouched for three years or more, she may be able to negotiate a preferential fee arrangement.

Performance fees are generally calculated at the level of the individual hedge fund investor, not the total fund. This is appropriate because different investors may have very different profit-loss situations, depending on when they made their investments in the partnership. Again, suppose that a manager loses money in year 1, then makes money in year 2, but does not surpass the valuation level that existed at the beginning of year 1. An investor who invested at the beginning of year 2 will owe a performance fee at the end of the year. But an investor who invested at the beginning of year 1 will not.

When we first broached the subject of performance fees, we asked whether these fees create an incentive for the hedge fund manager to assume undue risk. Although it may seem that, in theory, there is a substantial incentive to "go for broke," in practice, the answer is much more complicated. First, most managers will have a substantial amount of their own money at risk in the fund, which acts as a brake on risk taking. Second, most managers do not want to be "one-year wonders." They would much rather create businesses that will endure for a number of years and will generate a multiyear stream of investment profits that will create a substantial level of performance-related fees. To do this, the manager must strive to create a performance record that has fairly consistent returns and very low correlation with the standard markets. Since the hedge fund manager has to deliver consistent returns in order for his business to be a success in the long term, there is a powerful incentive *not* to take too much risk. If the hedge fund manager is driven entirely by short-term greed, then performance fees can create an incentive to take risk. But the better hedge fund managers are more focused on long-term greed than on short-term greed. The key due-diligence question, of course, is whether the candidate manager is long-term greedy or short-term greedy.

The psychology of performance fees becomes especially important when a hedge fund has been through a tough performance period. If a fund has been flat or down two years in a row, then no performance fees have been earned, and, if the partnership carries a high-water mark, then no performance fees will be earned unless the fund reaches the previous high. So it may turn out, for example, that no fees will be earned in the current year unless the fund is up 20 percent. This can create excruciating pressures on the manager of the fund, and it can increase the incentive to take risks to get out of the hole. Some managers will talk about singling and doubling their way out of a hole, but when the chips are down, sometimes what is really needed is a home run. Going for the home run can be perfectly prudent, but only if the risk-reward tradeoff is highly asymmetrical.

The performance fee has very important tax advantages for the hedge fund manager. If the hedge fund takes the form of a limited partnership, then the performance fee is not literally a fee, but an "allocation" of the partnership's realized and unrealized return. For the typical hedge fund, the total return will include some items that are taxed at high rates: interest, dividends, and realized short-term gains. But total return also includes realized long-term gains, which are lightly taxed, and unrealized appreciation, which is not taxed at all. When the general partner receives 20 percent of the partnership's return, that 20 percent allocation will have the same tax character as the partnership's total return. If the total return of the partnership consisted largely of long-term gains and unrealized appreciation, then the general partner's allocation will have the same tax-advantaged character.

If the hedge fund takes the form of an offshore corporation, then there is also a tax advantage. The asset-based fee and the performance-based fee both build up inside the offshore corporation and are not subject to taxes until they are explicitly repatriated back to the United States.

CHAPTER 14

Tax Issues

Some hedge funds are very "tax friendly," others are very unfriendly. The friendly funds have a long-term investment horizon and low turnover. A large portion of their total return is in the form of unrealized appreciation. These funds take advantage of the relative illiquidity of hedge funds to attract a cadre of long-term investors. In many of these funds, investors can redeem their funds only annually, perhaps even less frequently.

But most hedge funds are not like this. They engage in more active trading, generate a lot of realized gains and losses, and produce much more complicated tax reporting. In some of these funds, the limited partner may not receive his Schedule K-1 (Form 1065), which supplies all the information that the limited partner requires for a tax return—until a time very close to the standard April 15 filing deadline. If you are invested in a fund with high transaction volume and complicated strategies, you may not be able to file your own tax return by April 15.

Since a limited partnership is a "pass-through entity" from a tax point of view, the limited partner pays taxes on her share of the partnership's realized return, at her own personal tax rate. The limited partner owes taxes whether or not she receives a distribution from the partnership. The underlying realized return is taxed as follows:

1. *Income and expenses.* Stock dividends and bond interest are taxed at the usual rates. Dividends owed on short positions are net-

ted against dividends paid on long positions. Interest on short sale proceeds is part of income, and margin interest expense is netted against income.

2. *Realized gains and losses.* Realized gains and losses are taxed at the usual rates. Futures contracts and short sales receive special treatment. In each case there is a tax advantage and a tax disadvantage. With futures, the disadvantage is that there is no such thing as an unrealized profit. All futures positions are marked to market at the end of the year, and they are taxed accordingly. The offsetting advantage is that all futures profits are taxed as if they were 60 percent long term and 40 percent short term. In the case of short selling, the disadvantage is that all profits from short sales are taxed as short-term gains, no matter how long the position is held. The advantage is that if a stock sold short goes to zero (for example, in the case of bankruptcy), then there is no taxable gain if the short position is not covered.

Although many hedge funds are tax unfriendly, there is one mechanism that slightly mitigates this problem. In a limited partnership, every limited partner has a capital account whose balance reflects the limited partner's capital contributions plus the limited partner's proportional share of the partnership's accumulated total return. Each limited partner receives periodically an allocation of his portion of the partnership's return. The size of the allocation is determined strictly by the size of the limited partner's investment. But the tax character of the allocation can differ from one limited partner to another. In particular, many hedge funds allocate realized gains to those limited partners who are leaving the fund, or reducing the size of their investment. These limited partners will be realizing the gains anyway through the act of leaving the partnership, so they are not harmed by receiving a disproportionate amount of realized gain. The remaining limited partners thus receive a disproportionate amount of unrealized appreciation. So the limited partner who remains in a successful hedge fund for an extended period may find that he has built up a substantial amount of unrealized appreciation, even though the partnership itself has produced a substantial amount of realized gains. As new limited partners enter and old limited partners leave, the realized gains are allocated to the departing limited partners, so what remains in the partnership is unrealized appreciation that is spread across the limited partners who remain as long-term investors in the fund.

Although it is common to criticize hedge funds for their tax inefficiency, this criticism is not completely fair. The recent preoccupation with tax efficiency is a byproduct of a bull market that lasted almost 20 years. In an environment in which stocks are generally going up, appreciation is easy to earn, and unrealized appreciation is better than realized appreciation. But if appreciation is harder to achieve or if unrealized appreciation suddenly evaporates into unrealized depreciation, then investors will place a higher premium on putting real after-tax money in their pockets. Moreover, the standard preoccupation with tax efficiency is concerned mainly with *annual efficiency*, not *total efficiency*. The distinction between these two forms of efficiency is an essential part of the investor's long-term challenge.

Warren Buffett is fond of saying that his favorite holding period is forever. And sometimes investors are in a fortunate situation in which their expected holding period is forever. For example, an investor might buy a piece of property, or a portfolio of stocks, with the objective of holding the asset unto death, at which point the asset will pass into the hands of the investor's heirs. And, under current law, the heirs will receive a *step up in basis*. That is, if the heirs sell the property, their gain or loss will be calculated based on the value of the property at the time when they received it. The original cost of the property disappears from the tax calculation.

But most investors are not investing for the hereafter. For the typical investor, a time horizon of 10 to 20 years is very long. Most investors have much shorter horizons. Indeed, some studies suggest that the typical mutual fund investor has an investment horizon of only a few years. If you buy a tax-efficient fund and then sell it after 3 years, any unrealized appreciation in the fund becomes realized, and so you wipe out the tax advantage. To calculate the *total* tax efficiency of a fund, you have to take into account the tax impact of the final sale.

Mr. Goodwrench encourages us to take care of our cars on a regular basis. "You can pay me now, or you can pay me later." The same is true of the Internal Revenue Service. Holding a low-turnover, tax-efficient fund is a smart way to *defer* taxes, but it is not a way to *avoid* taxes. In a highly tax efficient fund, you pay less tax now, more later. In a high-turnover hedge fund, you pay more tax now, less later. The crucial question for the investor is how the two components of taxation add up. And that depends entirely on the details of the situation.

Suppose you buy a stock for $100 and hold it for 20 years. The stock pays no dividends but appreciates 20 percent every year for 20 years. You pay no tax at all within the holding period, and at the end you own a stock worth $3834. You sell the stock, for a realized gain of $3734. The 20 percent tax on the long-term capital gain is $747. Hence the net amount, after tax, is $3087. So the annually compounded return, after tax, is 18.7 percent. In other words, selling after 20 years reduces the return from 20 to 18.7 percent. Selling after 10 years reduces the after-tax return to 17.8 percent. After 3 years, the return goes down to 16.5 percent.

Now let's go to the opposite extreme. Consider a mutual fund whose return is fully taxable every year, at the highest rate. The fund return consists entirely of bond income, stock dividends, and short-term realized gains. Let's assume a tax rate of 40 percent, reflecting a high-bracket rate of 36 percent, plus a 10 percent surcharge. Thus a 20 percent pretax return becomes a 12 percent after-tax return. But there is no unrealized appreciation building up in the fund, so there is no special tax hit when you sell the fund.

Most real-world investments fall between the two extremes. Although there are stocks that pay no dividends at all, most equity mutual funds make taxable distributions as they go along. Even index funds, universally praised for their low turnover, make taxable distributions based on dividends and realized gains due to mergers, acquisitions, or changes in the composition of the index. In the case of the S&P 500, whose annual return is roughly 12 percent over the long term, the annual distribution might be roughly 3 percent. If that 3 percent is taxed at the 40 percent rate, then the tax is 1.2 percent, and the after-tax return is 10.8 percent.

As for hedge funds, although there are funds whose return is fully taxable every year, there are also funds that strive hard to build up unrealized appreciation. And there are lots of funds that fall in the middle.

To simplify the analysis, let's look at five different scenarios regarding tax efficiency. At one extreme are the stocks, or mutual funds, whose return consists entirely of unrealized appreciation. Here the annual after-tax return is the same as the pretax return: 100 percent tax efficiency. At the other extreme are funds whose total return consists entirely of ordinary income taxed at the highest rate: 40 percent. Here the after-tax return will be 60 percent of the pretax return. Let's call this 60 percent tax efficiency. Then there are three intermediate levels of efficiency: 70 percent, 80 percent, and 90 percent.

Table 14–1 considers an investment with a 12 percent pretax return. We look at four different holding periods: 3, 5, 10, and 20 years. And we look at the five levels of tax efficiency. To begin, notice that even if the investment is 100 percent efficient and you hold it for 20 years, the final sale still reduces the return from 12.0 to 10.9 percent. Selling after 5 years reduces the return to 10.0 percent. If we now assume that the fund is only 90 percent efficient and you sell after 20 years, then the return after all taxes slides down from 10.9 to 9.9 percent. If we assume 90 percent efficiency and a 5-year holding period, then the return after all tax is reduced to 9.3 percent. This figure is substantially below the annual after-tax return of 10.8 percent.

Now let's look at a hedge fund investment whose tax efficiency is below 90 percent. How well does the hedge fund have to do *before tax* to equal the 9.3 percent return after all tax? If the hedge fund is only 80 percent efficient, then it needs to deliver 13.0 percent pretax. At 70 percent efficiency, it needs to deliver 14.1 percent pretax. At 60 percent efficiency, the bottom of the scale, the hedge fund needs to deliver 15.5 percent pretax. Roughly speaking, the hedge fund needs 1 to 3 percent of extra pretax return in order to compete after taxes.

But now suppose that we are less optimistic about the return prospects for the index fund. Table 14–2 shows the results for a fund

TABLE 14–1

A Hypothetical Investment with a 12 Percent Pretax Return Considered at Five Levels of Tax Efficiency

Tax Efficiency	After-Tax Return, Annualized	Holding Periods, Years			
		3	5	10	20
		Annual Return after Liquidation			
100	12.0%	9.8%	10.0%	10.4%	10.9%
90	10.8	9.1	9.3	9.6	9.9
80	9.6	8.5	8.6	8.7	9.0
70	8.4	7.8	7.9	8.0	8.1
60	7.2	7.2	7.2	7.2	7.2

TABLE 14–2

A Hypothetical Investment with a 9 Percent Pretax Return
Considered at Five Levels of Tax Efficiency

Tax Efficiency	After-Tax Return, Annualized	Holding Periods, Years			
		3	5	10	20
		Annual Return after Liquidation			
100%	9.0%	7.3%	7.4%	7.7%	8.0%
90	8.1	6.8	6.9	7.1	7.3
80	7.2	6.4	6.4	6.5	6.7
70	6.3	5.9	5.9	5.9	6.0
60	5.4	5.4	5.4	5.4	5.4

with a 9 percent pretax return. If we assume 90 percent efficiency and
a five-year holding period, then the return after all taxes drops down
to 6.9 percent, which is well below the annual after-tax return of 8.1
percent. How well does a hedge fund have to do to compete? If the
hedge fund is only 80 percent efficient, the fund needs to return 9.7
percent pretax. At 70 percent efficiency, the fund needs to return 10.5
percent. At 60 percent efficiency, the fund needs to return 11.5 percent.

Tax efficiency is a good thing. Other things being equal, a tax-
efficient fund will be more profitable than a less efficient fund. But
other things are rarely equal. The ultimate after-tax return depends on
the pretax return, the efficiency ratio, and the length of the holding period. High tax efficiency is most valuable when the pretax return is high
and the holding period is long. Even if the efficiency ratio is 90 percent and the holding period is five years, you have already given up
several percentage points of total after-tax return. As you compress the
holding period and lower the pretax return of the tax-efficient investment, tax efficiency is no longer the dominating factor.

Here's another way of explaining this point: If you are very
confident that a highly tax efficient index fund will deliver 12 percent pretax returns over the next five years, then you probably
shouldn't spend too much time thinking about hedge funds. As you
form a less ambitious picture of index returns, other forms of investing become more interesting.

There is one other point worth emphasizing: All these calculations about after-tax returns make assumptions about tax rates in 5,
10, and 20 years. But the one thing we know about the tax code is that

it's always changing. If you focus too hard on the value of your unrealized appreciation in 20 years, you are implicitly assuming that the capital gains rate will not change. How much do you really want to bet on that assumption?

Since hedge funds tend to be actively traded, the ideal hedge fund investor is a nontaxable investor. The main occupants of this category are U.S. tax-exempt institutions (pension funds, endowments, foundations, and so on) and offshore investors (the mythical Belgian dentist). These investors are able to take advantage of offshore hedge funds. And the offshore hedge fund also offers a major advantage to the manager of the fund. The fund is a corporation that is based in an offshore tax haven. The manager of the fund receives some percentage of the total return of the fund, but this allocation is an allocation to an offshore entity. If the profit allocation is not repatriated back to the United States, it is not yet taxable to the U.S. money manager. So the U.S.-based manager of an offshore fund has the ability to allow her performance fee to grow offshore in a tax-deferred fashion.

When U.S. tax-exempt institutions invest in hedge funds, they face a tax issue concerning what is known as *unrelated business taxable income* (UBTI). The basic idea behind the taxing of UBTI is that a pension fund, endowment, or foundation may invest in securities, but it may not conduct an operating business. If the General Electric pension plan opened a chain of clothing stores, other clothing stores would complain, justifiably, that they were competing against a new chain of stores that did not have to pay taxes. When a pension fund (or other tax-exempt institution) borrows money to take on a leveraged long position, this is viewed as a departure from "normal investing," a step toward behaving like an operating company. So the Internal Revenue Service penalizes this activity by imposing a tax. The tax is calculated at the normal corporate rate, and applies to that portion of the return attributable to the leverage.

Needless to say, most tax-exempt institutions prefer not to make investments that generate UBTI. The format of the offshore fund provides a convenient route around this problem. An offshore fund is a corporation. The corporation may employ debt in its activities, but that does not mean that the investing pension fund is employing debt. After all, pension funds make investments every day in companies that have debt on their balance sheets. But the pension fund is not borrowing the money; hence there is no UBTI.

PART FIVE

The Menu of Hedge Fund Strategies

CHAPTER 15

An Overview of the Menu

We pointed out at the very beginning of this book that hedge funds, like mutual funds, are available in a bewildering variety of strategies, styles, and flavors. But the universe of hedge funds divides naturally into four main strategy groups: equity hedge funds, global asset allocators, relative-value managers, and event-driven managers. The object of this chapter is to take a general look at the broad menu of strategies. We will begin with a brief description of the main groups and subgroups. Then we will look at the historical performance of the various strategies, paying attention both to return and to the multiple dimensions of risk. The performance review is an aerial reconnaissance in two stages. We survey the five main strategies from 20,000 feet, then drop down to 10,000 feet for a closer look at the substrategies.

THE MAIN STRATEGY GROUPS

Equity Hedge Funds Equity hedge funds are active equity managers who have the ability to use leverage and to sell short. Like more traditional equity managers, they spend most of their time analyzing individual companies and individual stocks. Unlike traditional equity managers, they are not interested in beating the S&P 500 Index or some other passive equity benchmark. Their basic mandate is to produce an attractive positive return, independently of whether the market is going up or down.

The category of equity hedge funds divides into a number of subcategories, most of which are borrowed from the familiar world of traditional equity management. For example, there is the growth-value spectrum, which includes everything from very aggressive growth managers to deep-value managers. There is the capitalization spectrum, running all the way from "mega cap" to "micro cap." There are different geographical orientations: Some managers focus on U.S. stocks, others look mainly outside the United States, others are truly global. Some managers are sector specialists, focusing on technology, or media, or some other specific sector. Others invest across the full range of industries and sectors.

The most important new distinction relates to *directional bias*. It is useful to divide equity hedge funds into three main categories: long biased, short biased, and opportunistic. *Long-biased managers* will tend to be net long the market all the time. At our firm, the rule of thumb is that a long-biased manager will be at least 50 percent net long all the time, so a substantial portion of his return and risk will be determined by whether the market goes up or down.

We pointed out earlier that net exposure can sometimes be a misleading guide to risk. If a manager is 100 percent gross long and 50 percent gross short, and if the short positions really "hedge" half the long exposure, then the 50 percent net exposure figure is a pretty good risk proxy. As you move away from that simple case, the net number can be misleading. But the rule of thumb mentioned above still provides a helpful approximation.

Short-biased managers will be at least 50 percent net short at all times. The short-biased category includes the subcategory of *short-only* managers, or *short sellers*. These are the managers who focus exclusively on identifying overvalued stocks to short. We discussed these managers briefly in Chapter 9. Short selling was a great strategy in the 1970s and early 1980s, when interest rates were very high and stock prices were weak. So the interest on short sale proceeds was very high, and trading profits were plentiful. The bull market of the 1980s and 1990s has been a brutal environment for short sellers. There aren't many short sellers around, and those that remain are a tough band of hardy survivors.

Opportunistic managers are neither long biased nor short biased. This group divides into two subgroups. Some of these managers are aggressive managers who are sometimes more than 50 percent net long and sometimes more than 50 percent net short. Others are more defensive managers who prefer to remain inside the 50 percent exposure band at all times. (But, unlike the market-neutral equity managers, whom we will encounter shortly, these managers make no attempt to be fastidiously "hedged.") The defensive managers focus their effort entirely on stock picking. They do not want to be in a position where directional market movements will have an overwhelming impact on their returns. The more aggressive managers feel that there are times when stocks, in general, become undervalued or overvalued, and they want to vary their net exposure to reflect those changing circumstances. If this is market timing, then so be it.

In this chapter we divide the world of equity hedge funds into four main subgroups: U.S. long biased, U.S. opportunistic, global-international, and short sellers. The global-international group tends to be long biased. Since the short sellers have a high negative correlation to the stock market, we split them off into a separate category during our flight at 20,000 feet.

Global Asset Allocators While equity hedge funds are focused on individual stocks, global asset allocators are focused on broad markets and broad themes. The range of markets includes global stock and bond markets, currency markets, and the physical commodity markets (gold, oil, pork bellies, and so on). If the global asset allocator thinks that the U.S. stock market is a much better bet than the German stock market, she will be long a U.S. equity market index and short a German equity market index. But, in the pure case at least, she will not have long or short positions in individual stocks in the United States or Germany. Because global asset allocators are focused on whole markets and broad themes, they are sometimes called *macro investors*, to distinguish them from the *micro investors* who perform more detailed analysis at the level of individual companies. Many global asset allocators are *Commodity Trading Advisers* (CTAs), who invest only in futures contracts rather than individual stocks or bonds.

The global asset allocator will follow a very wide range of markets, and with respect to each market he may be long, or short, or have no position at all. Some global asset allocators operate with a fair amount of leverage and take very large positions in stock, bond, and currency markets. When the financial press refers to hedge funds that make "large leveraged bets in the global stock, bond, and currency markets," they are talking about the category of global asset allocators. George Soros is the most familiar example in this category.

The category of global asset allocators divides into discretionary managers and systematic managers. *Discretionary managers* formulate judgments that are based, at least in part, on fundamental analysis. *Fundamental analysis* looks at factors such as growth, inflation, and trade flows, which are part of the "real economy." *Technical analysis* looks at information that is purely market related: price, volume, and similar factors. *Systematic managers* have trading rules based on technical data, while discretionary managers have trading judgments that are typically based on some combination of fundamental and technical input.

Relative-Value Managers Relative-value managers operate *hedge* funds that try hard to be genuinely *hedged*. These funds are also sometimes referred to as *market-neutral funds*. A market-neutral fund is neither net long nor net short: It is neutral with respect to the market in which it invests. Imagine, for example, an equity manager who specializes exclusively in electric utility stocks. This manager takes long positions in utilities that she regards as undervalued and takes short positions in utilities that she regards as overvalued. She makes sure that the dollar value of the long positions and the dollar value of the short positions are the same, so that she is neither net long nor net short. If the long positions outperform the short positions, then the total portfolio will earn the performance spread plus the short-term interest rate earned on the proceeds of the short sale.

The basic idea behind hedged investing is to choose securities from within a relatively homogeneous universe, balancing long positions against short positions in such a way that the hedged portfolio will be relatively unaffected by the general movement up or down of the entire universe of securities. The dominant driver of total return will be the *difference* in performance between the long positions and the short positions.

Relative-value investing divides into four subcategories: (1) *Long-short equity managers* buy stocks in attractive companies and sell short stocks in unattractive companies. The two sides are balanced in such a way that, in theory, the portfolio will be unaffected by broad market moves. (2) The *bond hedger* buys attractive bonds and sells short unattractive bonds. The attractive bonds usually have a higher yield than the unattractive bonds, so the portfolio has *positive carry:* The income earned on the long side exceeds the income owed on the short side.

Adding leverage increases the income still further. (3) *Convertible hedgers* specialize in *convertible securities*, which are bonds (or preferred stock) that include a call option on the equity of the issuing company. The convertible hedger buys the convertible security, then sells short the underlying common stock. (4) *Multistrategy managers* build diversified portfolios using some combination of the strategies just mentioned, or other strategies with a similar hedged, or "nondirectional," quality.

Event-Driven Managers Event-driven strategies are company-specific strategies that are focused on transactions that affect the organizational structure of companies. There are two main substrategies: risk arbitrage and distressed debt investing. *Risk arbitrage* (also sometimes called *merger arbitrage*, or *deal arbitrage*) is a stock-oriented strategy that takes advantage of the special opportunities that arise when companies decide to buy, or merge with, other companies. If one company announces that it wants to buy another company, the acquirer will usually pay a substantial premium over the price that the target was trading at prior to the acquisition announcement. If the target was trading at $50, then the acquirer might be offering $70 per share. When the announcement is made, the price of the target will rise, but it may not rise to the full $70. After all, the deal may not happen, or it may get delayed, or other factors may intervene. Traditional equity investors are happy to sell their shares in the target company at $60 or $65, enjoying the recent "pop" in the price. The job of the risk arbitrageur is to buy the shares at some price below $70, and to *earn the spread* between that price and the offer price of $70. This, of course, is a highly idealized description of the strategy. We shall have a look at some of the details in Chapter 18.

 Distressed debt investing takes advantage of the special opportunities that arise when companies in financial distress undergo financial restructuring. In these situations, the equity investors in the company are typically wiped out altogether, while the various classes of lenders fight over who gets what in the reorganization. The distressed debt investor is betting that the debt that he buys today will be worth more at the end of the reorganization process.

 The event-driven category has three main divisions: risk arbitrage specialists, distressed debt specialists, and multistrategy managers who will invest in some mix of the first two basic strategies, with the exact allocation depending on market conditions. Event-driven investing is very situation specific and involves very intensive legal analysis of specific transactions. Returns often have a relatively low correlation with general equity returns since the returns depend on the outcome of specific deals and do not depend so much on such traditional variables as earnings growth, price/earnings (P/E) ratios, interest rates, and so forth.

THE HISTORICAL RECORD

The figures in this section display the performance record of the basic strategies for the period beginning January 1990 and ending December 2001. Since we are now at 20,000 feet, we show only the four main groups, with one twist: The short sellers are separated from the other equity hedge funds because of their distinctive risk-return profile. The data are based on the EACM 100® Index, which is described more fully in Appendix I.

Before we go any further, there are two caveats that must be emphasized. First, all the numbers that we are about to look at are based on past performance. And, as we saw at length in Chapter 6, you cannot blithely assume that the future will resemble the past. Future returns may be different from what you are about to see, and future risk characteristics may be different too.

Second, the numbers shown for each strategy are based on the performance of a group of managers. The main groups divide as follows:

Strategy	Number of Managers
Relative value	30
Event driven	15
Equity hedge funds	30
Global asset allocators	20
Short sellers	5

Each group of managers is a small portfolio, within which the returns of the various managers will not be perfectly correlated. So the standard deviation of the group will be slightly lower than the average standard deviation of the various individual managers. And the same will hold true for other risk measures: A single manager will be more risky than a group of many managers.

Figure 15–1 shows the basic return-risk tradeoff for the main strategies. *Return* is the annually compounded return, net of all fees.

FIGURE 15–1

Historical Risk-Return Characteristics
Annualized Rate of Return Versus Annualized
Standard Deviation

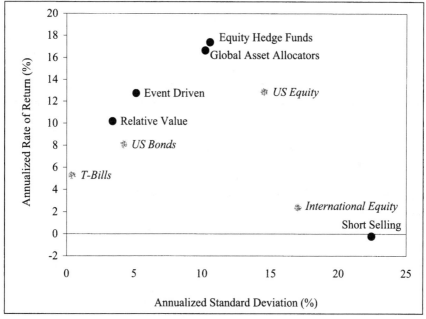

Calculations are based on monthly rates of return for January 1990 through December 2001. Hedge fund strategies (relative value, event driven, equity hedge funds, global asset allocators, and short sellers) are based on strategy components of the EACM 100® Index. Traditional assets are based on the following indexes: S&P 500 Index (U.S. equity), Lehman Brothers Government/Credit Index (U.S. bonds), Merrill Lynch 3-month U.S. Treasury Bill (T-bills), and MSCI EAFE USD (international equity).

Source: Standard & Poor's, Lehman Brothers, Merrill Lynch, Morgan Stanley Capital International Inc., and EACM.

Standard deviation is the volatility measure that we discussed in Chapter 7. Notice that four of the five strategies line up fairly straightforwardly. Relative value has had the lowest return and volatility, global asset allocators and equity hedge funds have had the highest return and volatility, and event-driven strategies have fallen in the middle. Short sellers have had the worst of both worlds: low return with high volatility. Notice that the imaginary line that connects the four main hedge fund strategies lies slightly above the imaginary line that connects the main traditional market benchmarks. Hedge funds have been very efficient in extracting return from risk.

Volatility tells us how much the returns vary around the average return. But, as we observed in Chapter 7, what investors really worry about is *downside volatility*: the risk of losing money. And this worry breaks into two questions: (1) How often will I lose? and (2) When I lose, how much will I lose? Figure 15–2 shows loss frequency against average loss for the various strategies.

In Figure 15–2, as in Figure 15–1, the most desirable neighborhood is in the northwest. (We have inverted the vertical scale in Figure 15–2 to make this work.) Relative value and event driven again appear as the more risk-averse strategies, with short selling at the other extreme. Equity hedge funds and global asset allocators

FIGURE 15–2

Historical Monthly Loss and Frequency
Average Monthly Loss Versus Frequency of Monthly Loss

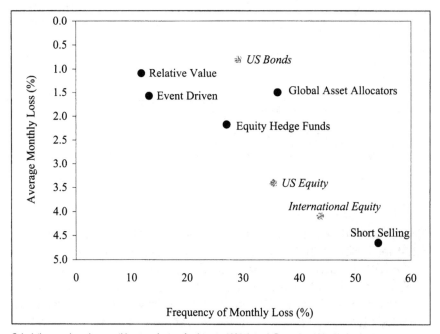

Calculations are based on monthly rates of return for January 1990 through December 2001. Hedge fund strategies (relative value, event driven, equity hedge funds, global asset allocators, and short sellers) are based on strategy components of the EACM 100® Index. Traditional assets are based on the following indexes: S&P 500 Index (U.S. equity), Lehman Brothers Government/Credit Index (U.S. bonds), and MSCI EAFE USD (international equity).

Source: Standard & Poor's, Lehman Brothers, Morgan Stanley Capital International Inc., and EACM.

are in between, but the two groups are further apart than they were in Figure 15–1. Global asset allocators lost money more often, but their average loss was less.

But losses are only half the picture. Figure 15–3 plots average loss against average gain. Gains and losses are roughly equal for three of the five strategies. (The line running from southwest to northeast shows where gains and losses are equal.) Short sellers and global asset allocators stand out for delivering gains that are noticeably greater than their losses.

Volatility, loss frequency, average loss, and average gain all relate to the risk of a strategy on a stand-alone basis. But, as we know from our earlier discussion of portfolio diversification, we also need

FIGURE 15–3

Historical Gains and Losses
Average Monthly Loss Versus Average Monthly Gain

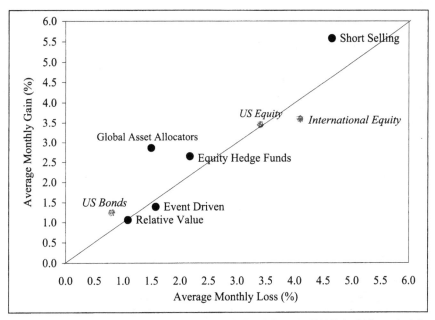

Calculations are based on monthly rates of return for January 1990 through December 2001. Hedge fund strategies (relative value, event driven, equity hedge funds, global asset allocators, and short sellers) are based on strategy components of the EACM 100® Index. Traditional assets are based on the following indexes: S&P 500 Index (U.S. equity), Lehman Brothers Government/Credit Index (U.S. bonds), and MSCI EAFE USD (international equity).

Source: Standard & Poor's, Lehman Brothers, Morgan Stanley Capital International Inc., and EACM.

to know how the various strategies interact with each other, and
with the standard market benchmarks. Table 15–1 shows the correlation matrix for the major strategies and major passive benchmarks.
Remember, correlations range from 1 to –1. When the number is
close to 1, the two strategies tend to move up and down together;
when the number is closer to –1, they tend to move in opposite directions; when the number is closer to zero, it means that there is little
relationship between the two strategies.

Notice that short sellers have a negative correlation with most
of the other strategies and most of the passive benchmarks. This feature makes short sellers very useful as part of a larger portfolio.
Notice also that both relative-value managers and global asset allocators have extremely low correlations with U.S. stocks.

The concept of correlation is very abstract. What investors really
worry about is downside correlation: How does investment A perform
when investment B is doing badly? This divides into two questions.

TABLE 15–1

Historical Correlation Matrix

	Relative Value	Event Driven	Equity Hedge Funds	Global Asset Allocators	Short Sellers	U.S. Equity	U.S. Bonds	U.S. T-Bills	International Equity
Relative value	1.0								
Event driven	0.4	1.0							
Equity hedge funds	0.3	0.5	1.0						
Global asset allocators	0.1	0.0	0.2	1.0					
Short sellers	–0.2	–0.6	–0.7	0.1	1.0				
U.S. equity	0.1	0.5	0.6	0.1	–0.8	1.0			
U.S. bonds	0.0	0.1	0.1	0.3	–0.1	0.3	1.0		
U.S. T-bills	0.0	–0.1	0.0	0.2	0.1	0.0	0.2	1.0	
International equity	0.2	0.3	0.5	0.0	–0.5	0.6	0.1	–0.1	1.0

Calculations are based on monthly rates of return for January 1990 through December 2001. Hedge fund strategies (relative value, event driven, equity hedge funds, global asset allocators, and short sellers) are based on strategy components
of the EACM 100® Index. Traditional assets are based on the following indexes: S&P 500 Index (U.S. equity), Lehman
Brothers Government/Credit Index (U.S. bonds), Merrill Lynch 3-month U.S. Treasury Bill (T-bills), and MSCI EAFE USD
(international equity).

Source: Standard & Poor's, Lehman Brothers, Merrill Lynch, Morgan Stanley Capital International Inc., and EACM.

How often does A make money when B is losing money? What is the average return of A when B is losing money? Figure 15–4 shows how the major hedge fund strategies are related to the S&P 500 Index.

In the period shown, the S&P 500 Index experienced a negative return in 35 percent of the months, with an average loss of 3.4 percent. Once again, the northwest corner is the most desirable neighborhood. Short sellers perform exceptionally well in down markets: Their average return is almost double the market's average loss. (Notice that the average *return* for the short sellers is not the average *gain*: It's the average return for *all* the months when the S&P 500 Index was down, including the few months when the short sellers were down too.) Relative-value managers and global asset allocators are also very

FIGURE 15–4

Performance in Down U.S. Equity Markets
Average Monthly Return Versus Gain Frequency

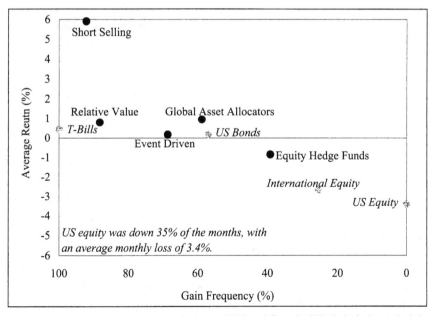

Calculations are based on monthly rates of return for January 1990 through December 2001. Hedge fund strategies (relative value, event driven, equity hedge funds, global asset allocators, and short sellers) are based on strategy components of the EACM 100® Index. Traditional assets are based on the following indexes: S&P 500 Index (U.S. equity), Lehman Brothers Government/Credit Index (U.S. bonds), Merrill Lynch 3-month U.S. Treasury Bill (T-bills), and MSCI EAFE USD (international equity).

Source: Standard & Poor's, Lehman Brothers, Merrill Lynch, Morgan Stanley Capital International Inc., and EACM.

resistant to down markets, consistent with the low correlation just noted. Event-driven managers just eke out a positive return in the down months; equity hedge funds are slightly down.

Given the relationships just noted, it becomes possible to construct a portfolio of hedge funds that has the potential to deliver attractive returns with reasonable volatility and very low correlation to the standard markets. There are two ways of doing this. One approach is a "common-sense" approach that takes advantage of some of the rough relationships noted above but makes no attempt to be ultraprecise. The second approach is the highly quantitative approach of the portfolio optimizer. If we use the returns, volatilities, and cross-correlations for the period 1990 through 2001, then we would construct the efficient frontier shown in Figure 15–5.

But the familiar caveats are in order. The inputs are based on a particular historical period and are not likely to hold in the future. As usual, some of the "efficiently diversified" portfolios look highly undiversified from a common-sense point of view. In the real world of uncertainty, it would be imprudent to invest in the portfolio that lies at the western end of the efficient frontier shown. That "efficiently diversified" portfolio is in fact a very aggressive bet on the accuracy of the underlying inputs.

Before we leave the topic of diversification, it is helpful to look at the relationship between a broadly diversified portfolio of hedge funds and the S&P 500 Index. Figure 15–6 shows the historical impact of adding a hedge fund allocation to a U.S. equity portfolio. We look at 11 portfolios: 100 percent in the S&P 500 Index, 90 percent in the S&P 500 Index plus 10 percent in the relevant hedge fund strategy, 80 percent in the S&P 500 Index plus 20 percent in hedge funds, and so forth. In each of the five cases, shifting some money from the S&P 500 Index into a hedge fund strategy reduced volatility. In two of the five cases, the shift also increased return.

The question is whether these relationships will also hold in the future. It is reasonable to assume that hedge funds can lower the risk of a portfolio, simply because hedge funds often have a low correlation with stocks and bonds. This point emerges from the historical data, but also makes intuitive sense. Hedge funds can take short positions in stocks and bonds, and they can use other hedging strategies. In addition, hedge funds can take long positions in commodities and other assets that have a low correlation with stocks and bonds.

FIGURE 15-5

Efficient Frontier, Historical Risk and
Return Characteristics

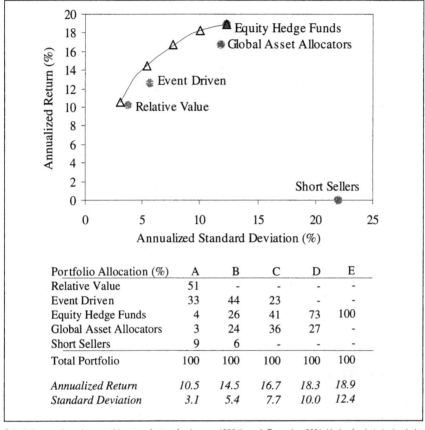

Portfolio Allocation (%)	A	B	C	D	E
Relative Value	51	-	-	-	-
Event Driven	33	44	23	-	-
Equity Hedge Funds	4	26	41	73	100
Global Asset Allocators	3	24	36	27	-
Short Sellers	9	6	-	-	-
Total Portfolio	100	100	100	100	100
Annualized Return	*10.5*	*14.5*	*16.7*	*18.3*	*18.9*
Standard Deviation	*3.1*	*5.4*	*7.7*	*10.0*	*12.4*

Calculations are based on monthly rates of return for January 1990 through December 2001. Hedge fund strategies (relative value, event driven, equity hedge funds, global asset allocators, and short sellers) are based on strategy components of the EACM 100® Index.
Source: EACM.

The return question is more difficult. If hedge funds continue to deliver returns in the low teens and U.S. equities resume the robust returns of the late 1990s, then hedge funds will look pretty tepid. But if U.S. equity returns revert to their historical norm, and hedge fund returns remain in line with the historical record, then hedge fund returns will be very competitive.

FIGURE 15–6

Portfolio Allocation, Historical Risk and
Return Characteristics

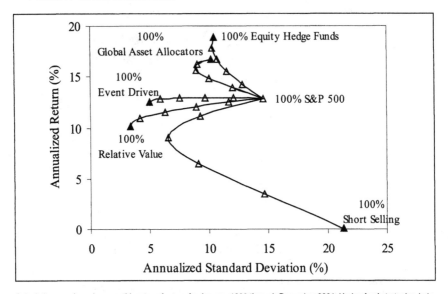

Calculations are based on monthly rates of return for January 1990 through December 2001. Hedge fund strategies (relative value, event driven, equity hedge funds, global asset allocators, and short sellers) are based on strategy components of the EACM 100® Index.

Source: Standard & Poor's and EACM.

A CLOSER LOOK

As we have just seen, relative-value and event-driven strategies tend to be the lower-risk strategies, while equity hedge funds and global asset allocators tend to be higher risk. But this is a generalization. There are high-risk relative-value managers, such as Long Term Capital Management. LTCM focused on relative-value trades, trying hard to avoid directional market risk, but the level of leverage was so high that the result was dangerously high risk. At the other extreme, there are global asset allocators who make directional bets in the global markets but use modest amounts of leverage and impose tight risk management disciplines. Still, as we look at the various substrategies, it makes sense to combine the relative-value managers with the event-driven managers, and to combine the equity hedge funds with the global asset allocators. We already covered the short sellers as a separate group, so we will omit them this time around.

Figure 15–7 shows that the multistrategy managers, both in the relative-value category and in the event-driven category, have delivered a very attractive return-volatility combination. The ability to vary the allocation across a short menu of related strategies has added value. The multistrategy managers also show up well in Figure 15–8, with low loss frequencies and fairly modest average losses. Long-short equity has been particularly successful in controlling loss. Figure 15–9 draws attention to risk arbitrage and bond hedging as short volatility strategies: The average loss is slightly higher than the aver-

F I G U R E   15–7

Historical Risk-Return Characteristics
Annualized Rate of Return Versus Annualized
Standard Deviation

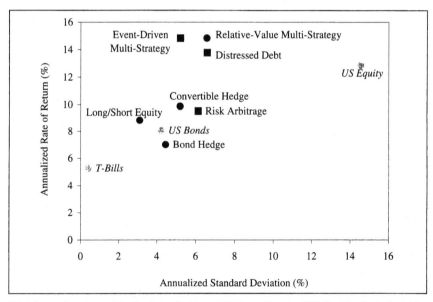

Calculations are based on monthly rates of return for January 1990 through December 2001. Specialized hedge fund strategies within the relative-value strategy group (long/short equity, convertible hedge, bond hedge, and multi-strategy) and the event-driven strategy group (risk arbitrage, distressed debt, and multi-strategy) are based on substrategy components of the EACM 100® Index. Traditional assets are based on the following indexes: S&P 500 Index (U.S. equity), Lehman Brothers Government/Credit Index (U.S. bonds), and Merrill Lynch 3-month U.S. Treasury Bill (T-bills).

Source: Standard & Poor's, Lehman Brothers, Merrill Lynch, and EACM.

FIGURE 15-8

FIGURE 15-8

Historical Monthly Loss and Frequency
Average Monthly Loss Versus Frequency of Monthly Loss

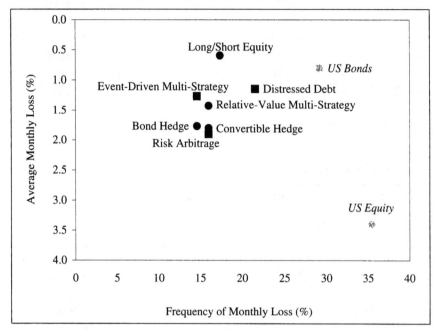

Calculations are based on monthly rates of return for January 1990 through December 2001. Specialized hedge fund strategies within the relative-value strategy group (long/short equity, convertible hedge, bond hedge, and multi-strategy) and the event-driven strategy group (risk arbitrage, distressed debt, and multi-strategy) are based on substrategy components of the EACM 100® Index. Traditional assets are based on the following indexes: S&P 500 Index (U.S. equity), and Lehman Brothers Government/Credit Index (U.S. bonds).

Source: Standard & Poor's, Lehman Brothers, and EACM.

age gain. Convertible hedging is, in theory, a long volatility strategy, but the historical figures, based on a group of about seven managers, have been pulled down by the results of one manager who experienced very disappointing returns. (This serves as another reminder of the importance of manager diversification.) Figure 15–10 suggests that event-driven strategies tend to have more equity-related risk than relative-value strategies. This makes intuitive sense since a risk arbitrage portfolio is a portfolio of stocks, and distressed bonds are sensitive to some of the same company-specific factors that drive equity prices.

Turning to the equity hedge funds and the global asset allocators, it is useful to focus on two differences: the difference between the long-biased and the opportunistic equity hedge funds, and the

FIGURE 15–9

Historical Gains and Losses
Average Monthly Loss Versus Average Monthly Gain

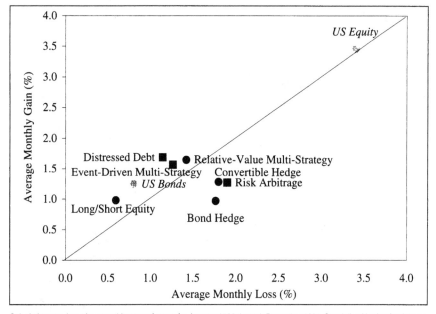

Calculations are based on monthly rates of return for January 1990 through December 2001. Specialized hedge fund strategies within the relative-value strategy group (long/short equity, convertible hedge, bond hedge, and multi-strategy) and the
event-driven strategy group (risk arbitrage, distressed debt, and multi-strategy) are based on substrategy components of
the EACM 100® Index. Traditional assets are based on the following indexes: S&P 500 Index (U.S. equity), and Lehman
Brothers Government/Credit Index (U.S. bonds).

Source: Standard & Poor's, Lehman Brothers, and EACM.

difference between the systematic and the discretionary global asset
allocators. Figure 15–11 shows that the systematic global asset allocators tend to be more volatile than their discretionary colleagues, and
the long-biased hedge funds tend to be more volatile than their
opportunistic colleagues. Similarly, in Figure 15–12 the systematic
global asset allocators have a higher loss frequency, and a higher
average loss, than their discretionary colleagues. The long-biased
equity hedge funds have roughly the same loss frequency as the
opportunistic managers, but their average loss is much higher. In
Figure 15–13, notice that the systematic global asset allocators have
been especially successful in delivering a "long volatility profile":
The average gain has been appreciably greater than the average loss.
The systematic managers also stand out in Figure 15–14 for their

FIGURE 15-10

Performance in Down U.S. Equity Markets
Average Monthly Return Versus Gain Frequency

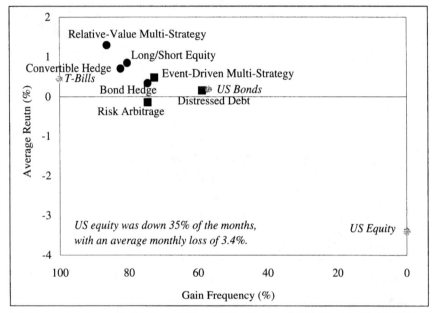

Calculations are based on monthly rates of return for January 1990 through December 2001. Specialized hedge fund strategies within the relative-value strategy group (long/short equity, convertible hedge, bond hedge, and multi-strategy) and the
event-driven strategy group (risk arbitrage, distressed debt, and multi-strategy) are based on substrategy components of
the EACM 100® Index. Traditional assets are based on the following indexes: S&P 500 Index (U.S. equity), Lehman Brothers
Government/Credit Index (U.S. bonds), and Merrill Lynch 3-month U.S. Treasury Bill (T-bills)
Source: Standard & Poor's, Lehman Brothers, Merrill Lynch, and EACM.

performance in down markets. Not surprisingly, the opportunistic
hedge funds perform better in down markets than the long-biased
managers. The long-biased hedge funds lose less money than the
index in down markets, but they do lose money.

BEFORE WE CONTINUE

To form an intelligent picture of the return potential and risk profile
of hedge funds, you need more than the historical numbers. You
need to get behind the numbers for a qualitative look at the personality of the various strategies. That is the object of the next three
chapters. We will spend more time on the less familiar strategies.

FIGURE 15-11

Historical Risk-Return Characteristics
Annualized Rate of Return Versus Annualized
Standard Deviation

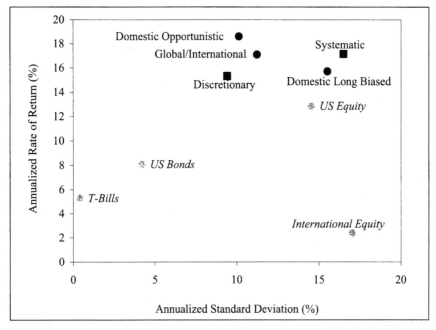

Calculations are based on monthly rates of return for January 1990 through December 2001. Specialized hedge fund strategies within the equity hedge funds strategy group (domestic long biased, domestic opportunistic, and global/international)
and the global asset allocations strategy group (discretionary and systematic) are based on substrategy components of the
EACM 100® Index. Traditional assets are based on the following indexes: S&P 500 Index (U.S. equity), Lehman Brothers
Government/Credit Index (U.S. bonds), Merrill Lynch 3-month U.S. Treasury Bill (T-bills), and MSCI EAFE USD (international equity).
Source: Standard & Poor's, Lehman Brothers, Merrill Lynch, Morgan Stanley Capital International Inc., and EACM.

This means a pretty quick look at equity hedge funds since their
activities are a natural extension of what goes on in the world of traditional equity management. And we will not spend a lot of time on
the discretionary global asset allocators, whose strategies are a natural extension of "globally diversified stock and bond management."
But the systematic global asset allocators require a little more time
because of their reliance on technical trading rules. Relative-value and
event-driven strategies will be the least familiar to the general reader, so we will devote the most time to these specialties.

FIGURE 15–12

Historical Monthly Loss and Frequency
Average Monthly Loss Versus Frequency of Monthly Loss

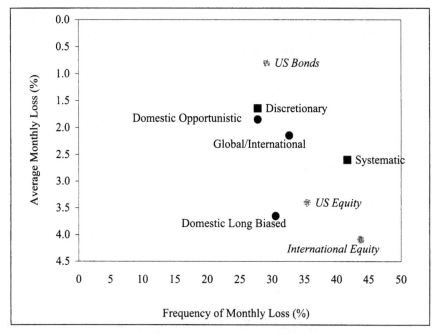

Calculations are based on monthly rates of return for January 1990 through December 2001. Specialized hedge fund strategies within the equity hedge funds strategy group (domestic long biased, domestic opportunistic, and global/international)
and the global asset allocators strategy group (discretionary and systematic) are based on substrategy components of the
EACM 100® Index. Traditional assets are based on the following indexes: S&P 500 Index (U.S. equity), Lehman Brothers
Government/Credit Index (U.S. bonds), and MSCI EAFE USD (international equity).

Source: Standard & Poor's, Lehman Brothers, Morgan Stanley Capital International Inc., and EACM.

FIGURE 15-13

Historical Gains and Losses
Average Monthly Loss Versus Average Monthly Gain

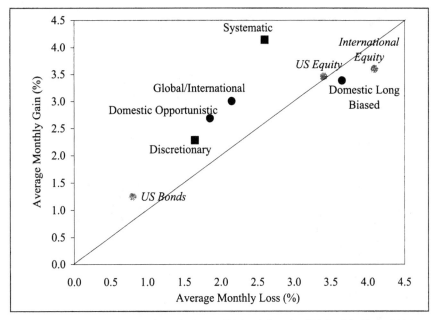

Calculations are based on monthly rates of return for January 1990 through December 2001. Specialized hedge fund strategies within the equity hedge funds strategy group (domestic long biased, domestic opportunistic, and global/international) and the global asset allocators strategy group (discretionary and systematic) are based on substrategy components of the EACM 100® Index. Traditional assets are based on the following indexes: S&P 500 Index (U.S. equity), Lehman Brothers Government/Credit Index (U.S. bonds), and MSCI EAFE USD (international equity).

Source: Standard & Poor's, Lehman Brothers, Morgan Stanley Capital International Inc., and EACM.

FIGURE 15–14

Performance in Down U.S. Equity Markets
Average Monthly Return Versus Gain Frequency

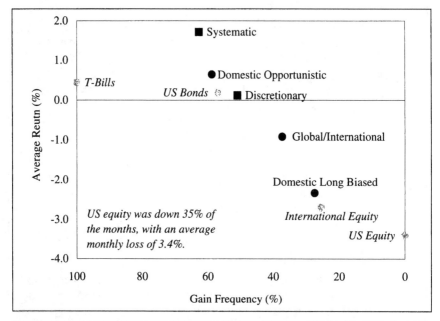

Calculations are based on monthly rates of return for January 1990 through December 2001. Specialized hedge fund strategies within the equity hedge funds strategy group (domestic long biased, domestic opportunistic, and global/international)
and the global asset allocators strategy group (discretionary and systematic) are based on substrategy components of the
EACM 100® Index. Traditional assets are based on the following indexes: S&P 500 Index (U.S. equity), Lehman Brothers
Government/Credit Index (U.S. bonds), and Merrill Lynch 3-month U.S. Treasury bill (T-bills), and MSCI EAFE USD (international equity).

Source: Standard & Poor's, Lehman Brothers, Merrill Lynch, Morgan Stanley Capital International Inc., and EACM.

CHAPTER 16

Equity Hedge Funds and Global Asset Allocators

People think of equity hedge funds as hyperactive portfolios that use liberal amounts of leverage and short selling. This is often the case but not always the case. Some equity hedge funds use essentially no leverage and no short selling, and they trade very sparingly. These funds are long term, low turnover, tax efficient investors. They take advantage of the fact that hedge funds have a limited number of investors, each of whom has much less liquidity than he would have in an ordinary mutual fund. If the investors in a fund can get access to their capital only once a year, or perhaps even less frequently, then the fund can have a longer investment horizon than an ordinary mutual fund, and it can invest in more illiquid positions. Benjamin Graham and Warren Buffett ran hedge funds of this kind, and such funds exist today.

The more typical equity hedge funds do use leverage and short selling, and they trade fairly actively. As we mentioned earlier, most of the style categories that apply to the world of traditional equity management apply also to the world of equity hedge funds. The distinction between growth and value deserves special attention because many people assume that hedge fund managers are very aggressive, growth oriented, and momentum driven. This is not true. The hedge fund community includes value managers of many different kinds.

GROWTH VERSUS VALUE

The basic distinction between growth and value is simple: Value investors like to buy cheap stocks, while growth investors like to invest in good companies. These two preferences usually conflict: Cheap stocks are usually not stocks of good companies. Life gets more complicated when we ask how to tell whether a stock is cheap, or a company is good. The standard measures of cheapness would include some of the following: low P/E (price divided by earnings) ratio, low ratio of price to book value, and high yield (ratio of dividend to price). The standard measures of high quality would include high earnings growth, high return on equity, high profit margins, strong management, and dominant industry position.

The value investor worries mainly about what he is paying; the growth investor worries about what he is getting. The problem is that usually you get what you pay for. If you're a real cheapskate, you wind up owning shares in lousy companies. If you like to invest in good companies, you aren't likely to buy them cheap. The challenge is to manage the tradeoff between what you're paying and what you're getting.

Warren Buffett is often revered as the dean of value investing, but Buffett has no interest at all in buying cheap stocks. He routinely makes fun of the "cigar butt school of investing" and is fond of saying that he would rather buy a great company at a good price than buy a good company at a great price. In the crunch, he is more interested in quality companies than in cheap stocks.

The hedge fund community, like the mutual fund community, includes managers from every point along the growth-value spectrum. At one end are deep-value managers who are so concerned with price that they often wind up investing in companies that look pretty unappealing. At the other extreme are aggressive growth managers who are so concerned with earnings growth or other measures of corporate excellence that they often pay very little attention to the price that they are paying. This is the "growth-at-any-price" approach. And then there are all sorts of managers in between, reflecting different ways of managing the tradeoff between cheap stocks and good companies. The growth-at-a-reasonable-price strategy is somewhere in the middle of the spectrum.

Growth-oriented investors are often momentum-driven, and value-oriented investors often have a contrarian view of the world. But there are exceptions. Some growth investors have a contrarian element in their approach: They like to buy growth companies when they are temporarily depressed. And some value investors have a momentum element in their style: They like to buy cheap stocks only when they are already beginning to show signs of turning around.

SKILL AND CAPACITY

The world of equity hedge funds is essentially the world of active equity management, enhanced with new tools: leverage, short selling, and other hedging techniques. In the right hands, those tools will add to return and keep risk under control. In the wrong hands, those tools will detract from return and increase the level of risk. So the skill of the manager is the crucial ingredient. There is no "natural source of return" for the equity hedge fund manager, no wind at her back. (We are excluding here the long-biased funds, which benefit from the fact that stocks tend to go up over the long term.)

As large institutions look to the world of equity hedge funds, they will need to focus on managers who can manage substantial pools of assets. This means a tilt toward managers who invest in large cap and mid cap stocks. Will those managers be able to absorb the new investment flows if they come?

The main reason for being optimistic is that hedge funds have the freedom to take short positions, so they should be able to avoid the classic problems that arise when too much money chases too few investment opportunities. When investors develop a passion for real estate, or emerging markets debt, or tech stocks, they bid up prices to unsustainable levels, and then the whole house of cards comes tumbling down. The buying interest creates a bubble, and then the bubble bursts dramatically and painfully. But the classic bubbles develop when all investors want to *buy*. Hedge funds are not limited to buying. Hedge funds can take short positions, so they *should* be able to take advantage of any market distortions caused by the influx of new money into hedge funds.

But *should* is not the same as *will*. Taking advantage of market distortions is not a riskless enterprise. Short selling presents special risks and requires special skills, especially in the area of risk management. Many portfolio managers have discovered, painfully, that shorting stocks is not just a natural extension of buying stocks. The transition from the long-only world to the long-or-short world is not as effortless as some people think. For example, many hedge funds that shorted overvalued tech stocks were hurt badly as the over-

valued became over-overvalued. Those who sold short were ultimately right, but they were early. And in the investment business
there's no sharp line between being early and being wrong.

GLOBAL ASSET ALLOCATORS

Equity hedge funds care about individual stocks and individual
companies. Global asset allocators care about broad markets and
broad themes. The global asset allocator will focus on stock market
indexes, long-term and short-term interest rates, currencies, and the
physical commodity markets: oil, gold, the agricultural commodities,
and so forth. With respect to each market, the global asset allocator
may be long, or short, or have no net position.

Discretionary global asset allocators make judgmental trading
decisions based on a broad array of factors, while systematic managers adopt definite trading rules or algorithms. *Systematic managers*
are often called *black-box managers*: Their investment strategy is
reducible to a set of rules that might be set up as a computer program.
Discretionary managers often follow rules of thumb, but they do not
follow hard-and-fast rules.

The distinction between discretionary and systematic managers
is related to the distinction between technical analysis and fundamental
analysis. *Technical analysis* focuses exclusively on information related
to markets: trends in price, volume, and so forth. *Fundamental analysis*
focuses on what is going on at the level of companies and economies.
What drives markets is investors' constantly changing beliefs, expectations, hopes, and fears regarding the fundamentals. The fundamental analyst believes that you cannot invest intelligently without understanding the fundamentals. The technical analyst believes that everything that you need to know about the fundamentals is already reflected in current prices and their relationship to past prices.

Most discretionary managers rely on some combination of fundamental and technical analysis. For example, a manager might rely
on fundamental analysis to decide whether economic trends in the
United States favor rising inflation or falling inflation. If the conclusion is that inflation should trend down, then the manager will get
interested in taking long positions in long-maturity bonds. At this
point, the manager might resort to some sort of technical analysis to
determine an attractive *entry point* for the trade. Technical analysis

can help the manager to identify the width of the current trading range, and where the *support* and *resistance levels* are. In a situation like this, fundamental analysis directs the manager's basic strategy, while technical analysis directs the tactics.

Other discretionary managers will rely almost exclusively on fundamental analysis, paying little or no attention to the technical situation. At the other extreme, there are discretionary managers who rely very heavily on technical analysis but who do so in a discretionary way. They will look at price trends and chart patterns to help shape their trading decisions, but they would reject the attempt to program a computer to replicate their trading decisions.

The systematic manager has a set of rules that are almost invariably based on technical analysis. The focus of the work is the detailed analysis of price data. And here we may distinguish multiple levels of detail. Some managers are content to deal with daily closing prices. Others will want open, high, low, and close. Still others will want *tick data*: trade-by-trade pricing information covering all the intraday movements. As for non-price-related data, the main items here would be volume, open interest, and similar information. For example, the combination of rising price and rising volume might be interpreted bullishly, whereas rising price and falling volume might be given a bearish interpretation.

DISCRETIONARY MANAGERS

The discretionary global asset allocator is a globally oriented manager who surveys the full menu of investment options: stocks, bonds, currencies, physical commodities, and so forth. The stocks and bonds may be in the United States or in other countries. He forms opinions about what is undervalued and what is overvalued and constructs long and short positions accordingly.

The typical global asset allocator will rely on some blend of fundamental analysis and technical analysis, but the key objective is always to form a reasonable investment *judgment* based on the evidence at hand. The discretionary manager believes that the world is a very complicated place, so any attempt to reduce that complexity to a set of rules is bound to lead to trouble.

The kind of fundamental analysis carried out by the global asset allocator is not at all unique to the hedge fund community. It is essen-

tially the same as the analysis that might be used by a more traditional manager who invests in global stock and bond markets. The
list of variables would include at least the following:

- Growth variables
  GDP growth
  Growth in corporate profits
  Employment and productivity growth

- Inflation variables
  Consumer price inflation
  Producer price inflation
  Price of energy and/or other key commodities

- Interest rates
  Level of short rates and long rates, both nominal and
     inflation adjusted
  Central bank policy

- Trade flows and capital flows

- Equity valuation variables
  P/E ratios, absolute level and relative to interest rates
  Price to cash flow, business value, other indicators

So, for example, during the late 1990s many global asset allocators thought that the U.S. and European economies were in much
better shape than the Japanese economy. The United States was experiencing good growth, low inflation, and a strong stock market fueled
by persistent positive inflows from both U.S. and non-U.S. investors.
Europe was less ebullient but nonetheless enjoying decent growth
and low inflation, and it was poised to reap the benefits of currency union. In particular, many managers anticipated that currency
union would trigger a wave of corporate mergers and acquisitions
as companies reorganized themselves to compete in the pan-
European market. Japan, by contrast, was the problem child of the
global economy, struggling with chronic economic weakness from the
time of the collapse of the "bubble economy" in the late 1980s.

Given this background, a natural reaction was to have long
positions in U.S. and European stocks and bonds, combined with
short positions in Japanese equities. But there were several gray
areas. Some managers were long U.S. equities, impressed with the

power and momentum of the U.S. bull market. Others were short or had very little exposure in either direction, because of chronic worries about the valuation of the U.S. equity market. Similarly, some managers were long Japanese bonds, reasoning that economic weakness would be good for the bond market. Others were short Japanese bonds, reasoning that Japanese interest rates were so low that the probability of an upward spike in rates was much greater than the probability of stable or falling rates.

The difference between a global asset allocator and a more traditional globally oriented manager is not in the style of analysis or the valuation conclusions. The difference lies in what the manager does with the conclusions. In the traditional money management world, the manager who worries about the state of the Japanese economy will simply be underweight in Japanese equities, and might even have zero exposure to Japan. In the hedge fund world, the manager has the ability to take a short position in Japanese equities. Similarly, if a traditional manager is worried that oil prices may be poised for a sudden upward move, then the only available option is to buy the stocks of oil-related companies that will benefit from that move. The hedge fund manager has the freedom to buy crude oil futures or to take a short position in bonds or other instruments that might be adversely affected by rising oil prices. The hedge fund manager paints in color, while the more traditional manager is confined to black and white.

SYSTEMATIC MANAGERS

The systematic global asset allocator follows definite rules for putting on and taking off positions. These rules will be based on technical inputs: information related to price and perhaps a limited number of other market-related variables (volume, open interest, and so on). Some of these trading systems will be very simple, based, for example, on moving averages of various sorts. Other systems will be impressively complicated, devised by "rocket scientists" with Ph.D.s and supercomputers. The common theme is to devise investment technologies that will "take the human emotion out of the picture."

Most trading systems are designed to be trend-following systems. The object of the game is to identify a price trend and then establish a trading position that will take advantage of that trend.

Notice that we said that the object was to *identify* a trend, not to *anticipate* a trend. If prices are beginning to trend upward, then the trading system will not identify the trend until after the trend has been in place for a while. And when the trend reverses, the trading system will not pick up the change until after the downtrend has been in place for a while. So the trend-following manager emphasizes from the start that she is not trying to buy at the bottom and sell at the top. Rather, she is trying to buy *after* the bottom, and sell *after* the top.

The simplest kind of trend-following system is a *moving average system*. For example, we compare today's price with the average price over the past 20 trading days. Or we compare the 10-day moving average with the 100-day moving average. If the short-term average is greater than the longer-term average, then prices are in an uptrend, and the system recommends a long position. If the short-term average is below the long-term average, then prices are in a downtrend, and the system recommends a short position.

Figure 16–1 shows the price of the eurodollar futures contract during 2000 and 2001. The eurodollar contract is a very liquid contract that serves as a proxy for U.S. short-term interest rates. Eurodollar deposits are U.S. dollar deposits held in large high-quality banks outside the United States. Eurodollar yields are usually slightly higher than Treasury bill yields, reflecting some element of credit risk. The price of the contract is calculated by subtracting the eurodollar yield from 100. Rising prices mean falling yields, and conversely. As you see clearly in Figure 16–1, yields were falling sharply as the Federal Reserve eased monetary conditions in response to a weakening economy.

Figure 16–1 shows the daily price of the contract as well as the 20-day moving average. (We chose 20 days because there are roughly 20 trading days in a month.) The main thing to notice is that sometimes the price trends nicely: The daily price stays consistently above, or below, the 20-day average. At other times the price action becomes more choppy: The daily price crosses above and below the moving average. Choppy periods are very tough for moving-average systems: The price moves above the moving average, you buy, then the price declines, you sell, and the price moves up again. You are whipsawed by the lack of a trend.

Figure 16–2 shows the cumulative profit that would have been earned by this very simple 1-day versus 20-day moving-average sys-

FIGURE 16–1

Price of the 90-Day Eurodollar Futures Contract
Daily Closing Price Versus 20-Day Moving Average
January 3, 2000 through December 31, 2001

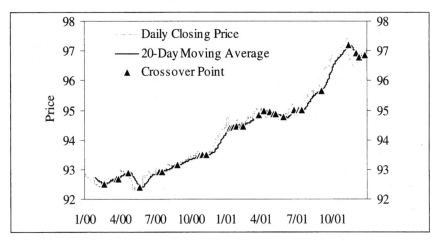

Source: Bloomberg LP.

FIGURE 16–2

Price of the 90-Day Eurodollar Futures Contract Trading
Systems: 1 Day Versus 20 Days
Cumulative Profit or Loss, January 3, 2000 through
December 31, 2001

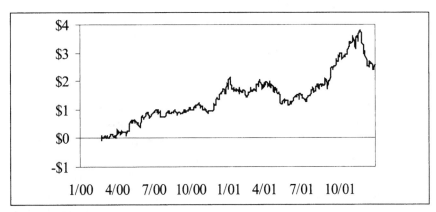

Source: Bloomberg LP.

tem. Sometimes you make money, sometimes you tread water, sometimes you lose money. The first half of 2001 is especially challenging, since buy and sell signals are tightly bunched, and whipsaw risk is high. The second half of the year features fewer signals, a more sustained trend, and greater profits.

We have been talking about a simple system that compares the daily price with the 20-day moving average. In the year 2000, the best results would have been achieved by comparing the 6-day moving average with the 21-day moving average. But that system would have lagged the 1-day versus 20-day system in 2001, and for the full 2-year period. The fundamental problem for the systematic trader is that a system that works well in one market, during one time period, may fail in other markets, and other time periods.

These very simple systems are reversal systems. The short-term average price is always either above or below the longer-term average price, so the system will always be either long or short. Other trend-following systems would allow for neutral positions. For example, maybe the system only flashes a buy signal if the short-term average exceeds the long-term average by more than a certain threshold amount. And the same threshold would be used on the short side. Using this approach, the system would have no position on if the difference between the prices did not exceed the threshold. Systems of this sort are sometimes called *breakout systems* because prices have to break out of a range in order to trigger a buy or sell signal.

Trend-following systems work beautifully when there are trends, but they get whipsawed when prices go into choppy, mean-reverting periods. We saw this clearly in the eurodollar example. Trend-following systems are momentum approaches, with broad similarities to dynamic trading strategies designed to replicate long options positions. Trend followers are thus usually more interested in winning big than in winning often.

There are also countertrend systems, which follow a more contrarian approach. Here the object is to identify periods when prices will trade within a narrow range, and then implement a strategy that buys on weakness and sells on strength. These approaches are short volatility strategies. Countertrend systems will do well when trend-following systems are doing badly, but both kinds of systems depend for their success on a certain kind of price behavior. Once the pattern of behavior changes, as it always does, the system will start to do badly.

Trend-oriented systems differ greatly with regard to their time horizon. Some systems are geared toward longer-term trends that might last as long as 9 to 12 months. Other systems are geared toward very short term trends, perhaps as short as a few days, or even a few hours. Still other systems are focused on medium-term trends that play out in a few weeks or months. Sometimes global asset allocators combine multiple time horizons into one program. For example, the manager trades the major currency and interest rate markets, and in each market he implements a short-term, a medium-term, and a long-term system. If all three systems flash a buy signal on the euro, then there will be three units of long exposure to the euro. If two systems flash a buy signal and the third flashes a sell, then there will only be one unit of net long exposure to the euro.

The universe of systematic traders is the universe that places the greatest emphasis on quantitative sophistication. Some of the trading strategies rely on mathematical techniques that will be understood only by specialists. Money managers in this category often pride themselves on the extreme complexity of their systems, so investor due diligence in this area can get very complicated. You have to hang onto a spirit of inquiring skepticism and not allow yourself to become intimidated by the appearance of extreme mathematical sophistication.

Although systematic managers like to emphasize that they have eliminated the harmful effects of emotion and judgment, in the real world there are two ways in which judgment can enter into the portfolio of even the most highly systematic traders.

First, many systematic traders reserve the right to reduce positions if, in their judgment, markets are behaving in a way that presents an unusually high level of risk. For example, during the stock market crash of October 1987, the Gulf War crisis of early 1991, and the Russian debt crisis of August 1998, many systematic managers decided not to follow all the signals dictated by their trading systems. Some managers put on the positions but in smaller size; some put on some of the positions but not all; some managers moved completely to the sidelines. The underlying thought here is that it is legitimate to use human judgment in *reducing* the risk of the portfolio, though it would not be appropriate to use human judgment in *adding* to the positions dictated by the trading system.

Second, many systematic traders use a very wide variety of systems in trading their various markets. They might have one system for trading the euro, another for trading U.S. interest rates, a third for trading oil. The various trading systems function, in effect, as a squadron of specialized portfolio managers. On any given day, some systems will be doing well, while others may be struggling. This creates room for a capital allocation function that might involve various elements of judgment. For example, the hedge fund manager might decide to allocate more capital to the medium-term oil system while taking some money away from the U.S. interest rate countertrend system. Or, if the gold market has suddenly become more volatile, the manager might decide to follow the basic signals of the gold-trading system but to reduce the position sizes. Thus the portfolio management function is broken into two components: There is a battalion of computer-driven "trading machines," but there is also a human being who controls the various machines, using discretion and judgment in allocating capital toward and away from the various machines.

CHAPTER 17

Relative-Value Investing

Relative-value managers are hedge fund managers who try hard to be hedged. The relative-value investor generally operates within one particular market and does not want to be net long or net short in the market in which she is operating. Her object is to focus on relative valuation within that market, taking long positions in what looks cheap and short positions in what looks expensive. The long and short positions are then balanced in such a way as to offset each other. In theory, returns will not be affected by whether the underlying market goes up or down. Returns will be determined entirely by the skill of the manager in making judgments of relative value within the market.

The simplest cases of relative value investing are "perfect hedges," where the long position and the short position are positions in identical instruments. If you have been long 100 shares of Microsoft and then you sell short 100 shares of Microsoft, you are now fully hedged. This is shorting against the box. If you have been short 100 shares of Microsoft and then you buy 100 shares of Microsoft, you are now fully hedged. This is boxing your short. If you buy gold in New York and simultaneously sell gold in London, you are fully hedged.

Even perfect hedges can get a little tricky. If the New York gold dealer fails to deliver the gold, and you still owe gold to the London dealer, then you have a problem. If your long Microsoft position is held at Merrill Lynch, and your short position is held at a small brokerage firm that goes bankrupt, then you also have a problem. Even when "investment risk" has been removed, there are various kinds of operational risk that can arise.

Hedge funds are usually not interested in being simultaneously long and short the same instrument. They are interested in being long and short in *related* instruments. So there is always some element of risk present, generally referred to as *basis risk*. Basis risk is the risk that the relationship may move in unexpected directions.

LONG/SHORT EQUITY

The simplest example of a relative-value strategy is what is often called *pairs trading*. For example, you think Cisco Systems is a fabulous company and that it is substantially underappreciated in the market. But you acknowledge that Cisco faces many risks, some related to markets and the economy in general, some more specifically related to the technology sector. So you are reluctant to take an outright long position in Cisco. However, you are very confident that Cisco is better positioned than Microsoft to weather whatever storms may develop. So you take a long position in Cisco, paired with a short position in Microsoft. You are no longer merely betting that Cisco will go up; rather, you are betting that Cisco will do better than Microsoft. Cisco may actually decline in price, but as long as Cisco declines less than Microsoft, the trade will be profitable. The following paragraphs describe three main categories of equity market-neutral hedge funds.

Single-Sector Fundamental Investors These are managers who specialize in a single sector of the stock market. The most common specialties are the utility sector and the financial services sector (banks, insurance companies, and related businesses). These managers spend a great deal of time on fundamental company analysis, and they gain a good understanding of the different trading patterns of the different stocks.

Multisector Fundamental Investors These are managers who follow the full range of market sectors and usually have quantitative techniques for "scoring" stocks based on a wide variety of factors. These scoring systems usually incorporate both growth factors and value factors. The *valuation factors* will include the stocks' price to earnings, price to book, price to earnings before interest, taxes, depreciation, and amortization (EBITDA), and so forth. The *growth factors* will be various indicators of business success: earnings growth, return on assets, profit margins, and so on. The ideal stock will score high on the success factors, while scoring cheap on the valuation factors. So every stock receives a combined numerical score, and the portfolio is constructed by buying the stocks that score high and selling short the stocks that score low. Because the manager is dealing with a very large universe of stocks, the manager typically does not know the individual stocks as well as the single-sector specialist.

Multisector Technical Traders These managers follow the full range of market sectors but are generally indifferent to the fundamental characteristics of companies. They have no interest in P/E ratios, earnings growth, or related fundamentals. All they care about is price movements and relative pricing. The manager is looking for situations in which prices have gotten out of line but are expected to go back in line within days, not weeks or months. So this strategy is a short volatility, countertrend, buy low–sell high strategy. The manager is betting that prices will revert to the mean. Most traders in this category are highly quantitative since they need to manipulate a vast amount of price information in order to discover trading opportunities.

Each of the three approaches has both advantages and disadvantages. The sector specialist is dealing with a single homogeneous group of stocks and thus has the opportunity to develop a detailed knowledge of the companies in which he is investing, both from the long side and the short side. So the manager can develop a good understanding of the company fundamentals and a good understanding of the trading behavior of the stocks. The main disadvantage of this approach is that it is very capacity constrained. Managers who operate in this area often find it difficult to manage more than a few hundred million dollars.

The multisector fundamental investors suffer from no such size constraints. They have the freedom to invest in large capitalization companies chosen from a wide spectrum of industry groups. The main disadvantage of this group is that it often has a definite *style bias*. Generally speaking, the long portfolio tends to look like a value-oriented portfolio, while the short portfolio looks like a growth-oriented portfolio. So the total portfolio is long value and short growth. While this posture may be market neutral, it is nevertheless a substantial bet. Sometimes the bet wins, sometimes it loses.

Figure 17–1 shows the historical relationship between large cap growth stocks and large cap value stocks, using the Russell 1000 value and growth indexes as proxies. The graph in this figure shows the difference in return: the return of the value index less the return of the growth index. The bar shows the monthly spread, and the line shows the spread on a trailing 12-month basis. Notice that 1998 and 1999 were particularly difficult for the long value–short growth bias, as tech stocks surged to outrageous levels of valuation and remained there longer than anyone expected. Some managers adjusted their systems to remove the value tilt and were then caught off guard when the relationship reversed with the bursting of the tech bubble.

The multisector technical traders are very capacity constrained, like their colleagues who specialize in single sectors. They are looking for small price discrepancies that will evaporate within a short period of time, so they need the ability to trade in and out of positions easily and almost invisibly. These traders buy on weakness

FIGURE 17–1

U.S. Equity, Value Less Growth
Monthly and Trailing Return Spread,
January 1995 through December 2001

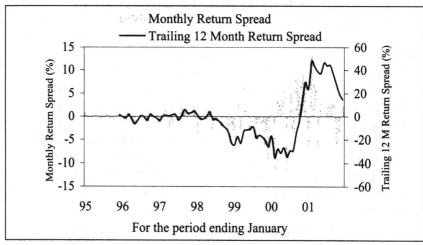

Based on monthly returns for the Russell 1000 Value Index and the Russell 1000 Growth Index.
Source: Frank Russell Company.

and sell on strength, betting against the short-term price trend. They are short volatility traders. These managers do well when there is a lot of noise and choppiness in price behavior, but they do less well when real trends emerge.

All market-neutral equity strategies depend ultimately on good stock selection. If the long portfolio outperforms the short portfolio, then the return differential is added to the risk-free rate, and the sum is the portfolio rate of return. But there is no "economic wind" at the back of the manager. There is no general principle of investing that says that if you buy a diversified portfolio of stocks and then sell short a stock portfolio of equal size, then you will make money over the long term. And even if one stock looks outrageously overvalued relative to another, there is no mechanism that will force the value of the two stocks to converge. There is no *forced* convergence, only *expected* convergence. And expectations can be wrong. Stocks that get out of line can stay out of line for a long time. Or it can turn out that the stocks only looked out of line because of a set of assumptions that are now obsolete. Market-neutral equity investing is pure active management: Whether or not you succeed over the long term will depend entirely on your ability to pick a portfolio of long positions that will outperform the portfolio of short positions.

This point holds even if we view the market-neutral investor as an important source of liquidity for the markets. The market-neutral equity investor tends to be a contrarian investor, buying on weakness and selling on strength, thus providing liquidity to the momentum investor who has the opposite trading pattern. So the market-neutral investor looks a little bit like a New York Stock Exchange specialist, making a market in a stock, and getting paid for her troubles. So it might appear that the market neutral investor is getting paid for providing a valuable economic resource: liquidity.

But this line of thought has to be taken with a grain of salt. Providing liquidity is a risky business. And the whole point about risk is that you don't always get paid for taking it. When momentum investors have the upper hand and prices go into periods of strong trends, the life of the contrarian investor becomes unpleasant and unprofitable. Buying low and selling high is not a risk-free strategy but a bet on trendless, mean-reverting, choppy markets. When prices don't behave that way, watch out.

BOND HEDGING

The market-neutral equity manager buys "attractive" stocks and sells short "unattractive" stocks, trying to take away the effect of broad market moves. The bond hedger buys attractive bonds and sells short unattractive bonds, also trying to remove the effect of broad market moves. The attractive bonds usually have a higher yield than the unattractive bonds, so there is a *yield spread* between the long portfolio and the short portfolio. If a high-quality corporate bond offers a yield of 6.0 percent while a Treasury of comparable maturity offers a yield of 5.8 percent, then the corporate bond offers a spread of 0.2 percent. If the bond hedger thinks that this is an attractive spread, then he will try to capture the spread by buying the corporate bond while shorting the Treasury.

We emphasized in Chapter 9 that hedging is not an infallible recipe for reducing risk. A hedged position is a bet that the long position will outperform the short position. In the world of bonds, if one bond performs better than another bond, then the yield spread between the two bonds *narrows*. To see this, suppose that a hedge fund manager has a long position in bond L and a short position in bond S. We assume that the yield on bond L is greater than the yield on bond S, so the hedged position captures a positive spread between the two bonds. If bond L performs better than bond S, then it may be that the price of L goes up while the price of S stays the same. But if the price of L goes up, then the yield of bond L will go down, and so the yield spread between the two bonds will narrow. Alternatively, it may be that L does better than S because the price of L remains constant while the price of S goes down. But if the price of S goes down, then the yield of bond S will go up, and so once again the yield spread between the two bonds will narrow.

Generally speaking, yield is an indicator of risk: If one bond has a higher yield than another, it is prudent to assume that the first bond has more risk than the second. Thus the basic position of the bond hedger is to own the higher-risk bond while taking a short position in the lower-risk bond. This means that bond hedging is far from riskless. In addition, yield spreads are often very small, typically less than 1 percent. So the bond hedger often applies large amounts of leverage in order to deliver the returns that he is after. Long Term Capital Management was a highly leveraged bond hedging operation whose spectacular failure is a vivid illustration of what can go wrong in bond hedging.

There are many different kinds of risk that can explain yield spreads. The four most common risks are inflation, credit, prepayment, and liquidity. Let's have a closer look at each of these risks.

U.S. Treasury obligations are a good example of *inflation risk* without *credit risk*. Credit risk is the risk of default: The borrower fails to repay the debt. In the case of a U.S. Treasury obligation, there is essentially no risk of default. After all, the government has the ability, in extreme circumstances, simply to print the number of dollars required to repay the debt. But this moves the spotlight to inflation risk. If you buy a $10,000 Treasury bond today that matures in 10 years, you can be certain that you will receive $10,000 in 10 years. But how much will $10,000 be worth in 10 years? What will you be able to buy for $10,000 in 10 years? The answer to this question depends on the level of inflation over the next 10 years. (Several years ago the U.S. Treasury began to issue special bonds whose interest payments and final maturity payment adjust to take into account the effect of inflation. These bonds solve the bond investor's main worry, inflation, but they have other complexities that have slowed their acceptance by the marketplace.)

When investors lend money for 10 years, their first worry is what the real value of a dollar will be in 10 years. When investors are worried about the possibility of rising inflation, they demand a high interest rate to compensate for the inflation risk. When investors are more optimistic about the outlook for inflation, they are willing to accept lower interest rates. The spread between long-term rates and short-term rates is thus a symptom of the level of anxiety surrounding the likely course of inflation. A wide spread means high inflation anxiety; a narrow spread means low anxiety. Figure 17–2 shows the history since 1990. Notice the very wide spreads that prevailed in the early 1990s and again in 2001. Both periods were periods of slow growth or recession in which the Federal Reserve was easing monetary policy aggressively.

Corporate bonds have inflation risk and credit risk. Credit risk is the risk of default, that is, the risk of not getting paid at all. Even very high quality companies sometimes default on their debt. And with lower-quality companies, the companies that issue high-yield debt, the risk of default is a major issue. When investors think that the risk

F I G U R E   17–2

Inflation Versus Yield Spreads
January 1990 through December 2001

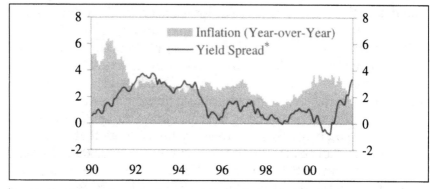

*The yield of the U.S. 10-year Treasury bond less the yield of the U.S. Treasury bill. Analysis based on monthly data, January 1990 through December 2001.

Source: Bloomberg LP.

of default is high, they will demand a very high yield on the money that they lend. When investors think that the risk of default is low, they will accept a lower yield. Figure 17–3 shows the history of yield spreads for both investment-grade bonds and high-yield bonds. Notice that yield spreads came in steadily from late 1990 until mid-1998 as investors grew more and more confident about the economy, then widened in the last few years as the economy weakened and investors perceived more risk in corporate bonds.

Prepayment risk is the risk that the loan will be repaid at a time when interest rates are lower, which creates the problem of reinvesting the funds in a lower-rate environment. Bonds backed by home mortgages provide the main example of prepayment risk. The main issuers are the Government National Mortgage Association (Ginnie Mae or GNMA), the Federal National Mortgage Association (Fannie Mae or FNMA), and the Federal Home Loan Mortgage Corporation (Freddie Mac or FHLMC). When a homeowner borrows money for 30 years to buy a house, she has the right to pay back the loan before the 30 years are up. This can be done without a prepayment penalty. If interest rates go down after the homeowner takes out a mortgage, the homeowner will be able to refinance the mortgage at the lower rates. The homeowner borrows money at the

FIGURE 17-3

Corporates and High Yield Less U.S. 10-Year Treasury Bonds
Monthly Yield Spreads, January 1990 through December 2001

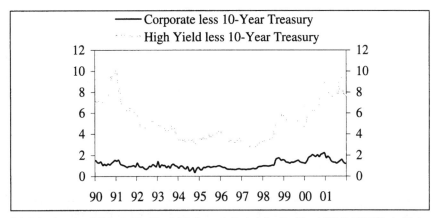

Calculations based on yields for the Merrill Lynch U.S. Corporate Master Index, Merrill Lynch U.S. High Yield Master II Index,
and 10-year U.S. Treasury bonds.
Source: Merrill Lynch and Bloomberg LP.

low rates that now prevail and uses that money to pay off the high-er-rate mortgage.

When a homeowner refinances a mortgage, the homeowner is buying back the original mortgage at face value. When interest rates go down, the value of the mortgage bond should go up, but this appreciation is limited by the fact that the homeowner holds a call option that enables her to buy back the mortgage at face value. The yield spread that separates mortgage-backed bonds from Treasury bonds is the price of the call option that the mortgage lender has granted the homeowner. Figure 17–4 shows the changing spread between mortgage-backed bonds and Treasury bonds.

The final risk is liquidity. *Liquid bonds* are bonds that are available in size, have a large daily trading volume, and command a great deal of investor attention. *Illiquid bonds* are smaller, they trade less, and they are not as close to the center of attention. Other things being equal, more liquid bonds will have higher prices, and lower yields, than less liquid bonds. For example, consider the difference between *on-the-run* Treasuries and *off-the-run* Treasuries. The U.S. Treasury issued a 30-year Treasury bond every quarter. The bond that was

FIGURE 17-4

Mortgage-Backed Bonds Less 10-Year Treasury Bonds
Monthly Yield Spread, January 1990 through December 2001

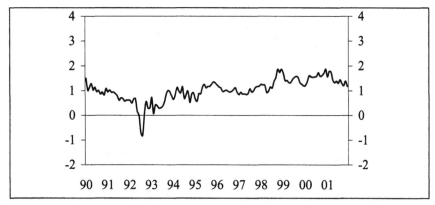

Calculations based on yields for the Merrill Lynch GNMA Master Index and 10-Year U.S. Treasury bond.
Source: Merrill Lynch and Bloomberg LP.

issued at the most recent auction is the *on-the-run 30-year Treasury*. The bonds that were issued at earlier auctions are the *off-the-run Treasuries*. The on-the-run Treasuries are consistently more liquid than the off-the-run Treasuries, and usually they trade at a slightly lower yield than the off-the-run Treasuries, even though the maturities are essentially the same.

So we have at least four different kinds of risk that can produce yield spreads attractive to bond hedgers: inflation risk, credit risk, prepayment risk, and liquidity risk. Now let's take a quick look at how to capture those spreads and what risks arise in the process.

Let's begin with the simplest case. Suppose that long-term interest rates are 6 percent, money can be invested short term at 3 percent, and money can be borrowed short term at 3.5 percent. If you buy long-term debt at a yield of 6 percent, and finance the purchase at a cost of 3.5 percent, then you are earning a positive spread of 2.5 percent. This is a *positive carry trade*: The yield on the long position is greater than the cost of financing the position. If you lever the trade 2:1, then the net yield (the yield on the full long position less the cost of financing) is 8.5 percent. If you lever the trade 5:1, then the yield goes up to 16 percent. Every unit of leverage adds 2.5 percent to the yield of the total position.

Does this mean that you should borrow a lot of money at 3.5 percent in order to buy bonds yielding 6 percent? Absolutely not. This trade has immense risk. If interest rates go up, then the cost of financing goes up, the price of the long position goes down, and you are in a position to lose real money. Consider the price and the yield of a 10-year bond. Prices go up as yields go down, and vice versa. Figure 17–5 shows the price and the yield of the 10-year bond that was issued in August 1999 and matures in August 2009. As the yield declined from 6.8 to 4.1 percent, the price increased from 94.50 to 112.88. In other words, a yield change of 2.7 percent translated into a 19 percent increase in the price of the bond.

But this works in the other direction too. In late 2001, the price dropped 7 points as the yield increased by 1 percent. In other words, an adverse price move is more than enough to wipe out the yield advantage of the longer-term bond. Moreover, the yield advantage will be earned over the course of a full year. For example, a 3.5 percent yield spread works out to about 0.3 percent per month. Price moves of that size are a dime a dozen. One bad day, or week, can destroy the yield advantage you were counting on for the entire year.

FIGURE 17–5

Daily Price and Yield of a 10-Year U.S. Treasury Bond
January 3, 2000 through December 31, 2001

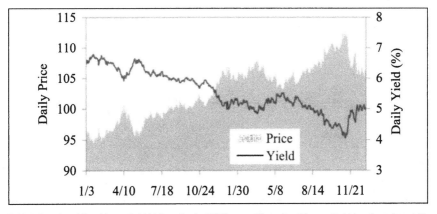

Analysis based on daily pricing and yield information for U.S. Treasury 10-year bond 6 percent yield, matures August 15, 2009.

Source: Bloomberg LP.

The trade we have just described is the classic *borrow short–lend long position*. This trade has wreaked havoc on banks, savings and loan (S&L) associations, and other lending institutions. An S&L borrows from its depositors and lends to homeowners. The S&L holds a portfolio of long-term mortgages, so the assets of the bank have a long maturity. But the bank deposits are a short-term liability. If interest rates go up, the S&L faces rising financing costs and falling asset values. Thanks to the S&L crisis of the late 1980s, lending institutions are generally much more careful in matching the maturity of their assets and their liabilities.

Because of these risks, the bond hedger is not likely to set up the simple borrow short–lend long trade. She may introduce various hedges to protect against falling asset values or rising financing costs. But all these protective measures will have a cost. The question at the end of the day is whether there is any return left after the relevant risks have been hedged away.

Figure 17–6 shows the background for hedging credit risk. The yield spread is the difference between high-quality corporate bond yields and government bond yields. The return spread is the monthly return of corporate bonds less the return of government bonds. If

F I G U R E 17–6

Corporate Bonds Less 10-Year Treasury Bonds
Monthly Yield and Price Spreads, January 1990 through December 2001

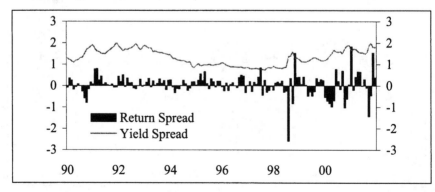

Calculations based on yields and monthly total rates of returns for the Merrill Lynch U.S. Corporate Master Index and Merrill Lynch U.S. Treasury Master Index.
Source: Merrill Lynch.

you're long corporates and short governments, you are betting that corporates will outperform governments, so you want the return spread to be positive. As the yield spread narrowed from early 1993 through late 1997, corporates generally outperformed governments. As the yield spread began to widen in early 1998, you begin to see months when corporates lag Treasuries by 1 percent or more. Yet the object of the hedge was to capture an annual yield spread of about 2 percent, which works out to about 0.15 percent per month. Again, one bad month of price action can destroy the yield advantage that was available over the course of a full year.

Figure 17–7 makes the same point with high-yield bonds against government bonds. As the yield spread widened from 4 to 8 percent, there are several months during which the long-high-yield/short-government "hedge" will lose 4 percent or more. One bad month wipes out the yield advantage that you were counting on for the whole year.

The bond hedger's basic strategy is to identify a wide spread, put on a hedge designed to capture that spread, and then apply a large amount of leverage to make the total return interesting. But this is simply the classic strategy of reaching for yield, with leverage added in to boost return, and risk. And that is a short volatility trade.

FIGURE 17–7

High-Yield Bonds Less 10-Year Treasury Bonds
Monthly Yield and Price Spreads, January 1990 through December 2001

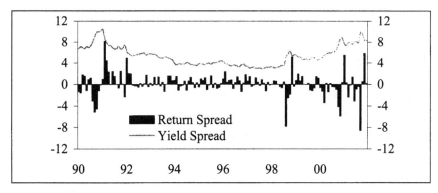

Calculations based on yields and monthly total rates of returns for the Merrill Lynch U.S. High Yield Master II Index and Merrill Lynch U.S. Treasury Master Index.

Source: Merrill Lynch.

The potential gain in the hedged position is finite, since the normal expectation is that the spread will return to its average level. In the extreme case, the spread might go to zero, or even turn slightly negative (in which case bond investors will say that the high-risk instrument is *trading through* the lower-risk instrument), but these scenarios are very unlikely. So the bond hedger seeks the high probability of earning a finite incremental yield, and must deal with the small probability of a large loss. The loss is large because liberal amounts of leverage are required to deliver the very small yield spread in a dosage that investors are likely to be interested in. Some of the most conspicuous blowups in the hedge fund world have been in the area of bond hedging since the required level of leverage may turn out to be fatal.

These cautionary notes are not meant to scare you away from bond hedging altogether. There are managers who are very sensitive to the risks involved and have displayed an ability to manage those risks intelligently. But this is an area that requires unusual levels of caution. When you're picking up nickels in front of a bulldozer, never take your eyes off the bulldozer.

CONVERTIBLE HEDGING

The market-neutral equity manager works entirely within the universe of stocks; the bond hedger works entirely within the universe of bonds. The convertible hedger has a foot in two worlds: the world of convertible securities and the world of common stock. Convertible securities are either convertible bonds or convertible preferred stock. Bonds, preferred stock, and common stock represent three different parts of the capital structure of a company. The three parts have different levels of seniority when it comes to paying out interest and dividends. Bonds are most senior, then preferred stock, and then common stock. Bond interest has to be paid before any dividends are paid to the preferred holders, and the preferred holders have to be paid before the holders of common stock get any dividends.

Convertible hedging is a form of *capital structure arbitrage*. Normally the hedger looks for situations in which the convert is *trading cheap* relative to the common. In these situations, the hedger buys the convert and sells short, in a disciplined way, the underlying common stock. (If the convert looks expensive relative to the common, the convertible hedger will short the convert and buy the common stock.) Shorting the common stock hedges some of the major risks of owning the convert and still leaves the potential for earning an attractive total return.

The total return has both an income component and a trading profit component. The income component is sometimes called the *standstill return*: It is the return that flows entirely from the underlying cash flows, before considering any price changes. The income component comprises the income from the converts that you own, plus the interest on the proceeds of the short sales. This income component will usually be well above the risk-free interest rate. Then you have to subtract any dividends that you will owe on the common stock that you are short, and you must also subtract any interest charges related to leveraging the long positions. The dividend expense will usually be a low number since companies that issue converts typically have a very low yield. So the total income will still be above the risk-free rate, and above the margin loan rate. Most convertible hedgers use leverage in their portfolios, sometimes as high as 6:1 or 7:1. (Convertible hedging funds will register as broker-dealers in order to employ these levels of leverage.) The final element of total return is the trading profits that might be generated as the bond price fluctuates and the short stock hedge is adjusted.

To understand convertible hedging, it is necessary to understand what convertible securities are. Convertible bonds are senior to convertible preferred stock, and they have a definite maturity date. Convertible preferred stock lasts into perpetuity. Many convertible bonds are issued by companies that have a simple capital structure, with no debt senior to the convertible bonds. To simplify the discussion in this chapter, we shall focus mainly on convertible bonds, ignoring convertible preferred stock.

The conversion feature works as follows: Each bond may be converted into, or exchanged for, a defined number of shares of common stock. For example, a bond with a face value of $1000 might be convertible into 40 shares of common stock. If the stock is trading above $25, then the bond can be converted into equity that is worth more than the face value of the bond. If the stock is trading at or below $25, then the face value of the bond exceeds the value of the underlying equity. So the convertible bond is like a conventional bond—a *straight bond*—with a call option attached. In this example, the call option has a strike price of $25.

Who issues convertible bonds, and who buys them? In the United States, the convertible market was dominated for a long time by companies of low credit quality that were unable to borrow using straight debt alone. In Europe and Japan, the traditional issuers of converts were higher-quality companies. The United States has recently seen an increasing amount of convert issuance on the part of higher-quality companies. A convertible bond is a straight bond with an *equity kicker*. So the interest rate on the debt is less than what it would be on nonconvertible debt. If the issuing company is a company with decent growth prospects and a volatile stock, then investors will be willing to *pay up* for the equity kicker, in which case the interest rate on the bond can get very low indeed.

If the company prospers, and the common stock appreciates above the strike price of the embedded option, then the lender earns extra return, and the borrower winds up paying off the debt using equity, not cash. If the stock falters, then the convert holder will receive his interest and the principal amount of the debt but no extra appreciation. And the issuing company will have to use company cash to pay off the debt. If the company experiences financial distress of some sort, then the convert holder may fail to get all the income to which he is entitled. If the company goes into Chapter 11 financial reorganization, then the convertible holders will be senior to the common equity but junior to any "straight debt" that might be outstanding.

The traditional buyer of convertible debt was a middle-of-the-road investor seeking a steady income stream with some potential for capital appreciation. Convertible securities were a common ingredient in balanced accounts, whose investment objective was to deliver some combination of growth and income. These accounts were *outright buyers*: They owned the convert, with no hedge in place. During the last several years the convertible hedgers have become the dominant players in the convertible market. Knowledgeable observers estimate that at least 50 percent of the convertible market is in the hands of hedgers. Although the convertible hedger is also looking for a combination of yield and capital appreciation, he does not want the appreciation to come from a rise in the value of the underlying common stock. Remember, the hedge fund manager is always looking for nondirectional risk. In this case, the hedger wants the appreciation to come from trading profits as he manages and adjusts his hedges. In the final analysis, the convertible hedger is more interested in the pure volatility of the common stock than in its potential for appreciation.

As convertible hedgers have become a more important factor in the convertible market, they have also become more important as a source of direct financing for the issuing companies. That is to say, the convertible hedger does not merely buy his converts from other investors: Rather, he often buys them directly from the issuing company. In this case, the money goes directly to the company, rather than going into the pocket of another investor. Thus the convertible hedger becomes a bank, lending money directly to the company. The convertible hedger is willing to do this because he enjoys terms that he regards as more favorable than those associated with straight debt. And the convertible hedger can hedge the risk of a decline in the stock. This sometimes leads to problems since the convertible hedger takes a short position in the common stock of the company that issued the convert.

(*Warning:* You are about to find out how convertible hedging really works. Parts will seem complicated, but the basic ideas are pretty simple. Relax, this will be over soon.)

Convertible hedging is essentially a form of delta hedging, which we discussed in Chapter 11. A convertible bond is a standard corporate bond plus a call option on the underlying common equity. The embedded option may be in the money, in which case the delta of the option will be close to 1, and the convertible bond will be very responsive to changes in the price of the stock. Or the embedded option may be pretty far out of the money, in which case the delta will be closer to zero, and the convert will be less responsive to changes in the price of the common stock. When the call is in the money, the convert is very stocklike; when the option is out of the money, the convert is very bondlike. In the extreme case, when the option is very far out of the money, the bond gets closer and closer to its pure *investment value*: The value it would have as a straight bond, without the conversion feature.

The convertible hedger has two tasks: He has to set up the hedge and then manage it as stock prices and bond prices bounce around. To set up the hedge, the convertible hedger has to estimate the delta of the call option embedded in the convertible bond. If the manager estimates that the embedded option has a delta of 0.5, and if the bond is convertible into 40 shares of stock, then he will sell short 20 shares of stock.

If the stock rises, then the delta of the option will increase, and the convertible bond will become more stocklike: The bond will become even more sensitive to further changes in the value of the stock. To maintain the hedged position, the hedger needs to increase his short position. Conversely, if the stock goes down, the embedded call has a lower delta, so the convertible bond becomes more bond-like: It is less responsive to further changes in the price of the stock. So the hedger wants to be short less stock, which means that he needs to cover some of his short position. Thus the trading pattern on the short stock side of the portfolio is the classic contrarian strategy: Buy on weakness, sell on strength.

In setting up the hedge and managing the hedge, the convertible hedger must constantly estimate, and reestimate, the sensitivity of the bond to changes in the price of the stock. It is important to emphasize that this is not a scientific process. Two hedgers who both want to be totally hedged (as much as possible) may disagree about what the appropriate hedge ratio is. Moreover, sometimes hedgers will give a slight *tilt* to their positions, being slightly bullish in some trades, slightly bearish in others.

If you look only at the short stock portion of the convertible hedger's portfolio, you will see the contrarian trading strategy. So you might think that convertible hedging is a short volatility strategy. But remember, on the long side of the portfolio there are real bonds with real options embedded inside them. So the bond side of the portfolio is definitely long volatility. That fact dominates the strategy.

To understand how the convertible hedger makes money, it is helpful to distinguish three different market situations. The worst market for the convertible hedger is a very quiet market. Imagine that the price of the underlying common stock does not change at all for six months. Then there will be no trading opportunities on the short stock side, and the call option embedded within the bond will gradually lose value. The drop in the bond's price will erode the standstill return, and it may even bring the total return into negative territory.

Now suppose that the price of the common stock begins to move a lot but moves within a range. The stock rises enough to trigger a change in the recommended delta, so the convertible hedger sells more common stock to bring the delta up to the required level. Then the stock falls back, so there will be incremental profit from the newly enlarged short position. If the stock falls back enough, then the hedger will cover some of his short position. If the stock then rebounds, there will be incremental profit from the appreciation of the reduced short position. So the short stock portfolio can earn trading profits in a "range-bound" market. Meanwhile, the value of the embedded call option will be declining. The trading profits on the short stock side may be enough to offset the decline in the value of the embedded call option, or they may not.

Finally, suppose that a major uptrend develops in the price of the stock, or that the stock gaps up due to some piece of good news. The convertible bond should be moving up in price, and the delta of the embedded option will be getting closer to 1. So the hedger will be shorting more stock as the stock price moves up. But the delta of the embedded option will be changing more quickly than the size of the short stock position, so the profits on the long convert position should exceed the losses on the short stock position.

If a major downtrend develops, or the stock gaps down on some piece of bad news, then the convertible bond will be moving down in price, and the delta of the embedded option will be moving closer to zero. So the hedger will be buying stock as the stock goes down. But the delta of the embedded option will be changing more quickly than the size of the short stock position, so the profits on the short stock position should exceed the losses on the long bond position.

Convertible hedging does rely on some element of *forced convergence*, not merely the *expected convergence* that drives market-neutral equity investing. No matter how cheap Ford gets relative to General Motors, there is no riskless arbitrage that can take advantage of the cheapness. In theory, Ford could go bankrupt while General Motors goes on to new triumphs. But if a convertible gets too cheap, there will be a riskless arbitrage. If a convertible bond priced at $1000 is convertible into 40 shares of common, each of which trades at $27, then the $1000 bond is immediately convertible into $1080 of common stock.

Despite these convergence relationships, convertible hedging is not a riskless machine for making money out of fluctuating stock prices. There are three principal risks that the convertible hedger faces, and they are related to the three risk exposures involved in a convertible bond. First, a convertible bond, like every other bond, is vulnerable to the risk of rising interest rates. Second, a convertible bond, like other corporate bonds, is exposed to the credit risk of the underlying company. Third, a convertible bond contains a call option, so there is risk related to the pricing of that option. The short stock hedge addresses the third risk more directly than the first two risks.

Interest Rate Risk If interest rates go up, then bond prices will go down. This will include prices of corporate debt, even convertible corporate debt. The short stock position may help in this situation because rising interest rates often put downward pressure on stock prices. But "often" is not the same as "always." The year 1994 provides a good example. Interest rates went up, bond prices went down, and convertible bonds declined as part of this broad phenomenon. But stock prices held up reasonably well, due to optimism about earnings growth. In effect, the positive impact of expected earnings growth was great enough to cancel out the negative impact of rising interest rates. So the convertible hedger had losses on his long bond positions, but the short stock positions did not produce enough profit to offset these losses. This came close to the hedger's worst-case scenario: The longs went down, and the shorts went up, or at least didn't go down enough.

Some convertible hedgers are fastidious about hedging the general interest rate risk of their portfolios. They might take short positions in U.S. Treasury bonds, or futures contracts on those bonds. But hedging has a cost, so the expected return from the hedged portfolio will generally be lower than that of the unhedged portfolio. In addition, it is always useful to bear in mind the negative scenarios, in which the long side of the hedge does worse than the short side. Suppose, for example, that interest rates decline on anxieties about recession. Meanwhile, corporate bonds fall on anxieties about worsening corporate credits, and option volatility falls as investors become less interested in the underlying common stocks. In this scenario, the converts would fall, but U.S. Treasuries would be rallying. This is what happened in the third quarter of 1998.

Credit Risk Corporate bonds are vulnerable to adverse developments in the fundamentals of the underlying company. Even if U.S. Treasury yields remain stable, the bonds of XYZ Corp. may decline for reasons entirely specific to XYZ. What happens is that the XYZ bonds are downgraded to a lower level of credit quality, so a bond that traded last week at 95 trades this week at 85. This may happen with or without an official change in rating from one of the credit rating agencies. Although it's likely that the stock price will decline when the bond is downgraded, the profits from the short stock position may not fully hedge the loss from the bond downgrade.

Some convertible hedgers address credit risk by using various credit hedging techniques, chief among which is the *credit swap*. The investor who owns the corporate bond gives up the incremental yield that flows from the credit risk and transfers that yield to another investor. Imagine two investors, John and Mary. John owns a corporate bond portfolio but doesn't want the credit risk. Mary owns a U.S. Treasury portfolio but wants incremental yield. So John and Mary engage in a swap transaction: John transfers the "incremental yield" of his portfolio to Mary, and Mary assumes the credit risk. So the incremental yield moves from John to Mary, without any bonds literally changing hands. The case is analogous to the case of the corn farmer selling corn futures to the cereal manufacturer, without any physical corn moving at all. Using credit swaps reduces the credit risk of the long convert portfolio but also reduces the yield of the portfolio, thus reducing the expected total return.

Volatility Risk The short stock position hedges the long call position that is embedded inside the convertible bond. Ideally, the convertible hedger will buy the bond when the *implied volatility* of the embedded option is cheap. That is, the hedger will buy when the market expects low volatility in the future. This is most likely when the actual volatility of the underlying common has been fairly low. When prices are quiet, investors have a natural tendency to assume that the quietness will continue, so options trade with low implied volatilities. If volatility then spikes upward, the convertible hedger has opportunities for incremental profit.

The worst market for the convertible hedger is the quiet market: The embedded call will lose value, and there will be no offsetting trading profits from the short stock positions. The convertible hedger needs price movement. If the stock goes into a wide trading range, then the countertrend behavior of the short stock hedge may produce enough trading profits to offset the eroding value of the embedded call. If there are big upward moves in the price of the stock, then the profits on the convert side should exceed the losses on the short stock hedge. And if there are big down moves in the price of the stock, then the profits on the short stock hedge should exceed the losses on the convert side.

The convertible hedging market has become especially inter-esting during the past several years. As we noted earlier, hedgers have replaced outright buyers as the dominant investors. This is a potential problem since markets tend to be most stable and most liq-uid when the participants have a variety of different motivations and risk-return profiles. But this risk is mitigated by the fact that convertible hedgers provide a pool of liquidity for the underlying stock. Since their trading pattern is to buy low and sell high, they offer a negative feedback mechanism for the underlying common stock, which is less destabilizing than having a market dominated by momentum-driven investors.

We also noted that convertible hedgers have become bankers to companies. The hedger buys a convertible bond from a company, which is a form of lending. The hedger then sells short the common stock of the company in order to hedge some of the risk of the bond position. So the company is borrowing money from a lender who is going to short the company stock. This leads to interesting public relations situations, in which companies complain that hedge funds are taking short positions in their common stock, and thus they have an incentive to see the price of the stock go down. But these com-plaints are disingenuous. When a company issues convertible debt, it should be aware that the debt will wind up in the hands of investors who will be short the common; hence, the transaction needs to be structured in such a way that the hedgers do not have too much incentive to see the stock decline. If the transaction is poorly struc-tured, the company is effectively giving away equity, or at least sell-ing it too cheap. And shareholders would have a right to complain.

Convertible hedging is a good example of a hedge fund strat-egy that is *not* entirely dependent on manager skill. Convertible hedging is a reasonably well defined strategy with reasonably well defined risks and reasonably well defined sources of return. Some of the returns come from providing liquidity to companies and to a niche market. Some of the returns come from credit and volatility exposures. The skilled convertible hedger will manage these risks intelligently, and the result will be a decent rate of return. But the returns are not generated from skill alone.

CHAPTER 18

Event-Driven Investing

Event-driven investments are investments in "special situations": investment opportunities that have a beginning, a middle, and an end. The world of special situations divides into two main strategies: risk arbitrage equity investing and distressed debt investing.

Risk arbitrage is an equity strategy totally different from any other equity strategy. Most equity investors are willing to reduce the frequency of winning in order to increase the amplitude of the wins. But the risk arbitrageur wants to increase the frequency of winning and is willing to reduce the amplitude of the win. The risk arbitrageur buys a stock today at $67 in the expectation that it will be worth $70 in six months. But the odds of getting anything beyond $70 are remote. And there is some risk that the stock will fall to $50. So the arbitrageur is risking $17 to earn $3. Risk arbitrage is a short volatility strategy that unfolds according to the schedule of an expected merger, acquisition, or other corporate transaction.

Distressed debt investing is a bond strategy totally different from any other bond strategy. Most bond investors seek a high frequency of winning so they accept a low amplitude. But the distressed debt investor wants to increase the amplitude of the wins and is thus willing to accept a lower frequency. The distressed debt investor buys bonds at steep discounts, sometimes as low as 25 cents on the dollar: He pays 25 cents for a bond that has a face value of $1. If he gets the dollar, he quadruples his money. Even if he gets only 50 cents, that's a double. Not bad for a bond. And, as in risk arbitrage, there is a definite time horizon imposed by the schedule of the financial reorganization process.

RISK ARBITRAGE

On January 16, 2001, Nestlé, Inc. announced its intention to buy Ralston Purina, Inc., at $33.50 per share. Ralston Purina had been trading between $24 and $26 immediately prior to the announcement, and it surged to close at $31.50 on the day of the announcement. Ralston experienced some weakness in May and June, but it then moved steadily upward toward the deal price of $33.50. Even the terrorist attacks of September 2001 had relatively little impact on the price of the stock. The deal closed on December 13, 2001, approximately 11 months after announcement. If you bought Ralston at $31.50 on January 16, then you made $2 on $31.50, which is a return of 6.3 percent. Earning 6.3 percent in 11 months is an annualized return of 6.9 percent. If you were able to buy stock at $30 on the day of the announcement, then your annualized return would be 12.7 percent. Leverage would increase that return, while also increasing the risk.

Figure 18–1 shows the price of Ralston Purina during the period in question, and Figure 18–2 shows the deal spread over this period. The *deal spread* is simply the percentage difference between the

FIGURE 18–1

Nestlé SA Bids for Ralston Purina Co.
Daily Price, January 2, 2001 through December 13, 2001

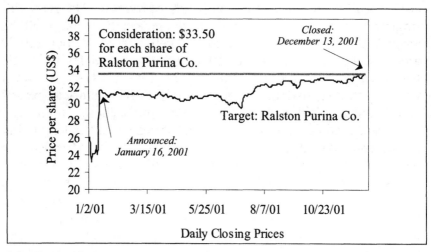

Source: Bloomberg LP.

FIGURE 18–2

Nestlé SA Bids for Ralston Purina Co.
Gross Deal Spread, January 16, 2001 through
December 13, 2001

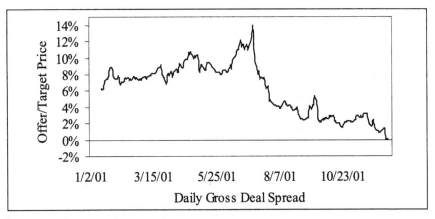

Source: Bloomberg LP.

Ralston price and the ultimate value of $33.50. For example, if the
stock is at $30 when the deal price is $33.50, then the spread is $3.50
divided by $30, or 11.7 percent. That spread is unannualized. The
spread begins at about 7 percent, gradually moves up toward 13
percent, and then steadily moves down toward zero as the closing
date approaches. Figure 18–3 shows the deal spread on an annualized basis, assuming that there are 250 trading days in a year. If the
gross spread is 1 percent with 25 days to go, then the annualized
spread is 10 percent. Notice that the annualized spread figures
become very volatile as the closing date approaches since we are
multiplying the gross spread by a very large number.

All these numbers have to be taken with a few grains of salt.
First, the figures are based on closing prices of Ralston Purina. But it
would not always be possible to buy large amounts of the stock at that
price, especially as the deal moved closer to completion. Second, the
annualized spread is calculated by using the number of days left until
the closing of the deal. In the real world, there will be some uncertainty
about the closing date, especially in the early stages of the transaction.

The Ralston Purina deal was a straightforward transaction in
which the deal moved ahead more or less according to schedule.

FIGURE 18-3

Nestlé SA Bids for Ralston Purina Co.
Annualized Deal Spread, January 16, 2001 through December 13, 2001

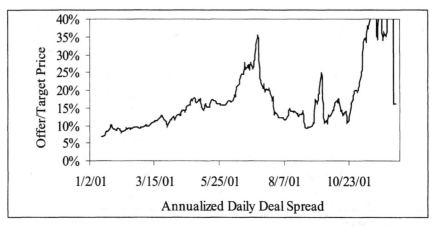

Annualized Daily Deal Spread

Source: Bloomberg LP.

But sometimes there are negative surprises, and sometimes there are positive surprises.

Positive surprises can emerge if two companies get involved in a bidding war for the third company, or if the original acquirer simply winds up increasing its offer. For example, consider Unilever's acquisition of Bestfoods. Unilever offered $66 per share for Bestfoods on May 2, 2000, causing the price of Bestfoods to jump from roughly $50 to a closing price, on the day of the announcement, of $61.25. The $61 price level represented a substantial discount to the $66 offer price. If you earn $5 on a $61 investment, then you have an 8.2 percent return. This is an attractive number, reflecting some perception of risk in the transaction. But then the Bestfoods holders got lucky: Unilever increased its offer from $66 to $73. If you bought Bestfoods at $61 and earned $12 on your investment, then your return is now 20 percent. Figure 18–4 shows the price history of Bestfoods over the period.

Negative surprises can emerge for many different reasons. As the two companies get into detailed negotiations, disagreements may emerge about who is going to run the combined companies. Or bad news may emerge about the target company, or perhaps there

FIGURE 18–4

Unilever NV Bids for Bestfoods
Daily Price, April 3, 2000 through
October 5, 2000

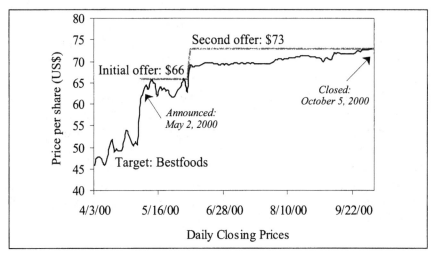

Source: Bloomberg LP.

are general market developments that give the acquirer second thoughts about the transaction. Or regulators may decide that the combined companies would stifle competition. In any case, there are three negative scenarios. First, the deal can get canceled altogether. Second, the deal may happen, but it is substantially delayed. Thus the annualized return goes down. Third, the deal may happen, but at a reduced price. These three risks—cancellation, delay, revaluation—are the main risks that the arbitrageur has to assess in deciding whether to take a position after the announcement of the transaction. And she has to reassess those risks every day thereafter.

As an example of negative surprise, consider General Electric's October 2000 bid for Honeywell International. GE offered 1.055 shares of GE for each share of Honeywell. When the bid was announced, Honeywell shot up from $35 per share to $52. But antitrust issues soon became very prominent. U.S. regulators approved the transaction in May 2001, but the European regulators dragged their feet. In February 2002 the Europeans indicated that they would be extending their review. In May 2001 there were further negative signals from the Europeans, and in July they blocked the transaction altogether. By the time the whole process was over, Honeywell had returned to its original price in the $35 to $40 range. Figure 18–5 shows the price of Honeywell compared to the price of 1.055 shares of General Electric.

Risk arbitrage is often described as a kind of *time arbitrage*: You buy something today at one price, in the expectation that at some defined time in the future, you will be able to sell at a defined higher price. This is a fine description, but the word *arbitrage* may suggest that the investor has somehow "locked in" a profit. This would be misleading. Risk arbitrage is not like buying gold today and then selling for delivery in six months. In risk arbitrage, the risk element is more important than the arbitrage element. Not surprisingly, the risk element is much more closely connected with uncertainty than with volatility. The challenge for the risk arbitrageur is to form an accurate picture of the various scenarios that may play out over the full holding period, which is quite different from estimating volatility within the holding period.

FIGURE   18–5

General Electric Co. Bids for Honeywell International, Inc.
Daily Price, September 1, 2000 through
October 31, 2001

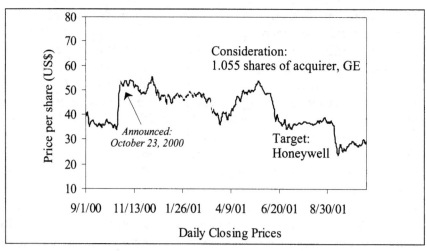

Source: Bloomberg LP.

THE M&A BUSINESS

The risk arbitrageur invests in situations created by the merger and acquisition business—that is, the M&A business. The arbitrageur feeds off the *deal flow* created by the fact that companies are often not content to grow "organically," by increasing their revenues, reducing their expenses, and so on. Rather, they grow by combining with other companies in transactions that are sometimes internally generated and sometimes generated by Wall Street investment bankers who are able to earn handsome fees by originating and structuring large transactions.

The motivations that drive the M&A business are many and varied. Sometimes the object is to increase revenues, which can be done in a wholesale fashion by acquiring entirely new product lines. Sometimes the object is to reduce expenses, by eliminating duplication. Sometimes the object is to reduce the number of competitors, which means that M&A transactions almost always attract the attention of antitrust regulators. In the early days of the business, the U.S. antitrust regulators were the only regulators that investors worried about. More recently, however, as economies and markets have become more global, the number of "cross-border transactions" has increased dramatically, and antitrust authorities in Europe and the United Kingdom have become a force to be reckoned with.

M&A transactions are often defended by appealing to important "synergies" between the two companies that will create dramatic opportunities for profit growth, either by increasing sales, reducing costs, or both. In many cases, these synergies are not realized, and the transaction that is greeted with enthusiasm today may turn out to be a major disappointment in three years. But even if the transaction eventually disappoints, this will be totally irrelevant to the risk arbitrageur, who will have moved on to other transactions long before the first one begins to lose its luster.

One major difference between the deal flow of the 1980s and the deal flow of the 1990s is that the 1980s were dominated by financial transactions, which were often hostile, while the 1990s were dominated by strategic transactions, which were generally friendly. The *financial transactions* were usually transactions in which a newly created company, sometimes literally referred to in documents as "Newco," would acquire a "real company" with enormous amounts of borrowed money, often provided by the Drexel Burnham Lambert junk bond group. The leveraged buyout of RJR Nabisco, in 1989, was the most dramatic example of such a transaction. Kohlberg Kravis Roberts and Co. acquired RJR in early 1989 for a purchase price of roughly $25 billion of which $20 billion was debt (either bank debt or Drexel-originated junk bonds). That transaction marked the peak of an era.

Strategic transactions are transactions in which one company acquires or merges with another company for legitimate business reasons. Although such transactions might involve some amount of debt, the levels of debt in the 1990s were nowhere near the levels seen in the 1980s. Often these transactions are part of a "wave" of consolidations that will grip various industries. In the 1990s, such waves were particularly dramatic in the financial services and telecommunications businesses. In the former case, banks, brokers, and insurance companies combined as the U.S. government loosened restrictions that had barred such combinations. In the telecommunications sector, U.S. and foreign companies combined to marshal strength in long-distance calling, local calling, and cellular communications. In the process, the breakup of AT&T almost turned into the putting back together of AT&T. Many of the mergers and acquisitions in the telecommunications sector came to grief after the bursting of the tech bubble. The travails of WorldCom are a conspicuous example of this phenomenon.

The risk arbitrage business is based on two important facts about the M&A process. First, when one company decides to buy another, the acquirer is often willing to pay a substantial premium over the price that the target was trading at prior to the announcement of the transaction. As shown in Figure 18–6, this premium often amounts to as much as 40 percent or more. Note the conspicuous rise in premium levels in the period from 1998 to 2001.

Second, when the deal is announced, the price of the target will typically rise toward the transaction price, but usually it will not hit that price since there is some risk that the transaction will not happen. As shown in Figure 18–7, the failure rate for much of the 1990s has been about 3 percent.

The first mystery of risk arbitrage is where the deal premium comes from. The acquirer may think that the target company is cheap or that the target will be worth more in combination with the acquirer than it is alone. But there is another force at work that is potentially

FIGURE 18–6

M&A Activity, Average Premium Offered*
Annual Results, 1991 through 2001

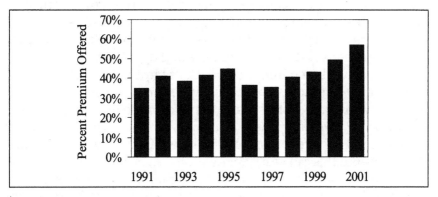

*Premium calculations are based on the seller's closing market price five business days before the initial announcement. These calculations exclude negative premium.

Source: *Mergerstat®*.

FIGURE 18–7

M&A Activity, Cancellations As a Percentage of
Gross Announcements
Annual Results, 1986 through 2001

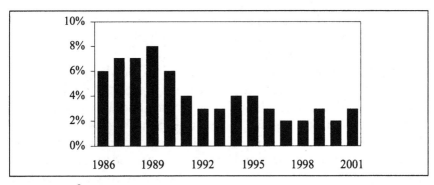

Source: *Mergerstat®*.

more important, which is the element of *control*. Most shareholders do not control the companies in which they invest. What they own is a minority, noncontrolling interest, which gives them a vote but not control. Even if the ownership interest is large enough to justify one or two seats on the board of directors, this position is not enough to grant control. Control is the ability to direct the future of the company, channeling resources in directions that are potentially more profitable than the directions that are currently being pursued. And control is worth paying for. The 40 percent premium is sometimes referred to as the *control premium* since it reflects the difference between the value of a passive minority interest and the value of a controlling interest.

The control premium has important implications for value-oriented equity investors. Many value investors will tell you that they try to buy companies at a substantial discount to their "private market value." *Private market value* is defined, roughly, as the amount that an informed private investor might be willing to pay for the entire company. But this can be a trap. As we have just seen, companies are routinely willing to pay a 40 percent premium in order to exert control, which means that companies routinely trade at a 29 percent discount ($40 on $140 is 29 percent) to their private market value. But the presence of this discount is not enough to make the company "cheap." To find real value, you have to look for much bigger discounts.

The risk arbitrageur is not able to capture the full amount of the control premium. That spread is available only to those who owned the stock prior to the announcement. The risk arbitrageur is content to try to capture the spread between the "postannouncement price" and the bid price.

Of course, if the risk arbitrageur has inside information to the effect that a $70 bid is forthcoming, she might buy company B at a price close to $50. But that is not risk arbitrage. That is insider trading, or, if the trade is based mainly on Wall Street whispering, *rumortrage*. Neither of these activities is risk arbitrage, and the first activity is illegal. During the late 1980s, when there was an enormous volume of deal flow related to the junk bond business of Michael Milken and Drexel Burnham Lambert, insider trading was a real issue, and a number of major insider-trading scandals unfolded. Once these excesses were dealt with, the M&A flow resumed with relatively little in the way of insider-trading problems.

Risk arbitrage is a perfect example of a *short volatility* strategy: The risk arbitrageur is attracted to the high probability of earning a small spread and thus has to manage the small probability of a larger loss. In our simplified example, perhaps there is a 90 percent probability that the investor will receive $70 in six months. And perhaps there is a 2 percent probability of getting lucky, in the form of a $72 final price. But there is also an 8 percent chance of the deal's falling apart, and in that case, the stock might fall back to $50. If we multiply the prices by the probabilities and then add up the results, we arrive at an expected value of $68.44. And then the arbitrageur has to figure out what she is willing to pay today for $68.44 in six months. The basic challenge for the arbitrageur is that the potential gain exceeds the potential loss. In round numbers, the risk arbitrageur is risking $20 to make $3.

Most equity investors do not like this return-risk tradeoff. Equity investors are attracted to the open-ended upside of equity investing. They expect to win less often than the bond investor, but they expect their wins to be bigger. Risk arbitrage has some analogies to selling calls against an equity portfolio. The investor caps her upside, while leaving intact most of the downside. So it makes sense for the conventional equity investor to get rid of stocks that become involved in deals. And this is precisely what creates an economic role for the risk arbitrageur. She performs a classic risk-transfer function, by taking on a type of risk that traditional investors are unwilling to assume.

Having said that *most* equity investors do not like the risk-return tradeoff in risk arbitrage, we should point out that some equity investors are willing to take deal-related risks in their portfolios. For example, when America Online (AOL) made its bid for Time Warner in early 2000, many equity investors held onto Time Warner. Some of them were investors who had owned Time Warner for a long time, and they liked the prospects for Time Warner even if the AOL deal never happened. Other investors liked Time Warner, liked AOL, and thought that holding Time Warner was a reasonable way to become owners of AOL shares. Thanks to the willingness of many traditional equity investors to hold onto their Time Warner shares, the Time Warner/AOL transaction never developed the kind of spread that some observers thought would be appropriate.

The Time Warner example is the exception, not the rule. Equity investors are usually happy to sell their stock to risk arbitrageurs since they are uncomfortable with the short volatility risk posture. This means that the returns to risk arbitrage investing are not driven entirely by manager skill. Skill is always helpful, but even without large doses of manager skill, there is a useful economic function to be performed. And it makes sense that there are returns to be earned from performing that function.

The successful risk arbitrageur must have, or must have access to, very substantial legal expertise. The merger and acquisition business is a game played according to very definite and very complicated rules. Risk arbitrage research often involves poring over long and complicated legal documents, looking for loopholes, warning signs, and hidden treasures. It's a green eyeshade business.

We have illustrated the risk arbitrage strategy with some simple examples. Now let's take a closer look at the details. To begin, we need to distinguish cash deals from stock deals. In a *cash deal*, the acquiring company offers to pay cash for shares in the target company. In a *stock deal*, the acquiring company uses its own stock to pay for the target company. The GE/Honeywell transaction was a stock deal, though never consummated. Here is an another example. When Chevron Corp. bid for Texaco, Inc., in October 2000, Chevron offered 0.77 shares of its own stock for each share of Texaco. Texaco jumped from $55 to $59 on the news, reflecting the price of Chevron at the time of the announcement. But the ultimate value of the transaction would depend on the price of Chevron at the close of the transaction.

Stock deals create a form of currency risk. In a stock transaction, the acquiring company is using its own stock as the currency with which to pay for the target. If you buy Texaco expecting to receive Chevron shares in payment, you don't know how much the Chevron shares will be worth when the deal closes. It's as if you had sold computer equipment to a European company for payment in euros in six months. But you don't know what the euro will be worth, in dollars, in six months. In each case, there is currency risk. The way to hedge the risk is to short the currency. You short the euro to hedge the risk in the computer example, and you short Chevron to hedge the risk in the Texaco-Chevron deal.

Hedging the currency risk leaves the risk of deal cancellation unhedged. Just as the European company might fail to pay for the computer equipment, so Chevron might fail to buy Texaco. Shorting the acquirer only addresses the specific scenario in which the deal goes through, but the stock of the acquirer goes down. When the transaction is an all-cash offer, there is no currency risk and nothing to hedge, and hence there is no need to take a short position.

The hedging activity of risk arbitrageurs is one reason that the stock of the acquiring company often goes down after a deal is announced. The price decline may reflect the market's judgment that the deal is not a good deal. But if the deal is a stock-for-stock transaction, the decline is partly the result of hedging activity on the part of risk arbitrageurs. For example, on the day that Chevron made its bid for Texaco, Chevron dropped from $84 to $82.

In some deals, the payment takes the form of some combination of cash and stock. In some stock deals, the transaction is structured as a collar. The *collar transaction* has some similarities to an option collar, in which the investor holds stock, sells an out-of-the-money call, and buys an out-of-the-money put. The investor still faces some uncertainty but has placed a limit both on the upside and the downside. In a pure stock-for-stock transaction, the owner of the target company will receive a fixed number of shares of the acquiring company. In a collar trasaction, the number of shares is adjustable. If the stock of the acquirer performs well, then the owner of the target company will receive fewer shares of the acquirer; if the stock of the acquirer performs badly, then the owner of the target will receive more shares of the acquirer.

For example, in April 2001 the insurance giant American International Group (AIG) announced a bid for American General Corporation, a smaller insurance company. AIG wanted to pay $46 per share for American General, but it wanted to pay that amount in stock, not cash. The deal was structured in such a way that the exact number of AIG shares to be received would depend on the average price of AIG during a "pricing period" prior to the close of the deal. If the average AIG price was greater than $76.20 but less than $84.22, then that average price would be used as the basis for calculating the relevant number of AIG shares. It turned out that the average price was $79.45, and each American General shareholder received 0.579 AIG shares. If the average price had been below $76.20, then each American General share would have been exchanged for 0.6037 AIG shares. If the average price had been above $84.22, then each American General share would have turned into 0.5462 shares of AIG.

When a collar is in place, the risk arbitrageur does not know exactly how many shares of the acquirer she will receive if the deal goes through, so the arbitrageur doesn't know how many shares to short. Hedging becomes more complicated, if not impossible.

In theory, the risk in risk arbitrage is totally deal specific, unrelated to what is happening in the stock market at large. And many hedge fund practitioners will tell you that risk arbitrage is a market-independent strategy, even market neutral. This is an exaggeration.

For one thing, risk arbitrage spreads are affected by the general level of interest rates. Moreover, the historical performance record clearly shows some level of correlation between arbitrage returns and stock market returns. This connection with the equity market makes intuitive sense. The factors that threaten stock prices in general can also threaten the orderly progress of an M&A transaction. Stocks do best in an environment of stable interest rates and growing corporate profits. The major threats to stocks are rising interest rates (which are sometimes accompanied by accelerating profits) and slowing corporate profits (which are sometimes accompanied by falling interest rates). But if interest rates go up, the increase may also put a damper on deal activity since deals are often financed with borrowed money. Similarly, if corporate profits are deteriorating, the decline will put pressure on companies that are involved in M&A activity. If A announces a bid for B in January, hoping to close the transaction in September, then B may report disappointing earnings at the end of the March quarter or the June quarter. So A may decide that B is no longer worth buying or is worth buying only at a lower price.

The risk arbitrage business is totally dependent on attractive deal spreads. Many arbitrageurs try to earn 20 percent per year, or 10 percent over six months. If a deal stock is trading today at $50, and if the deal is expected to close in six months at $55, then there is a 10 percent spread. If today's price were $53, then the target spread would be unavailable, and the arbitrageur would likely pass on the transaction. Sometimes, however, if the spread becomes too narrow, then the arbitrageurs may bet against the deal, arguing that the spread will get wider. In an all-cash deal, the move is to short the target company. In a stock-for-stock transaction, the move is to short the target while going long the acquirer.

It is vital to separate the availability of good deal *flow* from the availability of good deal *spreads*. Deal flow means that there are a lot of situations to invest in. Deal spreads are what ultimately drive return. In the ideal world, there will be good deal flow *and* good deal spreads. But sometimes good deal flow brings bad deal spreads: There may be a lot of deals, a lot of money chasing the deals, and narrow spreads. And sometimes good deal spreads are only available against the background of bad deal flow.

Because deal flow is changeable and unpredictable, risk arbitrage has to be classed as a *variable capacity strategy*. Sometimes it's possible to invest billions of dollars in deal stocks; sometimes the opportunities become much scarcer. As we saw in Chapter 4, Figure 4–1, deal flow increased strongly throughout the 1990s, both in terms of number of deals and total dollar amount, but then declined in 2001. The deal scene remains fairly quiet in 2002.

DISTRESSED DEBT

The distressed debt investor is mainly interested in two kinds of bonds: those that have extremely high yields and those that have no yield at all. The bonds with a very high yield might be called *stressed bonds*. The bonds with no yield are *defaulted bonds*. The category of distressed debt includes both the stressed and the defaulted.

The stressed bonds are still paying interest, but the underlying companies are struggling under excessive levels of debt. These bonds will be trading at a substantial *discount to par*: A bond originally issued at $100 may be trading at $80 or less. The buyer of the distressed bonds gets a higher *current yield* (coupon divided by price) than the buyer of the newly issued bonds. In addition, he gets an opportunity for capital appreciation. Some stressed bonds are bonds that started their lives as low-quality, high-yield bonds, and then became even lower quality. Other stressed bonds, the so-called *fallen angels*, started out as investment-grade bonds and then ran into financial problems that lowered both their credit rating and their price.

As the company's problems increase, the price of the bond gets lower and lower, perhaps getting as low as "25 cents on the dollar": A bond with a face value of $100 trades at $25. Eventually the company may file for bankruptcy in order to gain protection from its creditors. Now the bonds are defaulted bonds: They pay no interest at all. These bonds *trade flat*—that is, without interest. The purchaser of these bonds is interested only in capital appreciation.

Filing for bankruptcy protection does not mean going out of business. The distinction here is the distinction between Chapter 7 and Chapter 11 of the U.S. bankruptcy code. Chapter 11 enables companies to reorganize their finances while enjoying some level of protection from their creditors. Chapter 7 governs the process of liquidating a company. The companies of interest here are companies that have filed Chapter 11 but hope to avoid filing Chapter 7.

THE REORGANIZATION PROCESS

To understand distressed debt investing, you have to understand what happens when companies get into trouble and reorganize their financial structure. To understand the reorganization process, you have to understand the capital structure of companies.

In our discussion of convertible hedging, we pointed out that convertible securities have an intermediate position in the capital structure of a company, senior to the common equity but junior to the nonconvertible debt. And nonconvertible debt is available at different levels of seniority. At the top of the pyramid is *senior secured* debt, which is debt collateralized by a specific corporate asset. For example, an airline might issue debt secured by a specific aircraft, or an electric utility might issue debt secured by a power generation plant. Other senior debt is just a general obligation of the company, not secured by any specific asset.

The categories above apply to publicly traded bonds. But there is also nonpublic debt, of which the most important categories are trade claims and bank debt. *Bank debt* is simply money lent by a bank (or a syndicate of banks), which is often senior to the company's public debt. *Trade claims* are claims against the company presented by suppliers to the company. Suppose, for example, that you are a clothing manufacturer who has just sold merchandise worth $1 million to a chain of discount stores. You expect to get paid in one month. Then the retailer goes bankrupt. The retailer owes you money, and your claim against the retailer stands very senior in the pecking order. But the fact is that your claim is now tied up in the reorganization process, so you won't see any of that money for several years. If the retailer owes you $1 million, you might be happy to sell your claim to a hedge fund for a reduced price and let the hedge fund deal with the headaches. Although bank debt and trade claims are not literally publicly traded debt, recent years have seen the development of a reasonably liquid and well-organized market in these claims.

So there is a definite pecking order among the various creditors of a company, all of whom are senior to the equity holders. The equity holders stand at the end of the line, and their equity is usually wiped out in the financial reorganization process. (The Long Term Capital Management crisis is an example of this phenomenon. The investors in the fund were the equity holders; the major Wall

Street firms were the lenders. The equity investors lost virtually everything, and then the creditors reorganized the fund.) The various creditors then fight among themselves to determine how to divide the assets of the company. This process is a zero-sum game requiring high level negotiating skills and an appetite for brinksmanship. At the end of the process, the various creditors exchange their debt in the old company for new securities of the reorganized company. Creditors who are very senior—who stand at or close to the front of the line—are likely to get paid out mainly in cash or short-term debt. (These creditors may even recover a certain amount of postpetition interest, i.e., interest payments that were suspended when the company filed Chapter 11.) Very junior creditors—who stand at or close to the end of the line—are likely to get paid mainly in equity of the new company. Creditors who stand in the middle of the line will get some combination of equity and debt.

Professionals who invest in distressed companies wouldn't touch the common stock with a 10-foot pole. When companies get into trouble, their common stock will trade down to very cheap levels, $1 per share or less. These prices sometimes attract naïve investors who perceive bargain-basement prices and the opportunity to make a killing. This is classic long volatility thinking: You spend a dollar on a lottery ticket, not really expecting to win, but knowing that you will win big if you win at all. Professional investors in distressed companies assume that the equity is worthless, so their task is to decide which class of debt offers the most attractive risk-reward tradeoff.

The traditional high-yield debt investor is playing a short volatility game. When you buy high-yield bonds at par, there is virtually no upside—no chance at all of earning capital appreciation. Any surprises are much more likely to be negative than positive. The arithmetic gets more interesting when the market is worried about the financial health of the company. Prices go down, and opportunities for real capital appreciation emerge. Investors who buy defaulted debt may expect some of their bonds to double in the course of the reorganization process. Not bad for a bond investment.

Investors who buy very high yield stressed debt, or early-stage defaulted debt are value-oriented investors attracted by the lure of cheap prices. *Early-stage defaulted debt* is debt that is still at an early stage of the reorganization process. At this stage there is substantial uncertainty about how the reorganization will work out. As the reorganization process moves along, the investor is able to form a clearer idea of the outcome, and the orientation shifts from a value orientation to a risk arbitrage orientation. The investor owns a security that he will eventually exchange for some combination of debt and equity in the newly reorganized company. So the classic questions of risk arbitrage emerge. What package of securities will I receive? When will I receive it? What will it be worth?

Some of the hedge funds that invest in defaulted debt are activist investors, while others take a more passive role. The *activist investor* is not merely an active investor who tries to exploit special skills to generate superior returns. The activist investor is an investor who rolls up her sleeves and gets actively involved in the details of the financial reorganization. She will sit on one or more *creditors' committees*, which are committees formed to represent the various classes of creditors as the reorganization rolls forward. This gives the investor an important opportunity to try to advance her interests, but it also means that the investor is a company insider. Once you have inside information, you cannot sell your bonds to noninsider investors. You can trade only with other insiders. Some distressed debt investors are unwilling to accept this limitation, so they prefer not to serve on creditors' committees.

Distressed debt investing is not totally skill dependent. The distressed debt investor is making money partly because he is providing liquidity to more traditional bond investors who are often forced to sell bonds that still have good investment value. The phenomenon of forced selling is a classic creator of investment value. Forced selling arises because more traditional bond investors are usually investing for steady income, and they often must follow strict guidelines regarding credit quality. A mutual fund that is trying to deliver regular monthly income to its investors cannot afford to own defaulted bonds, which pay no income. A mutual fund that advertises itself as an investment-grade bond fund cannot own bonds that fall below investment grade. So these funds are often forced to sell, even if the portfolio manager feels that there is still substantial investment value in the bonds. The distressed debt investor provides liquidity to these sellers and picks up a bargain in the process.

Defaulted debt investors are sometimes referred to as *vulture investors*, perceived as predators struggling over the corpse of their prey. Vultures have a bad reputation, but remember: Vultures don't kill. They just clean up the remains. Similarly, distressed debt investors are not responsible for the financial distress of the companies in which they invest. But they are an essential part of the reorganization process.

Like risk arbitrage, distressed debt investing has some element of market-related risk. This emerges from the historical return data, and it makes intuitive sense. Corporate bonds are vulnerable to changes in the general level of interest rates but also vulnerable to changes in the fundamentals of the borrowing company. As you move from the investment-grade credits into the lower-quality credits, company-specific fundamentals become more important than the general level of interest rates. In effect, very low quality debt behaves almost like equity. And so the price of distressed debt can be very sensitive to factors that also influence the equity market: economic weakness, low or negative profit growth, and other factors that make investors worry about equities.

Distressed debt investors try to invest in good companies that have a bad capital structure. But sometimes it can be hard to tell the difference between a bad company and a good company that just happens to have unsustainable levels of debt. The distressed debt community is now looking at a tremendous amount of distressed paper created by the collapse of the so-called TMT sector: technology, media, and telecommunications. Many of the collapsed companies received equity and debt financing at a point when investors were irrationally exuberant, willing to invest in companies whose business plans were very dubious. So the challenge for the distressed debt investor now is to separate the companies that never made sense in the first place from the companies that just have too much debt. This is largely uncharted territory. Some brave pioneers will make killings, others will be killed. Still others will prefer to stay at home. This form of vulture investing is close in spirit to *venture* investing. In each case, the investor is a long-volatility investor who hopes that a few home runs will more than offset the strikeouts.

Capacity is an important issue for the investor in distressed debt. The distressed debt market is relatively small compared to the broader bond market, and its size is prone to major fluctuations linked to what is going on in the broader economy and market. When times are good, the amount of distressed debt is low; when times get tougher, the size of the market increases. As we saw in Chapter 4, Figure 4–2, the last several years have seen a sharp increase in bond defaults and a corresponding increase in the size of the defaulted debt market.

CONCLUSION

The preface offered a provisional definition of a hedge fund:

> A hedge fund is an *actively managed* investment fund that seeks attractive *absolute return*. In pursuit of their absolute return objective, hedge funds use a *wide variety of investment strategies and tools*. Hedge funds are designed for a *small number of large investors*, and the manager of the fund receives a *percentage of the profits* earned by the fund.

What do we know now that we didn't know when we began?

Hedge funds belong to the world of active investment management, in which managers try to use their skill to produce superior returns for their investors. The world of active management stands in sharp contrast to the world of passive management, in which managers use capitalization-weighted index funds to track various markets instead of trying to beat the markets.

The difference between hedge funds and other active managers is mainly a difference in objectives and strategies. The traditional active manager is trying to beat some passive market benchmark, such as the S&P 500 Index. If the benchmark is down 15 percent but the manager is only down 10 percent, then everybody is supposed to feel good. Hedge funds are trying to deliver a positive return, independent of the performance of the various standard markets. In pursuit of this objective, hedge fund managers use a wide variety of investment strategies and techniques: They use leverage, they sell short, and they engage in other hedging strategies.

Since hedge fund managers try to use investment skill, they are vulnerable to the critique of skill offered by the efficient market viewpoint. But this viewpoint is a complicated blend of insights and distortions. There are three main insights:

1. *Markets are efficient.* Investing is a ruthlessly competitive game in which all the players are seeking to achieve the highest possible return for the lowest possible risk. There are no free lunches, no return without risk.

2. *The past does not predict the future.* This point holds for individual securities, for markets, and for money managers. Trends don't go on forever, and there are all sorts of reasons why past success may sow the seeds of future failure.

3. *An investor should not put all his eggs in one basket.* The prudent investor will try to construct a diversified portfolio whose components will not all zig and zag together. The key to diversification is to identify investments that have a low correlation with one another.

Smart investors, including smart hedge fund managers, will never forget these three insights. But other elements of the efficient market viewpoint are not helpful. The problematic claims are these:

4. *Efficient markets are free of emotion.* False. Every investor is vulnerable to fear, greed, and all sorts of other emotions. Panics and bubbles are here to stay. The skilled investor does not banish the emotions, but channels them into useful directions. Greed drives the search for superior returns; fear drives the management of risk.

5. *Skill does not exist.* False. Some investors are more skilled than others. But skill is not merely brainpower. The investment world is filled with very smart people who produce mediocre results. This leaves room for a variety of "implementation" factors: focus, competitiveness, open-mindedness, and the like.

6. *Index funds are the best investment for the rational investor.* False. Although the index fund is a buy-and-hold portfolio, when you invest in an index fund, you are behaving like a momentum-driven investor: You are putting more money into the companies with better historical performance. So the cap-weighted index can become dangerously undiversified, as the tech bubble of the late 1990s clearly demonstrated.

   7. *Mean-variance optimization is the ideal technique for building a diversified portfolio.* False. To use the optimizer as a practical tool, the investor needs to forecast a long array of returns, standard deviations, and cross-correlations. The problem here is the eternal investment problem: Whenever you estimate the future, you might be wrong. And if you forecast the future by simply extrapolating the trends of the past, then you will *definitely* be wrong. Building a diversified portfolio takes some skill.

   Hedge funds take skill seriously, and they take diversification seriously. Indeed, the basic mission of the hedge fund manager is to use her investment skill to build a diversified portfolio that will produce an attractive absolute return. Some hedge fund managers use sophisticated optimization techniques to build portfolios, but most do not. Still, they all accept the principle that you shouldn't put all your eggs in one basket. So hedge fund managers are unwilling to confine themselves to long positions in stocks, bonds, and other financial assets. They want to be able to own nonfinancial assets too, like gold, oil, or pork bellies. And they want to be able to take short positions in both financial and nonfinancial assets. These extra layers of freedom are important precisely because they improve the money manager's ability to build an intelligently diversified portfolio.

   The hedge fund manager uses as much skill as she can muster. But hedge funds have no monopoly on skill, and skill is not the only source of hedge fund returns.

   The first point is the easier one. Some hedge fund enthusiasts will tell you that hedge fund managers are smarter, or more talented, or more skilled, than their colleagues in the traditional active management community. This is marketing hype. There are lots of skilled managers who have not joined the migration into the hedge fund world, and there are lots of hedge fund managers who are not as skilled as they think they are.

   The second point, that skill is not the only source of return, is a little more complicated. Hedge funds, as a whole, have multiple sources of return and risk. Some hedge fund strategies have a reasonably high level of *directional market risk*. The main examples here would be the long-biased equity hedge funds and the short sellers. At the other extreme are the relative-value hedge funds and the global asset allocators. The relative-value managers seek to be genuinely hedged at all times, with long and short positions offsetting each other. The global asset allocators can be long, or short, or neutral, depending on the circumstances, so the level of "chronic" directional risk is again very low. Risk arbitrage and distressed debt have modest levels of directional market risk since the forces that create weak equity markets also tend to create a headwind for these strategies.

But hedge funds are also influenced by factors that are *market related* but not *directional*. Some of these factors are *intramarket variables* that depend on relationships between two different parts of a market. Within the equity market, the growth-value distinction is especially important. If a hedge fund manager tends to be long value and short growth, then he will do well in some environments and will suffer terribly in others. Within the bond market, yield spreads are a critical factor. If a hedge fund manager tends to be long "spread product" (bonds that offer a yield premium over Treasuries) and short Treasuries, then the manager will thrive when spreads are narrowing and will suffer when they are expanding.

There are other important factors that are market related but not directional. The convertible hedger needs volatility. The momentum-oriented investor needs trends. The contrarian investor needs trendless, mean-reverting markets. The risk arbitrageur needs deal flow and decent deal spreads. The distressed debt investor needs a decent supply of opportunities and a congenial credit environment.

Since the different hedge fund strategies have different sources of return, and since these sources are often different from what drives a more conventional equity or bond portfolio, hedge funds can be a very powerful diversification tool. The best way to build a diversified portfolio is to blend multiple components that march to the beats of multiple drummers.

So it is no wonder that large institutions and wealthy individuals have been so interested in hedge fund investing. The appeal is not merely the appeal of the exotic or fashionable. It's the appeal of something that will behave differently from other parts of an investment portfolio. So the demand for hedge funds should remain strong, especially as investors get used to an age of diminished expectations. Once upon a time people thought that U.S. stocks were destined to deliver

20 percent annual returns. That confidence has disappeared. Some sophisticated institutions that used to assume 10 percent annual returns have lowered their expectations to 7 or 8 percent. In such an environment, it's natural to be interested in strategies that have the potential to deliver a decent return even in a lackluster equity environment.

So it makes sense for investors to be interested in hedge funds. And it makes sense for money managers to be interested in running hedge funds. The economics of the business are superb. The performance fees can be big, and the firms are usually small. So there's a lot of money to be spread among a small number of people. But money is not the only draw. The brain drain that takes people from big financial firms into hedge funds is also driven by the desire for greater investment freedom and less bureaucracy. At its best, the world of institutional money management offers an enticing combination of intellectual stimulation and financial reward. At its worst, it's a bureaucratic straitjacket that is totally obsessed with beating the passive benchmarks by 1 percent.

But the world of hedge funds does present some unique risks, both for the money manager and for the investor. The wannabe hedge fund manager needs to remember that the failure rate is high. And this has consequences for the investor. If you're looking at relatively young and unseasoned hedge funds, think of them as young technology companies. There may be one or two winners in the batch, but there's room for lots of losers. And even when a hedge fund is more seasoned, the typical fund is still critically dependent on one or two key people. Knowledgeable investors always worry about "the bus problem": What happens if the key investment person is hit by a bus? The bus problem is a bigger problem in hedge funds than elsewhere. So diversification across managers is more important in the hedge fund world than elsewhere.

Hedge funds are still exotic investments. But this is likely to change as institutional and individual investors continue to explore styles of active management that are not so dependent on the performance of the standard benchmarks. Large institutional investors are conspicuously stepping up their activity in the hedge fund arena, and the mutual fund business is taking steps to make hedge fund strategies available to smaller investors. So it seems almost inevitable that hedge funds will gradually become more visible, more "institutionalized," and less mysterious. We may even see regulatory changes that will make it easier for hedge fund strategies to move closer into the investment mainstream.

Many of those who are currently invested in hedge funds would prefer that hedge funds remain exotic and mysterious. They worry that the new investors will ruin the opportunity for the established investors. Once you've discovered the perfect tropical island retreat, you don't want big cruise ships calling there every week. So there are many hedge fund investors who quietly rejoice whenever a hedge fund disaster hits the headlines. They figure that the disaster stories will keep the tourists off their island.

The real question here is whether hedge funds have the capacity to absorb the additional capital that would result from increasing investor attention. Some strategies have very limited capacity; others (principally risk arbitrage and distressed debt) have capacity that ebbs and flows depending on deal flow and economic conditions. Strategies that focus on the very large and liquid markets have, in theory, very large capacity, but the question remains whether managers will be able to absorb the capacity successfully. Since hedge funds can take short positions, they should be able to avoid the classic bubble problems that arise when everybody wants to buy the same thing. But, as we have seen, short selling is not just an effortless extension of long-only investing.

The key to successful investing is to form realistic expectations. Many people used to believe that investors could throw money at stocks and make 20 percent. That naïve confidence is now gone. But it is also naïve to believe that you can throw money at hedge funds and make 10 to 15 percent. Investing in hedge funds is like any form of investing. You work through the research and the analysis, you think about how the future might be importantly different from the past, and then you place your bets. But you have to construct a diversified portfolio of bets, and you must be constantly alert to signs that your analysis might be wrong.

Hedge funds generate strong feelings from their defenders and from their detractors. This book was designed to present a balanced portrait of the world of hedge funds, steering a course between the exaggerations on both sides.

Many people will tell you that *hedge funds are bad*. They will say that these funds are secretive, unregulated investment vehicles that make highly leveraged speculative bets in the global financial markets. The investors are either wealthy individuals with more money than sense, or large tax-exempt institutions who should know better. The hedge fund managers are investment cowboys who are interested solely in earning fat performance fees. If the performance is not good enough to generate attractive fees, then the hedge fund managers simply steal the money, using various forms of fraud and deception. Considered as a whole, hedge funds are momentum investors who add volatility and instability to the markets. In extreme cases, such as the case of Long Term Capital Management, hedge funds have the potential to create a meltdown of the global financial system.

Even if you manage to avoid the frauds and the cheats, the fact remains that hedge funds are just ultra-active funds. But active management requires investment skill, and skill is an illusion. Markets are efficient, there are no free lunches, and past success does not predict future success. So the sensible investor will own a portfolio of capitalization-weighted index funds constructed in accordance with the principles of mean-variance optimization. Hedge funds have no place in this scheme.

On the other side of the debate are those who will insist that *hedge funds are good*. Hedge funds have the ability to deliver steady, consistent returns that have no correlation at all with stocks, bonds, or anything else. So hedge funds are a powerful tool for portfolio diversification because hedge funds have sources of return and risk that are totally unrelated to the standard markets. The key source of return is the skill of the manager. The hedge fund community is the "smart-money" community, the beneficiary of the massive brain drain that moves talented investors away from the huge investment bureaucracies into small and nimble investment organizations. But skill is not the sole source of return. Some hedge funds take advantage of market inefficiencies created by the behavior of the large investment organizations. Other hedge funds get paid for delivering liquidity to the marketplace or performing other valuable services.

Both of these extreme views are wrong. Hedge funds are not a scam designed for the unwary, nor are they the answer to all investment problems. They are an important and essential part of the investment landscape. They appeal to investors because they offer the possibility of attractive returns that do not depend on the performance of the conventional market benchmarks. They appeal to money managers because they offer the possibility of wide-ranging investment freedom and very impressive financial rewards.

The key word here is *possibility*. The fledgling hedge fund manager may be driven by visions of dazzling success, but the failure rate is high. The eager investor in one or two hedge funds may have visions of 15 percent annual returns with no down quarters, but that expectation is almost certain to be dashed. In other words, hedge funds contain risk, both for the money manager and for the investor. Some of these risks are very general risks that are attached to any form of investing, while others are specific to hedge fund investing. The colorful newspaper stories about the inevitable hedge fund disasters call attention to some of these risks but deflect attention from other risks and they deflect attention from the larger forces that make hedge funds an essential part of the investment community and an essential part of many investment portfolios.

The prudent investor will not turn up his nose at hedge funds, nor will he rush headlong into them. The prudent investor will do the research and approach the area with caution, an open mind, and realistic expectations.

APPENDIX I

The EACM 100® Index

In January 1996, Evaluation Associates Capital Markets, Inc. (EACM), launched the EACM 100® Index as a benchmark for alternative investment strategies. The index is an equally weighted composite of unaudited performance information provided by 100 private investment funds chosen by EACM to represent 5 broad investment strategies and certain niche substrategies. Strategy weightings are determined by EACM and are subject to change at EACM's discretion. Investment manager allocations are rebalanced at the beginning of each calendar year. Within the index there are 5 broad strategies and 13 underlying substrategy styles:

Relative Value Managers structure balanced or hedged portfolios with long and short positions that attempt to generate performance results independent of market direction. Four styles: long/short equity specialists, convertible hedgers, bond hedgers, and multistrategy managers that combine different relative value styles.

Event Driven Managers focus on corporate transactions and special situations, including deal arbitrage and distressed debt. Three styles: deal arbitrageurs, distressed debt specialists, and multistrategy managers that opportunistically combine different event-driven styles.

Equity Hedge Managers invest in long and short positions with varying degrees of exposure and leverage. Three styles: domestic long biased, domestic opportunistic, and global/international managers.

Global Asset Allocators Managers invest opportunistically, long and short, in a variety of U.S. and non-U.S. financial and/or nonfinancial assets. Two styles: systematic traders and discretionary managers.

Short Selling Managers short specific U.S. equities based on the fundamental characteristics of a company or current market trends, with the expectation of a decline in the share price.

Investment managers in the index are selected based on guidelines established by EACM, and EACM has the sole discretion to revise these guidelines. EACM seeks investment managers that genuinely represent an appropriate investment style and meet eligibility requirements regarding minimum track record and assets under management. The investment vehicle and/or manager also must be open to new investment and agree to provide EACM accurate and timely performance data. All investment managers have agreed to be included in the index and may at any time decide to leave the index at their discretion. EACM agrees not to disclose individual manager names, and publicly disseminates information and performance results only on the index and its strategy components.

Performance results for the period 1990 to 1995 are based on the historical performance of those managers whose funds were still in operation and included in the index as of January 1996. These results therefore reflect some degree of *survivor bias*. For example, certain hedge funds that ceased operations prior to January 1996 were unavailable for inclusion in the index at its inception. Such funds may have been included (or considered for inclusion) had the index been launched on an earlier date. Performance results for the period 1996–2001 are relatively free of survivor bias.

All underlying performance data reflect the performance of investment vehicle(s) represented by the investment managers to be representative of all accounts managed pursuant to a designated investment strategy and is net of such managers' stated fees, but does not reflect any pro forma calculation of EACM fees. None of such performance data and representations are independently verified or approved by EACM, and EACM makes no representations as to their accuracy. Recent manager performance information is likely to be in the form of a preliminary estimate and is therefore subject to revision by the respective manager(s). Although EACM is under no obligation to correct or to update this index or such information in any way, EACM may, in its discretion, modify any portion of the index's return figures (including component strategy and substrategy figures) in order to reflect such manager revisions.

Suggestions for Further Reading

BOOKS: GENERAL

Crerend, William J., *Fundamentals of Hedge Fund Investing: A Professional Investor's Guide.* McGraw-Hill, New York, 1998. Bill Crerend is the founder of Evaluation Associates, which is the parent company of Evaluation Associates Capital Markets, Inc. His book is a natural sequel to this book, designed for the professional investor.

Swensen, David F., *Pioneering Portfolio Management: An Unconventional Approach to Institutional Investment.* The Free Press, New York, 2000. Swensen has overall investment responsibility for the Yale University endowment, a $10 billion portfolio that was an early investor in hedge funds.

BOOKS: EFFICIENT MARKET VIEWPOINT

Bernstein, Peter L., *Against the Gods: The Remarkable Story of Risk.* Wiley, New York, 1996. A historical account of the attempt to quantify risk.

Malkiel, Burton G., *A Random Walk Down Wall Street.* W.W. Norton, New York, 1973. Malkiel, professor of economics at Princeton University, is an eloquent advocate of the efficient market viewpoint. This extremely readable book is an investment classic.

BOOKS: HISTORY AND PEOPLE

Although most hedge funds try to stay out of the press, George Soros and Long Term Capital Management are now clearly in the public domain.

Books about Long Term Capital Management

Dunbar, Nicholas, *Inventing Money: The Story of Long-Term Capital Management and the Legends Behind It.* Wiley, New York, 2000.

Lowenstein, Roger, *When Genius Failed.* Random House, New York, 2000.

Books about George Soros

Kaufman, Michael T., *Soros: The Life and Times of a Messianic Billionaire.* Knopf, New York, 2002.

Slater, Robert, *Soros: The Life, Times and Trading Secrets of the World's Greatest Investor.* McGraw-Hill, New York, 1996.

Soros, George, *The Alchemy of Finance: Reading the Mind of the Market.* Simon & Schuster, New York, 1987.

More General Books about Hedge Fund Personalities

Ellis, Charles D., *Wall Street People: True Stories of Today's Masters and Moguls.* Wiley, New York, 2001.

Schwager, Jack D. *Market Wizards: Interviews with Top Traders.* Simon & Schuster, New York, 1989.

ARTICLES: HISTORY AND PEOPLE

The following articles chronicle the early history of hedge funds:

Loomis, Carol J., "The Jones Nobody Keeps Up With." *Fortune*, April 1966.

Loomis, Carol J., "Hard Times Come to the Hedge Funds." *Fortune*, January 1970.

The next two articles deal with more recent market history:

Cassidy, John, "Striking It Rich." *The New Yorker*, January 14, 2002. A very readable account of the last days of the recent bull market.

Gladwell, Malcolm, "Blowing Up." *The New Yorker*, April 22 and 29, 2002. A colorful account of the difference between selling options and buying options.

PERIODICALS

In addition to these books, there are various periodicals that enable the interested person to remain current with what's going on in the hedge fund arena.

Barron's. This weekly periodical often has interviews with hedge fund managers.

Financial Times. Features regular coverage of developments within the hedge fund community.

MAR Hedge. Monthly publication that covers news in the hedge fund community, along with performance results.

Journal of Alternative Investments. An academic journal, edited at the University of Massachusetts—Amherst, which focuses on the hedge fund universe. Although it is an academic journal, many of the articles are written in such a way as to be accessible to the general public.

GLOSSARY

active management See *efficient market viewpoint.*

at the money See *options.*

basic tools Hedge funds have the freedom to take either *long positions* or *short positions* in stocks, bonds, other financial assets, or nonfinancial assets (such as physical commodities). A *long position* is a position that will make money if the price of the asset goes up; a *short position* makes money if the price of the asset goes down. A long position can be either leveraged or unleveraged. A *leveraged position* is partly financed with borrowed funds. *Unleveraged positions* involve no borrowing. Short positions automatically involve borrowing since the short seller borrows the asset that he plans to sell. If an investor begins with $100,000 in cash and sells short stocks worth $100,000, the position would generally be viewed as an unleveraged short position since the value of the short position is no greater than the net assets in the account.

broker See *financial institutions.*

buy and hold See *dynamic trading strategies.*

call See *options.*

capitalization See *efficient market viewpoint.*

contrarian See *dynamic trading strategies.*

correlation See *statistics.*

dealer See *financial institutions.*

delta See *options.*

diversification See *efficient market viewpoint.*

dynamic trading strategies These are trading strategies according to which changes in the price of an asset signal the investor to increase or decrease his position in the asset. Dynamic trading strategies contrast with *buy-and-hold* strategies, in which the investor does not respond at all to changes in price. The chief example of buy-and-hold investing is a *capitalization-weighted index fund.*

    The main dynamic strategies are *momentum investing* and *contrarian investing.* The momentum investor buys when prices are rising and sells when prices are falling; the contrarian investor has the opposite strategy. The trading behavior of a momentum investor is similar to the behavior of an investor who is trying to replicate the effect of owning a put or call, while the trading behavior of a contrarian investor is similar to the behavior of an investor who is trying to simulate the effect of selling a put or a call.

efficient frontier See *efficient market viewpoint*.

efficient market viewpoint This body of thinking includes two main ideas: Financial *markets* are efficient, and the rational investor should hold a *portfolio* that is efficiently diversified. The claim of *market efficiency* is based on two points: (1) You have to take risk in order to beat the risk-free rate of return ("there are no free lunches"); and (2) the past performance of a security, or a money manager, does not predict the future performance. These points lead to the problem of *manager skill*: How can you tell whether a money manager is skilled or just lucky? And that problem leads to the idea that the best portfolio is a *capitalization-weighted index fund*. An index fund is a portfolio that offers a "slice" of the underlying market: The weight of each company is determined entirely by the weight of the company in the market at large.

An efficiently diversified portfolio is a portfolio that offers the maximum return for a given level of risk, or offers the minimal risk for a given level of return. This idea is made more specific by using *standard deviation* as a measure of risk and then calculating the standard deviation of a portfolio from assumptions about the standard deviations of the components and the *correlation* among the components. (See *statistics*.) The mathematical ideas were originally laid out by Harry Markowitz, who received the Nobel Prize in Economic Science for his work in 1990.

financial institutions The distinction between a *broker* and a *dealer* is crucial for understanding how Wall Street institutions work. A broker acts as an agent, or intermediary in bringing buyers and sellers together. The broker earns a commission for her work. A dealer acts as a principal, buying and selling for his own account. The dealer maintains an inventory of positions and earns the spread between the bid price (the price at which the dealer is willing to buy) and the ask price (the price at which the dealer is willing to sell).

hedge fund An actively managed investment fund whose objective is to earn a positive rate of return that does not depend on the return of the standard market indexes. Hedge funds use a variety of investment strategies and tools, such as leverage, short selling, and options. Hedge funds are typically designed to serve a small number of large investors, rather than a broad market of retail investors. The manager of the hedge fund typically earns a percentage of the profits generated by the fund.

index funds See *efficient market viewpoint*.
in the money See *options*.

leverage See *basic tools*.
liquidity A liquid market is a market in which willing buyers and willing sellers can find each other relatively easily.
long position See *basic tools*.

margin See *basic tools.*

momentum See *dynamic trading strategies.*

options An option is a right to buy or sell an asset at a specific price within a specific time period. A *call option* is a right to buy, while a *put option* is a right to sell. For example, the Microsoft $60 call option of September 2002 gives the owner of the option the right to buy Microsoft shares at a price of $60 per share up until September 2002. The *strike price* of the option is the price at which the owner of the option may buy or sell the underlying asset. The Microsoft option has a strike price of $60.

Options are either in the money, at the money, or out of the money. An option is *at the money* if the current price of the asset is the same as the strike price of the option. An option is *in the money* if the option gives its owner the right to do something that has immediate economic value. A call option is in the money if the strike price of the option is below the current price of the asset: In this case the owner of the call has the ability to buy the asset at a below-market price. Conversely, a put option is in the money if the strike price of the option is above the current price of the asset. An option is *out of the money* if the option has no immediate economic value: The strike price of the call is above the current price of the asset, or the strike price of the put is below the current price of the asset.

The *delta* of an option measures the sensitivity of the option price to changes in the price of the underlying asset. Delta is the change in the price of the option divided by the change in the price of the asset. Call options have deltas between zero and 1; put options have deltas between zero and –1. As an option gets further out of the money, the delta moves close to zero; as the option gets further in the money, the delta gets closer to 1 (or –1, in the case of puts). This fact is the basis of various *dynamic trading strategies.*

out of the money See *options.*

passive management See *efficient market viewpoint.*

put See *options.*

short position See *basic tools.*

standard deviation See *statistics.*

statistics Professional investors use the concepts of *standard deviation* and *correlation* in assessing the risk of a single investment or a portfolio of investments. The standard deviation of a return series is a measure of the *volatility,* or variability, or dispersion, of the returns. If the returns of a money manager have a low standard deviation, then the manager's returns are tightly clustered around the manager's average return. High standard deviation means that the returns are much more widely scattered around the average. High standard deviation is usually regarded as a sign of high risk.

Standard deviation is related to probability. In a normal bell-shaped distribution, there is a 68 percent probability of achieving a return within 1 standard deviation of the mean and a 95 percent probability of achieving a return within 2 standard deviations of the mean. (See Figure 7–3.)

Correlation measures the degree to which two series of returns move together. Correlations range from 1 to –1. A correlation close to 1 means that the two assets, or money managers, tend to move up and down together. A correlation close to –1 means that the two assets, or managers, tend to move in opposite directions. Correlations close to zero mean that the two series of returns move independently of one another.

The theory of portfolio diversification is based on the fact that the standard deviation of a portfolio depends on two factors: the standard deviation of the individual components and the level of correlation among the components. If a portfolio includes components that have a low or negative correlation with one another, then the standard deviation of the total portfolio will be lower than the average standard deviation of the components. In other words, don't put all your eggs in one basket, and try to find pairs of baskets that have a low correlation with one another.

strike price See *options*.

volatility See *statistics*.

INDEX

ABOUT THE AUTHOR

Robert A. Jaeger is vice chairman and chief investment officer of Evaluation Associates Capital Markets, Inc. (EACM), which invests in a broad variety of hedge fund strategies on behalf of institutional clients. Bob is also executive vice president and chief investment officer of EACM's parent company, Evaluation Associates (EAI), which provides investment consulting services to U.S. tax-exempt institutions. Bob joined EAI in 1983, prior to which time he was a member of the faculty of Yale University and the University of Massachusetts at Amherst. He holds a B.A. from Princeton, a B. Phil. from Oxford, and a Ph.D. from Cornell.